Acta Universitatis Upsaliensis

Studia Uralica Upsaliensia 32

T0413392

Susanna Fahlström

Form and Philosophy in Sándor Weöres' Poetry

UPPSALA 1999

Dissertation for the Degree of Doctor of Philosophy in Finno-Ugric languages presented at Uppsala University in 1999

Abstract

Fahlström, S., 1999: Form and Philosophy in Sándor Weöres' poetry. Acta Universitatis Upsaliensis. *Studia Uralica Upsaliensia* 32. 243 pp. Uppsala. ISBN 91-554-4614-0.

Dissertation written in English
This dissertation, by presenting comprehensive analyses of six poems by the Hungarian poet Sándor Weöres, investigates the poetical forms and the poetical philosophies in these texts. The poems represent specific philosophic spheres of Weöres' poetry. The analyses emerge from the formal elements, and aim to shed light upon the structural coherences between the texts and their philosophical contexts. This method of analysis also complies with Weöres' views on the aesthetics of poetics and his method of writing, where form and structure always played an outstandingly important role. The complex methods used in the analyses are very much influenced by the views and methods of a text stylistics that looks at the literary work as a global entity. Taken together, these analyses illustrate the focal points of a remarkable poetical form and a most profound philosophical context in the poems of an outstanding Hungarian poet.

Key-words: Sándor Weöres, Hungarian literature, Hungarian poetry, Hungarian language, Rhetorics, Stylistics, Text analysis, Text stylistics, Poetical form, Poetical structure, Philosophy in poetry, Religion in poetry.

Susanna Fahlström, Department of Finno-Ugric Languages, Uppsala University, Box 527, SE-751 20 Uppsala, Sweden

The figure on the cover is based on an original photograph by U. T. Sirelius in the possession of the National Museum of Finland.

Cover lay-out: Jerk-Olof Werkmäster

ISSN 1101-7430
ISBN 91-554-4614-0

Distributor Uppsala University Library, Box 510, SE-751 20 Uppsala, Sweden

Printed in Sweden by Akademitryck AB, S-590 98 Edsbruk, 1999

Contents

Acknowledgements

Acknowledgements

When at last it was time to decide what this thesis would be about, I did not hesitate too long. Why would I not write about Sándor Weöres? Surely, his poetry is such an internal part of my life that even in my self-imposed emigration his melodies perpetually resound in my mind. The middle verses of the *Harmadik szimfónia* 'Third symphony' are very important for me in this connection. However, during the five years at the Teacher's training college at Pécs, when my name still was Zsuzsa Fényes, and where I, among other subjects, studied Hungarian language and literature, my childhood's bewitchment from Weöres' poems matured in a more scientific way.

Here I wish to thank my old and new colleges at Pécs for all the help they gave me during writing this thesis: Dezsőné Vera Zemplényi, with whom I taught Hungarian at the Janus Pannonius Gymnasium at Pécs, and who also gave me useful advice regarding this work; Antal Bókay, especially for his excellent book *Irodalomtudomány a modern és posztmodern korban* 'Theory of literature in modern and post-modern period'; and my old friend, Katitsné Zsuzsa Balatincz, for the never-to-be-forgotten hours when we read poems to each other, including Weöres', aloud. I want to thank Beáta Thomka at the Janus Pannonius Tudományegyetem at Pécs, who gave me many tips regarding material helpful to my thesis, and also the Department of Finno-Ugric Languages at Uppsala University for the financial help with the one months' long journey to Pécs. During my second journey to Hungary I met Borbála Keszler, Erzsébet Fehér and Zoltán Kenyeres at Eötvös József Tudományegyetem at Budapest, to whom I send my deepest thanks for reading several chapters of my manuscript. I am also grateful to Svenska Institutet from whom I received a scholarship for one month for the journey to Budapest.

Still, I am most thankful to my tutor Professor Lars-Gunnar Larsson. He trusted and encouraged me during these last four years, and his appreciative attitude meant much to me. He gave me valuable pieces of advice drawing on his vast knowledge. I thank him also for accepting my thesis in his series.

I am very grateful for Pamela Marston who checked the English version of this work. She always "felt" what I wanted to say, and did the language editing rapidly and correctly. Rolf Lundén's seminars on American literature improved aspects of my English, and also gave me new and interesting perspectives on literature studies. I am also grateful to Rolf Lundén and Liz Kella for their advice to one of the chapters of the thesis.

I also would like to express my thanks to Bengt Landgren for the opportunity to participate in his seminars on literary methodology. I thank Mária

Dugántsy Becker for her encouragement and advice, and I also thank Ágnes Mélypataky for kindly lending the Hamvas books to me. I will also send my thanks to Ilona Várhelyi for her response to two chapters of this work. To Chistina Wernström who helped me with the illustrations, my sincere thanks.

For moral support and much good advice I would like to express my thanks to Virve Raag. She had always time for listening to my broodings and she often encouraged me as well. Though mostly from far-off places, Manja Lehto gave me her friendly support, too.

Many thanks to the post-graduate students at the Department of the Finno-Ugric Languages of Uppsala University for fruitful discussions of several chapters of my thesis in Professor Lars-Gunnar Larsson's seminars. I will especially thank Matti Hellberg, André Hesselbäck, Mika Ojanen, Torbjörn Söder and Lennart Unga.

I am much obliged to my "own" library, the Uppsala University Library. Without the help of its outstanding staff it would have been difficult to carry out this work.

It is, however, to my family, Ulf, Tessan and Mikael, I owe the deepest debt of gratitude. They were always there when I needed them. Ulf also helped me with the bibliographical research and he often was the first reader of my English translations. Tessan took my place many times in the kitchen and in doing the housework, too. The deep involvement in the "book" that Tessan and Mikael showed through their many questions was exceedingly inspiring. I dedicate this work to my family, especially Ulf, Tessan and Mikael.

Uppsala in September, 1999.
Susanna Fahlström

1 Introduction

1.1 Background and Aims

There is no doubt that Sándor Weöres is one of the most debated and controversial Hungarian poets of the 20th century. There are three basic reasons for a continued keen interest in his poetry: first, his entrance into literary life as an infant prodigy; second, his passivity concerning the socialist reforms after the Second World War; and third, the final definitive approval of his poetry among the most outstanding poets of Hungary. These three basic reasons, naturally, gave birth to many studies. Thus, there is a great abundance of sources, which I hope I can sort out according to the aims of this work.

The main monographs about Weöres are, as follows, in chronological order of publishing: Attila Tamás' work with the title *Sándor Weöres* in 1978; *Weöres Sándor közelében* 'Closely to Sándor Weöres' of Imre Bata in 1979; and Zoltán Kenyeres' monography entitled *Tündérsíp* 'Fairy Whistle' in 1983. These monographs all contain a chronological rendering of Weöres' life and work and also a thematical grouping of the chapters. Thus, for example, Tamás in several chapters deals with Weöres' general view of life, and Bata and Kenyeres write on the sonnets in greater detail. In Kenyeres' work we can find two larger chapters about the so-called *hosszúénekek* 'long-songs' and *játékversek* 'play-poems' of Weöres, while Bata and Tamás discuss the dramas and the translations in separate chapters. All three monographers refer to or go into the details of certain poems and cycles, such as the forty sonnets of the *Átváltozások* 'Metamorphoses' cycle or the poems *Az elveszített napernyő* 'The Lost Parasol' and the *Harmadik szimfónia* 'Third Symphony'.

In addition to these three monographs there are also three main anthologies dealing with Weöres: firstly, the volume *Magyar Orpheus* 'Hungarian Orpheus', published in 1990; and secondly, the volume *Egyedül mindenkivel* 'Alone with Everybody', published in 1993. Both these volumes were edited by Mátyás Domokos. The third volume, entitled *Weörestől Weöresről* 'Of Weöres, about Weöres', also published in 1993, was compiled by Tibor Tüskés. These three anthologies, principally containing interviews, letters, articles, are mostly concerned with an introduction of Weöres as an individual.

Unlike the authors of the three monographs mentioned above, I have no intention of discussing Weöres' works in a chronological order, but of instead analyzing the poems in their philosophical context, which emerges from the formal elements. More specifically, I am interested in giving a comprehensive analysis of poetical texts and I also want to find structural coherences between the texts and the world of the texts in order to shed light upon the focal points of the poetical form and the philosophical context. The analysed poems represent specific philosophic spheres of Weöres' poetry, and the selection aims at giving a complete picture of each specific philosophic sphere. Nevertheless, realizing the fundamental profundity of this poetic philosophy, this effort of mine must be content with only being a step towards completeness.

1.2 Material and Methods

My investigations are based on the third, enlarged edition of the three-volume *Egybegyűjtött írások* 'Collected Writings' of Sándor Weöres, published in 1975. All the analysed poems are taken from these volumes, and in each case I refer to the pages where these poems are to be found. My translations of Weöres' poems into English are mostly rough translations. The most obvious reason for this is the method applied in the analyses, a structural investigation which is based on the formal elements of the poems. Unfortunately, rough translations usually do not mirror the most essential formal qualities, such as the rhythm and the rhyme. This fact especially makes itself felt when dealing with Weöres. In many of his poems form is of primary importance. Consequently, the Hungarian texts of the poems must also be kept in mind. In order to facilitate comprehension, all the Hungarian quotations are also translated into English, even if this means being accused of repeating oneself. An adequate rendering of the figures of speech, metaphors and tropes is another example of the almost insoluble problems when translating Weöres' poems. In these cases, however, the original meaning of the word is given when it appears for the first time. I have translated the original Hungarian and Swedish quotations into English, but quotations from German and French have not been translated.

The method applied in the analyses is closely connected to the subject matter indicated by the title of this work, and also to the intent of explaining correspondences between the poetical form and the poetical philosophy.

There is, however, one more substantial circumstance which influenced my view on the methodology: as I believe that an analysis of any poetical work must be based on the poem itself, my starting-point for the analyses, without exception, is the text itself. This belief is supported by Weöres' views on the aesthetics of poetics, as well as the following statements referring to his own poetry: "Several structures, several scopes of movement appeared all the time, which are only casually connected to a literary theme, or not at all" (Simon 1993:275). "[...] I was much more attracted by the form, the structure, the brushstrokes, than those contents which might become poetry" (Mezey 1993:430). Or as Kenyeres (1978:73) put it: "The concentration on the linguistic function, the appearance of the form as a task, is the point where we reach the very essence of Weöres' view of literature". This, however, as Kenyeres also points out in the same place, is not identical with any kind of formalism, as the form is not the aim but the means "which by shaping the language and the form, contributes towards the common purpose, namely the language-conquest of the world". Consequently, my method of analysing is very much influenced by Weöres' method of writing.

Weöres' poetry, as it unfolded in the thirties, is also embedded in that period of changed paradigms which, during the time of the successive decline of the avantgarde movements, simultaneously with other European poetries, inspired poets to write in their own, individual ways. These new paradigms, as regards Weöres, have much in common with T. S. Eliot's poetry, a circumstance he declares in the following way: "I should like to belong to those, who, like Eliot, without any poetic doctrine, follow their own best bents, who strive for maximal values, who stubbornly fight against any weakening, but who do not have any high-flown or obstructive theories. They are sometimes traditional, sometimes innovatory, sometimes comprehensible, sometimes incomprehensible, according to what best answers to the actual subject he wants to express" (Weöres 1993a:43). The innovations emphasize the significant role of Weöres' experimentation with language (Szathmári 1977:194-203).

Szathmári (1983:320-355) also points to the fact that a stylistic analysis of a given text cannot be confined to the sentence, but that a global analysis must originate from the whole text. Nevertheless, as Ferenc Kiefer (1976:199) also made clear, a literary analysis of a text, in spite its obvious connection to linguistics, makes use of the theories of the science of literature in the first place.

A contextual approach of a given text must be based on complex analysis, which necessarily makes use of other methods of analysis, as, for example, that of the "explication de textes", the genetical, psychological, structuralist, generative, mathematical-statistical and the contrastive methods (Szathmári 1983:335). In his analyses Szathmári (1990) distinguishes between the following levels:

1. the acoustical level
2. vocabulary and expression-level
3. syntactic level
4. figurative level
5. textual level
6. extralingual level

As all these levels include a natural level of understanding, there is no need for a semantical level, in Szathmári's opinion.

Bengt Landgren (1985:35) also has a complex interpretation method in view: "Therefore the biographical and comparative aspects must be completed by a structural analysis, which aims at uncovering other text-levels, than attention hitherto had been paid to. In this connection, it becomes necessary to split the entire text in levels (layers) and separate elements, in order to reconstruct – study the relations, the interplay between these elements on several language levels later on". When analysing a poem by Johannes Edfelt, Landgren attaches great importance to the semantical level, as the special meaning of the poem gives some kind of a "semantical dyeing" (Landgren 1985:37) to all the other levels. His analyses of two poems by Erik Lindegren are based on the following levels (Landgren 1983a; 1983b):

1. typographical-visual level
2. syntactic level
3. rhythmical structure
4. phonetical level
5. grammatical level
6. semantical level

Elemér Hankiss (1985), describing the structural model of the poem, points out the levels as follows:

1. the level of the linguistic relations
2. the level of the relation of the reality-elements and the meaning these stand for
3. the level representing the relation of positive and negative semantic values
4. the level of compositional relations, based on the function of the linguistic signs.

Zoltán Szabó's (1985; 1988) analyses, much influenced by that of Teun A. van Dijk, Peter Cassirer, János Petöfi S., Michael Alexander Kirkwood, Maria Renata Mayenova and Ruqaiya Hassan, are based on a main principle which defines all the parts of the text, and which he calls the text organization principle. The cohesion between the elements of the text is related to this text organization principle, usually expressed by a single sentence in which the substantial values of the given works are focused. Szabó's analyses begin with the establishment of the text organization principle, which is followed by the unravelling of the focal sentence, the content of the work, the treatment of the elements of the represented reality and the stylistic means.

Klára Széles (1996:99) writes as follows about the methods of literary analyses: "every analysis of some literary work is restricted by the fact that it must comply with the laws of its object, its material, the literary work". According to Széles (1996), the literary work is a system of linguistic and extra-linguistic networks grouped around a particular focus. This focus can be concrete, such as a trope or a sentence with integrating qualities, but it can also be more abstract, involving prosodical or social-historical factors. A given work may have several focuses, as Széles points out, and the analysis might begin with any one of these. It is most essential, however, that the networks belonging to the focus chosen are described according to their actual functional interdependencies.

These complex analyzing methods, briefly presented above, which look at the literary work as a global entity, have had a strong influence on the development of my own type of analysis. I intended to combine parts of these methods with the subject indicated in the title and with Weöres' views on his own aesthetics of literature. My method is based upon two main elements: the text, forming the basis of the analysis, and the world of the text, disentangling itself from the text. Each section of the analysis aims at enlarging the sphere of the relations between the elements of the text and also the world of the text, in order to improve the results in every consequent part of the analysis. Through these means, the last section dealing with Weöres' philosophy of poetics becomes a sort of a synthesis, making sense of the text and the world of the text embraced in the same entirety. The conclusion of this work will also offer a kind of synthesis between the levels of analysis of the different poems.

1.3 Sándor Weöres. A Short Biography

Sándor Weöres was born on June 22, 1913 in Szombathely, a little Transdanubian town near the Austrian border. He spent his childhood at Csönge, a village not far from Szombathely. His father was an army major, and during the Horthy-regime, was deprived of his rank and became discharged with a pension. He then withdrew to the family-estate in Csönge and ran his farm there. Sándor Weöres's mother, Mária Blaskovich, was a very well-educated woman, who, very early on, taught her son German and French and also acquainted him with the works of Shakespeare, Goethe and other classic writers. She even took him to the meetings of the Anthroposophical Society at Csönge and the contact with Steiner's ideas unmistakably influenced Weöres' life-work. He was a precocious child with not many comrades of his own age but with a strong interest in reading and writing poems.

As he was often sick as a child, during his first school-years he had a

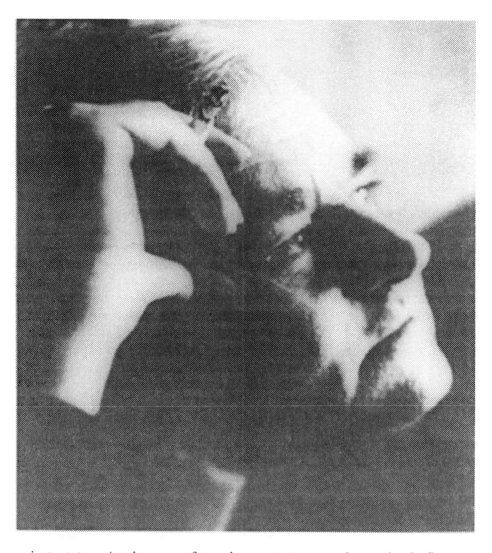

private tutor. At the age of ten he went to secondary school, first to Szombathely, then to Győr and Sopron. He said as follows about these years in several secondary schools in an interview: "My relation to school was very strange. My teachers were very engaged in me on the one hand, but on the other hand I made the secondary school a little bit like a university, often I rather went beside the school than into it. Then in spite of the fact that the teachers partly liked me and thought well of me, they still kicked me from one school to another like a football. I was not an amenable schoolboy at all. I had a slight problem with alcohol already at that time and I didn't learn very much. I only learned things I was interested in" (Moldován 1993:192-193).

It was Ágoston Pável, a teacher, a newspaper editor and the founder of the town library in Szombathely, who first sent Weöres' poems to Budapest newspapers and before long these poems were published in 1928. These first poems instantly drew public attention to the schoolboy and the critics spoke about an infant prodigy. Adorján Bónyi (1990:41), for example, wrote as follows: "With the music of this Hungarian child it is good to lean our heads over to the mysterious, cruel and wonderful Hungarian fate, which also in our loneliness, in our poverty, again and again presents us with some very good surprises". Zoltán Kodály took note of a poem with the title *Öregek* 'Old Ones', which he then composed into a choral work. From 1932 Weöres' poems were frequently published in the legendary literary magazine *Nyugat* 'West' and he also began to correspond with the most outstanding poets connected to it, such as Mihály Babits and Dezső Kosztolányi.

In 1933 Weöres moved to Pécs in order to start his university studies. At first he attended lectures in history and geography, then became a law student but ultimately he decided on the subjects of philosophy and aesthetics. In 1939 he even wrote a dissertation thesis in aesthetics with the title *A vers születése* 'The Birth of the Poem'. This is, obviously, not a very usual topic for a thesis and especially not when it deals with an author's own way of writing. All the same, it was written under the encouragement of his supervising professor József Halasy-Nagy, which is a circumstance that clearly shows the keen interest in his poetry. In this thesis Weöres particularly emphasizes the significance of the formal elements, like rhythm, when he declares that many of his poems are based on a primary metrical pattern which suddenly came to his mind and which only later was followed with a possible meaning.

His first poetry volume, titled *Hideg van* 'It is Cold', was published in Pécs in 1934, which gave him the Baumgarten prize, his first literary prize. The autumn of that year he spent at the hospital of Szombathely, where he was treated for neurasthenia. Here he composed the poem *Valse Triste*, one of his best. His second volume with the title *A kő és az ember* 'The Stone and the Man' was published in Budapest in 1935, followed by *A teremtés dícsérete* 'The Praise of Creation' in 1938, which again was published in Pécs. In the years 1936-37 he stayed a long time in India, China and Ceylon.

His first mentor, as he called those who influenced him most, was Lajos Fülep, lecturer in history and philosophy of art at the university of Pécs. His second mentor, Nándor Várkonyi, director of the University Library of Pécs, initiated him into the editing of the literary journal *Sorsunk* 'Our Fate', which already in its first issue published a drama of Weöres with the title *Theomachia*. It was also at Várkonyi's request that Weöres translated the Sumerian-Babylonian ancient *Epic of Gilgamesh*. This translation is applied in Várkonyi's work about ancient, vanished cultures, with the title *Sziriát oszlopai* 'The pillars of Seiris'.

After taking his doctor's degree in 1939, Weöres first worked at the

University Library of Budapest and from 1941 at the Town Library of Pécs as a librarian. He lived in Pécs for two years but in 1943 he finally moved to Budapest. According to Várkonyi's (1976:388) autobiography, it was mostly the attraction of the literary life of Budapest including, of course, the *Nyugat*, Babits and Kosztolányi, that caused the move.

The same year he moved to Budapest a play appeared with the title *Bolond Istók* 'Crazy Istók' and in 1944 the volume *Medusa*. This last volume brought him into connection with the philosopher and the novelist Béla Hamvas, Weöres' third mentor. Hamvas' (1990:213-217) criticism of the *Medusa* volume encouraged him in finding his own way by giving up the literary traditions of the *Nyugat* and returning to the only true poetry of Orpheus, that is, the Orphic poetry (Kenyeres 1990:165-174). When Hamvas rejected the lion's share of the poems of the *Medusa* volume due to their unduly individual concern and also encouraged a descent to the irrational experiences, then he also set an individual lyric against a sort of lyrics which declared the idea of completeness in life, the search for the Absolute. How deep an impression this criticism of Hamvas made on Weöres is clearly seen in his next volume published in 1945, with the title *A teljesség felé* 'Towards the Absolute', in which Hamvas' thoughts are easy to trace. In opposition to Hamvas, however, Weöres kept what Hamvas rejected, that is, the deliberately conscious formal experimentations on poetic language. The most striking examples of this ambition are the *Rongyszőnyeg* 'Rag-carpet' cycle with the significant subtitle *Dalok, epigrammák, ütempróbák, vázlatok, töredékek* 'Songs, Epigrams, Rhythm-experiments, Sketches, Fragments' in this volume and the *Magyar etüdök* 'Hungarian Etudes' cycle, first published in the volume *A hallgatás tornya* 'The Tower of Silence'. These rhythmical pieces, though originally not written for children, are to be found in volumes published for them. Music has been composed to many of these poems and they are on the whole the most popular of Weöres' works. They are, however, as Kenyeres (1984:48) pointed out, impossible to translate and that is why they "must remain Hungarian secrets", as Miklós Vajda (1987:50) put it.

During the years of the Second World War Weöres lived for the most part in Csönge, under circumstances he wrote about in a letter to Gyula Takács, a fellow-poet in Pécs: "The main thing is that we are alive. Neither my parents nor myself have any whole clothes left, our home is temporarily occupied by the army, we hardly have any food" (WW:109). Nothwithstanding, there are three volumes published in 1946: *A szerelem ábécéje* 'The Alphabet of Love', *Elysium* and *Gyümölcskosár* 'Fruit-Basket'.

The poems written during the years of the war and right after it bear witness to a very deep pessimism. He had no confidence in the future of a socialistic reform of society and his poems also reflect this disconsolation and hopelessness he felt then. A characteristic title which exquisitely expresses the fundamental feeling of these years is *A reménytelenség könyve* 'The Book of Hopelessness', written in 1944. Weöres, who early recognized the Fascist threat and who already in 1933 wrote a condemnatory poem about Hitler, also gave voice to his fear and worry in the poems written in the war-years. In 1947 he published two volumes with the titles *A fogak tornáca* 'The Portico of Teeth' and *Testtelen nyáj* 'Bodiless Herd', but after this, up until 1955, he couldn't issue any of his poems. During these years when even literary life had to conform to the tenets of the Marxist-Leninist ideology, many Hungarian writers were sentenced to silence. A schematic set of descriptions which strived to cover up the real social problems became strictly required from every author who desired to be published. No poetical experimentations on language were accepted in a time when literature should contribute to the building of socialism. Weöres' lyrical production was "reduced to nothing", as Bata (1979:29) put it. Critical essays on his poetry at that time also accused him of showing an inadmissible passivism concerning societal matters.

A great event in his private life was in the year 1947, when he married Amy Károlyi, who was also a poet. In an interview he spoke as follows about the marriage: "Before our marriage I was a country loiter, I lived once in Pécs, once in Fehérvár, once in Csönge, I had no permanent address. And the first fixed point in life came with this marriage." (Bertha 1993:149). In the same year they both got a scholarship to Rome and because of this could stay nearly a whole year in Italy.

When they returned to Hungary the next year, Weöres began to work at the library of the Hungarian Academy of Sciences, but he was dismissed from this employment very soon. Amy Károlyi also lost her job. When it became impossible to publish their own works, they both began to take translation-work provided by friends like Zoltán Kodály. Though he left them in his desk-drawer, Weöres also wrote poems during this time, with the longer ones connected to mythology and stories from the Bible, as for example the poems *Mahruh veszése* 'The Fall of Mahruh', *Medea, Orpheus, Minotaurus* and *Mária mennybemenetele* 'The Ascension of Mary'. Translating now became not only a means of subsistence for Weöres but also provided a broad perspective concerning the literature of other peoples and thus it was an exceptionally good inspiration and challenge for his own poetry. Furthermore, his exquisite translations made remote, less-known literatures popular in Hungary. Between the years 1952-54 the works of the Chinese poets Po Chü-i and Ch'ü Yüan, the Russian poet Taras Hryhorovych Shevchenko and the Gruzian poet Shota Rustaveli appeared in Weöres' translation. A collection of his translations with the title *A lélek idézése* 'The Raising of the Soul' was published in 1958 in the same year as the translation of the main work of Taoism, the *Tao-te Ching*. His translations of Shakespeare, Dante, Petrarch, Blake, Eliot and Mallarmé are among the best in the Hungarian language.

19

His first collection of poems after the eight years of silence appeared in 1955, a children's book entitled *Bóbita*. These poems are small, rhythmical pieces mostly from the *Rongyszőnyeg* 'Rag-carpet' and the *Magyar etüdök* 'Hungarian Etudes' cycles. By this time the political climate had become much more relaxed and after Stalin's death the government also began to eliminate the unlawful acts of the past years. The many writers who were silenced during the years of a dogmatic ideology, now in a new era when the demand of a schematical rendering metamorphosed to a demand of realism, could again be published. A collection of poems by Weöres with the significant title *A hallgatás tornya* 'The Tower of Silence' appeared in 1956. This title is from Lajos Fülep, who was also the publisher's reader for the volume. In spite of a very careful selection (Kenyeres 1986:340), the critics were not very considerate this time either. Though somewhat milder than the critiques Weöres was subjected to after the war and even pointing to the real value of Weöres' poetry, Miklós Szabolcsi (1957:183-192) still rejects it, accusing the poet of being irrational and anti-intellectual: "Still its most characteristic feature is the sense of dehumanization, devoid of the human, a passive contemplation, a cultural pessimism, behind which, as a subjective motive for his actions, maybe a deep affection for the human, a search for a colorful reality is hidden, but the result, the realization, the poetry that may be read is one of the keenest, the most hopelessly disillusioned in the history of Hungarian poetry".

Presumably, this review by Szabolcsi and other reviews comparable to it, was the reason why his next volume, a *Tűzkút* 'Well of Fire' wasn't published until 1964. This volume is called the volume of synthesis, owing to the fact that poems written earlier, together with the newer ones give a summary of the poet's general view on life and the several ways of poetically expressing it. Characteristic of this is the structural balance regarding both the arranging of the poems within the volume and the inner composition of them. According to Imre Bori (1984:476-483), this composition of the poems is concordant to that of music and he also draws a parallel between these poems and Bartók's compositions in his latest period.

Two dramas of Weöres, *A holdbeli csónakos* 'The Oarsman in the Moon', written in 1941 and the *Octopus, avagy Szent György és a sárkány históriája* 'Octopus, or the History of Saint George and the Dragon' were published in 1967 in a composite volume with the title *Hold és a sárkány* 'Moon and the Dragon'. At the request of the National Theatre in Pécs in 1972, he also wrote a tragi-comedy with the title *A kétfejű fenevad, azaz Pécs 1686* 'The Two-Headed Beast, or Pécs in 1686'.

The next volume, *Merülő Saturnus* 'Saturn Submerging' was published in 1968. Unlike the previous volumes there are several poems in this volume which deal with personal topics, but examples of experiments on poetical form, such as automatic writing, can also be found.

In 1970, ultimately in a reformed cultural climate, he received the greatest appreciation from the government for his poetry, the Kossuth-prize. The two-volume *Egybegyűjtött írások* 'Collected Writings' was also published during this year, which increased to three volumes in 1975.

Without doubt, the volume *Psyché,* with the subtitle *Egy hajdani költőnő írásai* 'The Writings of a Poetess from Before', published in 1972, is the most remarkable work of Weöres. As both the main character and the language seem authentic although it is pure fiction, this work is the greatest metamorphosis a Hungarian poet ever produced in literature. Psyché, or Erzsébet Lónyay, who according to Weöres lived between 1795-1831, is an imaginary person, and consequently, her poems and letters are also imagined. The language of the work is a true imitation of the early 19th century Hungarian language, that is, the period of Ferenc Kazinczy's language reform. Kazinczy's new words and grammar are discussed in the dialogues and Psyché's poems give evidence of a renewed Hungarian language in the making, all of which makes the reading of this work a fantastic adventure in the history of a language. However, this is a hard period in Hungarian history, when Austrian absolutism and the censorship of the press strove to suppress all national intellectual activities. Poetry, as so many times before in Hungary, is guided by a political vocation, which in this period is the struggle for the national independence from the Habsburgs. This most essential political programme determined what poetry was from a thematical point of view. Psyché, however, is not concerned with these themes, she writes about another topics, about her private life. Or as Kenyeres (1986:355) put it: "The work Psyché is the subsequent composing of those poems which necessarily were omitted from our literature in the last century. [– – –] In this context, the work Psyché is the ephemeral vision of that poetry which lives and develops in a medium where literature is not obliged to bother with political troubles of society because the task of mobilization is managed by other institutions".

The volume *Tizenegy szimfónia* 'Eleven Symphonies' was published in 1973. In the *Egybegyűjtött írások* 'Collected Writings' of 1975, this number expanded to twelve. They are really earlier poems arranged in a new way, that is, according to the composition principles of the symphony. Bringing musical structures to poetry was not a new endeavor for Weöres and this fact may also be illustrated by titles as *Canzone, Fughetta, Bagatell, Suite, Rumba, Rock and Roll.* The regular structural pattern of the second part of the poem *Négy korál* 'Four Corals' inspired the painter Ferenc Lantos to sketch the arrangement of the six words composing the poem. According to Lantos, the combination of these six words, similar to the permanent and altering parts of a choral work shows a regular structure, which can be illustrated as some kind of a visual composition (Fábián 1977). These particular poems can be analyzed using the musical and visual principles Attila Tamás (1978:148-168) called musicalartistical language products.

Három veréb hat szemmel 'Three Sparrows with Six Eyes' is the title of a volume published in 1977. This is a result of a collection of works written over many decades. Poems of past and long-forgotten Hungarian writers, such as László Tóth Ungvárnémethy, are published in this volume, for the reason that Weöres phrases in the following way: "These poets have totally foundered in time, that is why I feel it necessary to bring them back to surface again. That is to say, it is a great luxuriousness that there are about twenty notable figures according to our way of looking at literature, we are only engaged in them, though there are twenty or thirty others whose merits only fall a little bit behind these notable figures" (Havas 1993:346).

His last volumes are the following ones: *Áthallások* 'Interferences', *Harmincöt vers* 'Thirty five Poems', *Ének a határtalanról* 'Song about the Boundless', *Kézirásos könyv* 'Book Written by Hand', *Posta messziről* 'Post from Far Away', *A sebzett föld éneke* 'The Song of the Wounded Earth and *Kútbanéző* 'He Who Looks into the Well'. These last poems are mostly of a more private character talking about the decline of the body and the soul. He died, or as Amy Károlyi worded it in the obituary notice, returned home on January 22, 1989. In the newspaper *Svenska Dagbladet* in Sweden János Csatlós (1989) says his farewells to Sándor Weöres with the following words: "Everybody in Hungary followed his last years with anxiety and compassion when his physical and mental health slowly broke down. He was a legend already during his lifetime to all layers and all age-groups of the society. Once I went home with him in a taxi and while his frail figure faded away in the thickly wooded garden of the house up on the Buda-hills, the driver asked me: 'Wasn't that Sándor Weöres?' At my confirmation, he smiled: 'God bless his soul!'".

2 The Forms of Impersonality

2.1 Becoming Another in Second Person Singular

A hársfa mind virágzik,
a csíz mind énekel,
a lomb sugárban ázik,
csak szíved alszik el.

Nyílnak feléd a lányok
mint ékszer-ládikók –
nem is figyelsz utánok,
kedved beszőtte pók.

Már csak hitet szeretnél,
szolgálnád Ég-Urát,
minden hiút levetnél,
viselnél szőrcsuhát.

A hársfa mind virágzik,
a csíz mind énekel,
a lomb sugárban ázik,
csak szíved alszik el.

All the limetrees are in blossom,
all the siskins are singing,
the leaves bathe in sunshine,
only your heart goes to sleep.

The girls open themselves to you
like cases for precious stones –
you don't even watch them,
a spider has spun your pleasure.

Nothing else but faith you'd want
to serve the Lord above,
vanity you'd get rid of
to wear a monk's habit.

All the limetrees are in blossom,
all the siskins are singing,
the leaves bathe in sunshine,
only your heart goes to sleep.

(*Rongyszőnyeg 76* 'Rag-carpet 76'. In: EI I:410)

2.1.1 The Text

2.1.1.1 The Structure and Shape of the Writing

The poem in its entirety is characterized by steadiness, symmetry and proportionality. There are four strophes in it, each with four lines. These lines are approximately of the same length, but the first and third lines in every verse are obviously longer than the second and fourth lines. There is consequently a regular and symmetrically proven contrast as to the length of the lines. Each line is a syntagm and there is not a single enjambement throughout the poem. Each line builds a sentence with regular punctuation: commas at the end of the first three lines, and periods at the end of the fourth. There is only one exception from this rule: the second verse where the comma is missing in the first line and where it is replaced by a dash in the second. Simple, clear, concluded thoughts are formed in a simple, clear, concluded shape. The shape is like Hungarian folk-songs or folk poetry with motifs of nature that frame the poem to a rounded whole.

2.1.1.2 The Represented Elements of Reality

The first and the fourth verses of the poem show a perfect formal congruence and by this means function as a frame for the two middle verses. These two identical strophes visualize the contrasting forms of the outside and inside reality. The outside reality appears by means of views of nature, the inside reality is expressed by the *szív* – 'heart'– motif. Opposing the bright, positive pole of the outer world, the inner world stands as a negative pole of the spirit. The three lines presenting nature show a semantically symmetric structure according to figure 1. The verbs in the end of the first three lines also show the same symmetry on the basis of semantics, as we can see in figure 2.

Contrary to these tropes the last line represents the negative pole of the inner world: *csak szíved alszik el* 'only your heart goes to sleep'. A parallel

Figure 1

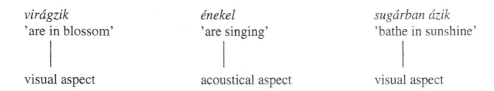

Figure 2

structure can be noticed between the three words of this line, with the exception of the adverb *csak,* 'only', which introduces a content with a different meaning, and the three lines denoting motifs of nature, as illustrated in figure 3.

Studying the second verse, we see that the positive pole of the world outside is expressed in the first and second lines as a comparison between the

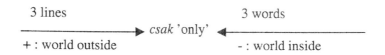

Figure 3

human and the material: *lányok – ékszer-ládikók* 'girls' – 'cases for precious stones'. Through a regular alternation of two opposite poles of the four lines – lines 1-2 on the one hand and lines 3-4 on the other hand – a new example of the principle of symmetry can be proved.

All the four lines of the third verse represent a world inside. The elements of reality are mostly positive: *hit* 'faith', *Ég-Ura* 'Lord above', even the poles of negative quality: *hiú* 'vanity' [lit. 'vain'], *szőrcsuha* 'a monk's habit' appear as positive qualities determined by the verbs: *levetnél* 'you'd get rid of, *viselnél* 'to wear' [lit.: 'you would wear']'.

The represented elements of reality in the global structure can be divided in equal parts based on a kind of proportional symmetry. Eight lines visualize the world outside: three lines in the first verse (1-3), two lines in the second verse (1-2), and three lines in the fourth verse (1-3). The world inside is likewise represented in eight lines: one line in the first verse (4), two lines in the second verse (3-4), four lines in the third verse (1-4), and one line in the fourth verse (4). This being so, an obvious formal realization of the esthetical discipline of proportionality and symmetry among the represented elements of reality can be proved.

I think that contrast, the bipolarity of the positive and negative qualities, is the primary structuring principle of the text. Parallelism between poles of the same positive or negative quality can be noticed too, but its significance, compared to the principle of contrast, is secondary.

In the syntagm *csak szíved alszik el* 'only your heart goes to sleep' – in my opinion – the content of all the other syntagms are combined into a whole. Therefore it is a sentence with an integral power and has a focal quality in the structure of the represented elements of reality. The lines of nature scenes appear as many times as the syntagm *csak szíved alszik el* 'only your heart goes to sleep' occurs in the poem, that is, twice. Though the arrangement of these two poles of positive and negative qualities are constant, they do not have a focal quality. This may be due to their coordinate character: the same positive pole is represented by them no less than three times. However, as an obvious consequence of the concept of focus quality, there may be only one single sentence implying this specific feature. The negative pole of the syntagm *csak szíved alszik el* 'only your heart goes to sleep' increases in semantic complexity as a result of its constant repetition. Furthermore, the first three lines of nature scenes are preparatory, when they, by the mechanism of retardation, create an expectation, increase tension and concentrate attention on the opposite context of the line following. As the syntagm *csak szíved alszik el* 'only your heart goes to sleep' is the last line in both the first and fourth verse, its placing is essential: these lines set the poem in a frame.

2.1.1.3 The Rhetorical-Stylistic Structure

When regarding the text as a global structure, parallelism, also understood as a rhythmical figure of thought, is likely to be initially studied in the relationship of the first and last strophes. The fourth strophe is a word-for-word repetition of the first strophe and functions as a refrain of it. Clauses with similar grammatical structure in every strophe make the parallelism even clearer. The fact that the very same articles occur in the very same position in each syntagm reinforces the significance of the figure. As trope the detailed describing of natural phenomenon can be considered as *demonstratio*. This way of relating to nature scenes in the first lines is common in many Hungarian folksongs. In Hungarian it is called *népdalküszöb*, i.e. an image of nature initiating a folksong. Its use is motivated by a certain wish to express a particular feeling. Nature becomes a mirror of the poet's impressions and emotions. In this poem of Weöres the *népdalküszöb* is even a source of the opposition which determines the structure of the whole.

A profusion of tropes can be found in a detailed examination. The 'leaves that bathe in sunshine', *a lomb sugárban ázik* that connects different kinds of sense-impressions together can be attributed to *synaesthesia*; the last line *csak szíved alszik el* 'only your heart goes to sleep' can be described as a personification.

The verb *nyílnak* 'open themselves' in the first line of the second verse appears to be of an even broader complexity. In its syntagmatic context the trope is a comparison between *lányok – ékszer-ládikók* 'girls' – 'cases for precious stones'. The verb *nyílnak* 'open themselves', however, also has another meaning in Hungarian, namely 'are in blossom' and then it might only secondarily correlate with girls, because the concept of blossoming primarily refers to flowers, plants or trees, that is, the first line of the first verse: *A hársfa mind virágzik* 'All the limetrees are in blossom'. This complex trope binds the two first verses together, especially in their first lines. Paralleling the trope of the last line of the first verse, the last line of the second verse is a personification, too: *kedved beszőtte pók* 'a spider has spun your pleasure'.

Even the tropes we meet in the third strophe show a certain symmetry in placement. The four syntagms of the strophe build the trope of coordinated *congeries*, but when considering how the thoughts advance in intensity of content, from trust to a monk's habit, this trope can even be classified as a *climax*. There are two *chiasmi* in the strophe in a parallel relationship to each other. This parallelism is illustrated in figure 4. *Ég Ura* 'Lord above' in the second line of the third verse is, in its figurative use, another name for God. The same manifestation of metonymy can be found in the expression *szőrcsuha* 'a monk's habit', where *szőrcsuha* as a matter of course denotes the

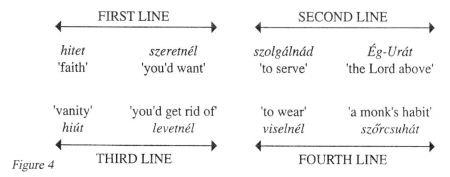

Figure 4

monk himself. The phrases *Ég-Ura* 'Lord above', *szőrcsuha* 'a monk's habit' are in both cases placed at the end of the lines. They rhyme with each other – which confirms their close relationship even more.

2.1.1.4 The Metrical Structure

The composition of the metrical structures is also characterized by a clear arrangement and steadiness. The last verse is a refrain of the first one, and the placing of the alternate rhymes are symmetrical: *abab* in the first and the fourth verses, *cdcd efef* in the two middle verses. Feminine rhymes (lines 1 and 3) alternate regularly with masculine rhymes (lines 2 and 4) except for the two feminine rhyme-words: *Ég-Urát* 'Lord above' and *szőrcsuhát* 'a monk's habit' in lines 2 and 4 in the third verse. All rhymes are end-rhymes. It is characteristic of the rhyme pattern that all the rhymes are full rhymes at their most perfect, i.e. *rime riche* in the two frame-verses. In the two middle verses, however, the rhymes are mostly *assonances*. One exception, however, may be found: the full rhymes of *szeretnél* 'you'd want' and *levetnél* 'you'd get rid of', also in the third verse.

    The lines of the poem are symmetrically constructed when considering the number of syllables as well: all the first and third lines of the strophes are made up of seven syllables, whereas there are always six syllables in every second and fourth line.

    Such a restriction in the number of syllables, a strictly regulated rhythmical recurrence, and a tendency for a definite and consequent setting of stress always on the first syllable of the word may all indicate that this poem of Weöres' is written according to the rules of the peak-counting accentual-syllabic metric system:

```
x x̌ | x x̌ || x x̌ | x        4-3
x x̌ | x x̌ || x x̌           4-2
x x̌ | x x̌ || x x̌ |          4-3
x x̌ | x x̌ || x x̌           4-2
```

There is, however, another possibility of rhythmical identification according to the rules of the quantitative metric system:

```
∪ – | ∪ – | ∪ – | ῡ
∪ – | – – | ∪ ῡ
∪ – | ∪ – | ∪ – | ῡ
– – | ∪ – | ∪ ῡ
```

The four feet lines build an iambic, broken tetrameter which alternates with iambic trimeters. Consequently, both the peak-counting, peak-accented and the quantitative metric system are represented in the poem at the same time. As it can be included in both categories, this poem of Weöres' can be seen as an excellent example of simultaneous verse.

The peak-counting or syllabic metric system of Hungarian is generally characterized by a balanced construction of the metric units of the line. According to this rule of equal metres, each metre is of the same length, independent of the individual length of the syllables that belong to it. Let us illustrate this rule by András Hajdú's example (1990:312):

⏑ ⏑ ⏑ ⏑ | – –   4-2
Gerencséri utca

⏑ ⏑ ⏑ ⏑ | – –   4-2
utca gerencséri

That is, the length of the metres depends not on the absolute length of a syllable but on a relative length determined by the position of these syllables within the structure of the poem. András Hajdú gives a summing-up of Weöres' versification in the following way: "The main point for Weöres' method is the backing up of the length of the syllables when placed in the structure of the poem with the absolute length they originally have" (Hajdú 1990:312). Ildikó A. Molnár (1977:78) comes to the same conclusion. Since many poems of Weöres' show a pattern of similar simultaneous versification as a result of using ancient colons and metres in such an individual way, he brought about a real "revolution in metrics" in Hungarian poetry as István Szerdahelyi (1996:329, 331) put it.

It may be interesting to mention that the iamb in its original Greek form was often used in a sarcastic sense in satiric poems (Henrikson 1982:80). Such a use of it has naturally lost its significance long ago. Nevertheless, perhaps as a kind of Empsonian ambiguity, this ancient context appears anew. Whom this mockery mostly concerns may become a question for the reader and it may presumably be answered with the same ambiguity.

From what she considers a rhythmic plainness of the iamb, Ildikó A. Molnár (1977:45) comes to the realization of a certain poetic function. She writes as follows about this poem of Weöres: "[...] these easy, tender, fast iambs, nearly scurrying as if in dance, express a gentle, familiar atmosphere" (Molnár 1977:50). This is certainly true. When, however, I lay more stress upon content than she does, in the monotonous alternation of the short and long metric feet or metres, I feel some kind of resignation, a frame of mind without any hope. The structure of the poem may support this belief of mine: the deep sigh of desire in the third verse is barely answered by the echo of the first verse and gives no solution.

2.1.1.5 The Grammatical Structure

All four strophes consist of a single sentence. These are all compounded sentences. The structural pattern of these coordinations is that of copulative sentences except for the last lines in the first and fourth verses, which are contrasted to the three preceeding lines as adversative sentences. The last two lines of the second verse are opposed to the two first lines with an absent conjunction *de* 'but', as an example of the trope *asyndeton*. Each of the four sentences of the four strophes are affirmative. The discipline of parallelism asserts itself perfectly in the relation of the first and last verses, as they are identical.

Compound sentences, that is, repetitions of certain syntactic units are characteristic of the impressionistic style. Descriptions of nature reflect different levels of perception, that is, seeing and hearing in *Rongyszőnyeg 76* 'Rag-carpet 76'. The lack of conjunctions, another characteristics of impressionism, is striking in Weöres' poem, too. The missing conjunction is *és* 'and', in this case, connects the clauses of the copulative sentence. A further impressionistic trait is an intense musical rhythm (Szathmári 1990:167) which this poem of Weöres conclusively has.

There are two attributive compounds in the poem placed parallel to each other: *ékszer-ládikók* 'cases for precious stones', the last word in the second line of the second verse, and *Ég-Urát* 'Lord above', the last word in the second line of the third verse. Both nouns begin with the same vowel. This alliteration creates a sort of oscillation between different fields of meaning. As a result *ékszer-ládikók* 'cases for precious stones' belongs not only to the trope of *lányok* 'girls', but also to the trope of *Ég-Ura* 'Lord above'. The image of a case containing some very valuable stones may, in a contextual relationship to *Ég-Ura* 'Lord above', even lead one to think about another case, namely the case for the stone tablets with the Ten Commandments. Content, then, may obviously be influenced by form.

The study of the phonetic features in a poem which establish coherences between form and content, like the study of a metrical structure, can for the same reason easily lead to a dead end. The fact that phonemes have no immanent meaning of their own is worth emphasizing. That is to say, in different words or text-environments the very same phoneme may carry an altogether different logical or emotional content. Phonemes also have, however, as any other part of speech, a stylistic value. Consciously used phonemes lend color to a style and become style markers. They can even become the most essential units of a given individual style, and as parts of a global structure should be studied with the concept of sound-symbolism (Szathmári 1983:343; Begemann 1994:25) in mind.

Consciousness in all respects is a clear characteristic of Weöres' poetry. My investigation of the phonemes in the *Rongyszőnyeg 76* 'Rag-carpet 76' will begin with an examination of the consonant *sz* in the structure. This voiceless spirant is an integral part of the following words: *szíved* 'your heart'; *alszik* 'goes to sleep'; *ékszer-ládikók* 'cases for precious stones'; *figyelsz* 'watch'; *beszőtte* 'spun'; *szeretnél* 'you'd want'; *szolgálnád* 'to serve' [lit 'you would serve']; *szőrcsuhát* 'a monk's habit'. We notice a certain regularity in terms of their placement, and a clear and obvious symmetry: *sz* occurs twice in the first and the last verse, and three times in each of the two middle verses. The consonant *sz* can also be found once in the last lines of each verse. The words which contain *sz* represent a negative pole of an inner world.

The significance of the sentence *csak szíved alszik el* 'only your heart goes to sleep', earlier declared as the sentence with integral power and focal quality, can be further reinforced and motivated by the role of the consonant *sz*. When we look closer we find that this syntagm is the only one in the poem containing two *sz*-phonemes in the same line, appearing even in words adjoining to one another.

If one is familiar with Weöres' poetry in general, one can easily demonstrate how this phoneme, when consciously used, mostly with a tone-painting purpose, may influence meaning. Associations are freely made to a wind blowing, and an illusion of flying, floating and moving. Some examples may illustrate it:

Őszi éjjel
izzik a galagonya
izzik a galagonya
ruhája.

Zúg a tüske
szél szalad ide oda,
reszket a galagonya
magába.

An autumn night
glows the hawthorn's
glows the hawthorn's
dress.

Thorns are rustling

wind is running to and fro
the hawthorn is trembling
all alone.

(Rongyszőnyeg 99. 'Rag-carpet 99'. In: EI I:420)

Hogyha kijössz, messzire mégy,
hogyha maradsz, csípdes a légy.
Habzik az ég, mint tele tál,
tarka idő szőttese száll.

If you come out, you go far,
Flies will bite you, if you stay.
The sky is in foam, as a filled dish,
the homespun of colorful time flies.

(Magyar etüdök 54. 'Hungarian Etudes 54'. In: EI II:89)

These phonetical occurences will be studied on the basis of an intertextual cohesion. There is a relationship between the poems cited above and piece 76 of the *Rongyszőnyeg* 'Rag-carpet' series. A special sort of connection is created by the *sz*-sound. The image of flying may even associate with a different dimension of one kind of descending, that is, falling asleep. Flying, however, is dynamic, contrary to the purpose and aim of going to sleep and the state of sleeping, which is static. When we grasp the contrast between the verb *alszik el* 'goes to sleep' with the negative static pole of steadiness in it and the verbs *szeretnél* 'you'd want', *szolgálnád* 'to serve' with the positive dynamic pole of an individual world inside, then we will see a new proof of opposition, as the main structuring principle realized.

A new contrast can be established to the positive pole world outside. Compared to the positive and the negative pole of the individual world inside, there is not a single *sz*-sound here. On the other hand, a high frequency of vowels is striking: *i* occurs twelve times and *á* eleven times. The number of the nasals *m, n* och *ny* is high, too. They occur a total of nineteen times. My intent is to say that there is a difference concerning sound-qualities in the two different poles of an outside and inside world.

Contextuality between parts of a text can be created by rhymes, but even alliteration can denote meaning. A majority of the alliterations can be found in the third verse. The semantically-based opposition between *hit* 'faith' and *hiú* 'vanity' is a new example of the primary structuring principle; while *szeretnél* 'you'd want' [lit.: 'you would like'], *szolgálnád* 'to serve', *szőrcsuhát* 'a monk's habit', with the same context of expressing a longing for pureness and innocence, are examples of the principle of parallelism. At the same time there is a connection between *szeretnél* 'you'd want', *szolgálnád* 'to serve', and *szőrcsuhát* 'a monk's habit'. This connection is a positive counterpole to the syntagm *csak szíved alszik el* 'only your heart goes to sleep'. According to these facts, contrast, as a primary structuring principle, can even be followed within a field of the very same sound.

Hangcsoportok 'Sound-groups' (EI I:614-615) is the title of one of Weöres' poems. It is written in an imaginary language. Vowels and consonants representing different sense-impressions are collected in corresponding groups. The sounds *i, m* and *n* are classified in no less than three groups: first in the group of soft and fervent, secondly in the group of quick, sparkling and merry, and thirdly in the group of flowing and shining sounds. The vowel *á* fits in two groups: as soft and fervent and as flowing and shining voice. The unique role of the consonant *sz* is underlined by the fact that it belongs to only one group: that of the flowing and shining sounds.

2.1.2 The World of the Text

2.1.2.1 The Theme

"Every poem lacks the content, as a logical fact, all the more it is a poem, all the more organical is its sprouting from the ancient mould of words. Its content is just being as it is. [– – –] Poetry is a sensorial wonder" (Kosztolányi 1957:99). This quotation is taken from a chapter dealing with poetry and poets, from a work with the title *Ábécé* 'ABC' by Dezső Kosztolányi. According to these words, poetry is incomprehensible and for this reason unexplainable. Every form of understanding depends exclusively on our senses, without any contribution from the human intellect.

Se tartalom, se forma – hát mi kell?
A jó vers élőlény, akár az alma,
ha ránézek, csillogva visszanéz,
mást mond az éhesnek s a jóllakottnak
és más a fán, a tálon és a szájban,
végső tartalma, formája nincs is,
csak él és éltet. Vajjon mit jelent,
nem tudja és nem kérdi. Egy s ezer
jelentés ott s akkor fakad ki belőle,

mikor nézik, tapintják, ízlelik.

Neither content, nor form – what then?
A good poem is a living being, like an apple,
when I look at it, it looks back at me,
and it says different things to the starving and to the satisfied
and is different on the tree, the dish or in the mouths,
it has no definite form or content either,
it only is and keeps you alive. What it means,
it doesn't know and doesn't ask. One and thousand
meanings spring from it there and then
when it is seen, touched and tasted.

> (*Vázlat az új líráról*. 'A Sketch about the New Lyrics'. In: EI
> III:164)

Weöres gives voice to the same thing through poetry that Kosztolányi does through prose. Content and form, in a dialectical sense of the word, are united in our senses and are therefore, in this connection, eliminated when, in a new combination, they change into meaning. Interpretation is individual and subjective and, like poetry, ambiguous too, saying different things to different interpreters.

In a letter, written in 1943 to Nándor Várkonyi (1976:189), Weöres declared that one shouldn't seek the meaning in the lines of a poem, but in the "associations that thoughts let flash through the mind". Applying this method "all elements become an equal and an undissolvable unity".

To discuss poetical form, the elements of an inner contextuality as a function of defining theme itself, may only be done in this particular sense. The theme appears in the structure of the work, in a poetical form where "the binding materials are no longer the links of logic, but a gravitation like that of the stars", as Weöres put it (Bozóky 1993:236). This star-like gravitation is created by the formal elements and that is the reason why a thematic research of the poems of Weöres can basically refer to formal and structural categories.

Our starting-point then, in order to define the theme, is the structure. As pointed out on several occasions, contrast is the most significant feature of the structure of this poem. A shiny, happy nature of a world outside is opposed to the emptiness of an individual world inside. Whose world inside? Possibly, as indicated by the second person singular, it can be the world of the reader. Certainly, the most suitable literary genre to which the poem might belong would be the lyrical song. The lyrical song, as is well known, expresses pure and simple feelings of the individual. Primal scenes from nature reflecting innermost feelings and moods, as mentioned before, are characteristic of many Hungarian folksongs.

Evidently, there is a connection between the lyrical song and Eliot's objective correlate, the New Critics' image-concept and the Hungarian objective-intellectual style of the twenties-thirties. Expressing innermost feelings as forms of an objective reality is common to both concepts. Weöres' way of showing a frame of mind by means of scenes from nature was not unfamiliar to them. What is different, however, is his contest to identify himself with it, which creates the conflict between the world outside and the world inside. Moreover, there is no identification with the second person singular either, as shown by the grammatical form. This second person singular, when he gets rid of all vanity and puts on a monk's habit, wishes to undress his personality. This is the point where the first person singular and the second person singular meet, that is, in a total revealing of the self. In other words, the poem is a kind of personal lyric in an impersonal form, that is, subjective lyric in an objective form. Referring to the opposition between personal and impersonal, Ákos Szilágyi (1984:690) writes as follows: " [...] a general and common human content as visualized in lyrics can never be impersonal, because being general and common doesn't necessarily make it impersonal, just not focused on the individual. Unwillingly, all the same, here the main point comes to light, the problem that it is just impersonality Weöres is about to express".

Another dimension of the theme becomes clear if we consider the structure of the frame-like composition more closely. The repetition of the lines of the first verse within the last verse is related to the context. The refrain is an answer to the desire expressed in the third verse: there is no hope for change, no hope for you to become another, your destiny is fulfilled between the two lines of the first and last verses: *csak szíved alszik el* 'only your heart goes to sleep' – you are surrounded by hopelessness from every side and in every form.

The abandoning of a world outside and the desire for another human meaning of life, expressed by the motifs of undressing, opens up a new way of interpretation: a person who seeks himself. He refuses any identification with the world outside and desires a world of deeper dimensions, a world so profound that it can only be found in the self. The search is at the same time the pursuit of this other person who, like a monk, wears the other world. The refrain, echoing the words of the first verse, doesn't show any way out. Parts of the poem *Harmadik szimfónia* 'Third Symphony' (EI I:348) come to mind:

Kereplőként űzöd körbe magad,
rab vagy, de keserved álma szabad
s igazad az álom, a röpke!

Like a rattle, you chase yourself around,
you are a slave, but the dream of your grief is free
and your truth is the dream, the fugitive!

Summing up the most essential components of the theme of the poem, they are
in my opinion as follows:

1. Abandoning a world outside.
2. A wish for a more complete world inside.
3. Searching for the self, which fruitlessly turns to impersonality.
4. There is no way out of the self.

2.1.2.2 The Poem as Part of Weöres' Lifework

The cycle *Rongyszőnyeg* 'Rag-carpet' was first published in a volume with
the title *Medusa* in 1943. It was no less than Zoltán Kodály who was the driv-
ing force of the birth of the poems included. To start with, in 1933 he set music
to *Öregek* 'Old Ones', one of the poems of Weöres' (Kenyeres 1983:37) and
after that he continually asked for new pieces. Most of these poems are found
in the cycles *Rongyszőnyeg* 'Rag-carpet' and *Magyar etüdök* 'Hungarian
Etudes'. The majority of them were written in 1941 in Budapest in a period of
exceptional creativity when poems were born in unbelievably quick succession (Várkonyi 1976:384).

The poem beginning *A hársfa mind virágzik* 'All the limetrees are in
blossom' was also written in 1941. According to Weöres, it was written in the
following way: "On some poems, consisting of merely a few lines, I have
worked for more than ten years, *Galagonya* 'The Hawthorn' may be an example of this; and there are some poems that I wrote on the spot, without any
correction, for instance *A hársfa mind virágzik* 'All the limetrees are in blossom'" (Simon 1993:275).

The *Medusa* has been treated by the critics as a book that represents
Weöres' cross-roads (Kenyeres 1974:276). It was a critique by Béla Hamvas
(1990: 213-217) in 1944 that gave rise to this opinion. Weöres' cross-roads
involved the choice between the individual lyrics of a deeply-rooted *Nyugat*
'West'-tradition and a type of lyrics that are impersonal and have no traditions
in Hungarian literature. In Hamvas' opinion the first volumes of Weöres –
Hideg van 'It is Cold', *A kő és az ember* 'The Stone and the Man', *A teremtés
dícsérete* 'The Praise of Creation' – ought not to be published at all. "On the
big roads one would go lonely, alone, without witnesses or public, unknown
and ascetic; to grow before the public is, if not impossible, much more difficult", as he wrote (Hamvas 1990:213). Hamvas resolutely rejects all kind of

individual, introverted lyrics. For him lyrics manifest an innermost existence, and the period of returning to Orpheus' true poetry, the orphism. "This poetry has no knowledge of the great poetic arsenal that has been developed since Homeros' days, that is, the metre, the rhyme, the comparing, the tropes, the structure, the sounding and the clanging, the varnish, the spectacular side-show and the magic play. In the poetry of Orpheus all depends on the super-human power of inspiration. This poetry is rather obscure than shining, rather stuttering than rhythmical, rather untamed than playful" (Hamvas 1990:217).

Hamvas' critique had a crucial effect on Weöres. At the cross-roads of the personal and the impersonal, he chooses the one which suits his personality the best: the impersonal. Still, he doesn't accept Hamvas' critique in every respect. That is also his personality. He doesn't accept and ought not to accept Hamvas' refusal of the magical language experimentation, since he would deny himself by doing so. And certainly it would be a pity being without such pieces, despite their individual character, for instance the poem with the title *Füst* 'Smoke' (EI I:81) expressing a matured philosophy of life:

Cigarettázom az árokparton.
Húsz fillér az össz-vagyonom,
de az egész föld a hamutartóm.

I smoke on the bank of the ditch.
Twenty pennies is all my riches,
but the whole world is my ashtray.

Even the poems where tropes are united by a kind of humor of unusual associations would be missed. The pieces of *Suite burlesque*, are of this type, where the sun "belches for the last time" or Nietzsche enjoys himself whooping "sej-haj-hacacáré", an expression without equivalence in English, roughly: hallo holla (EI I:94):

Régen elmúlt immáron a bronzkorszak,
kedves rózsám, a világért nem adlak.
Nem leszek én többé
a falu bolondja,
Sej-haj-hacacáré,
ahogy Nietzsche mondja.

Long ago the Bronze-age passed away,
Not for the world would I give you away, my dear rose.

I won't be
a parish-fool any more.
Sej-haj-hacacáré,
as Nietzsche puts it.

This articulated native poetry of Weöres' does not resemble anything in Hungarian poetry and scarcely even in world literature.

The subtitle of the *Rongyszőnyeg* 'Rag-carpet' *cycles* is: *dalok, epigrammák, ütempróbák, vázlatok, töredékek* 'Songs, Epigrams, Rhythm-experiments, Sketches, Fragments', which illustrates a way of writing that Imre Bata (1979:86) describes as follows: "A peculiarity for many of these pieces is that there is a reflection which moves the forming instinct, but the shape that is created by that doesn't get far". The piece 14 in the cycle, where the first verse runs back into itself, is in this way (EI I:381-382):

Rózsa, rózsa, rengeteg,
lányok, lepkék, fellegek,
lányok, lepkék, fellegek,
illanó könny, permeteg.

Roses, roses, a lot of roses,
girls, butterflies, clouds,
girls, butterflies, clouds,
evanescent tears, sprinkling.

The many *l*s in the words denoting floating and flying are associated with mortality. Opposed to this, the static idea of staying behind appears in the third verse. The identical first and last verse makes the main thought doubly sure: all things will disappear and *csak az Isten érti meg* 'only God understands' why it is so.

Piece 27 in the cycle (EI I:387) does not get particularly far when it adapts a similar structure to piece 76. There is a symmetry caused by an identical first and last verse and the basic structuring principle is the contrasting element in this case too:

Száz ponton zörget a kezem
s megakad egy kilincsen:
a Van mindig bizonytalan,
csak egy biztos: a Nincsen.

On a hundred places I rap on the door
and get stuck on a door-handle:
Being is always uncertain,
the only certainty is: Nothingness.

These strophes frame a philosophy characteristic of Weöres. A comprehensive view of hopelessness is common to all of these poems.

Many believe piece 99 (EI I:420) to be the most beautiful in the circle. Zoltán Kenyeres (1974:295; 1983:192) is one of them, and another is Béla Hamvas when writing that Weöres, in this poem, "wrote something so extraordinary that the heart of the earth began to tremble" (Hamvas 1990:214):

Őszi éjjel
izzik a galagonya
izzik a galagonya
ruhája.
Zúg a tüske,
szél szalad ide-oda,
reszket a galagonya
magába.
Hogyha a Hold rá
fátylat ereszt:
lánnyá válik,
sírni kezd.
Őszi éjjel
izzik a galagonya
izzik a galagonya
ruhája.

An autumn night
glows the hawthorn's
glows the hawthorn's
dress.
Thorns are rustling,
wind is running to and fro,
the hawthorn is trembling
all alone.
If the Moon lets its veil
fall down:
a girl she becomes
and begins to cry.

An autumn night
glows the hawthorn's
glows the hawthorn's
dress.

The similarity of this piece to piece 76 lies not only in the parallel structure, but also in the function of the structure in defining the meaning. The same frame-like composition is an expression of the same sadness and hopelessness even here. The change, merely a wish to become somebody else in piece 76, is much more than a wish in piece 99. When the hawthorn turns into a girl, we have a total metamorphosis. Nevertheless, this transformation happens only at night and the last verse repeating the first seems to declare an atmosphere of the unchanged and unchangeability itself: the hawthorn remained a hawthorn. The contrasting principle between hawthorn and girl is shown within the structure of this metamorphosis.

Similar to the poems mentioned above, the last strophe of piece 119 repeats the first (EI I:429):

Víz-torlasztó hegyfalak,
szél botlasztó bércfalak
mit bánják, ha mállanak,
mit bánják, ha porlanak.

Walls of hills that drift the water,
walls of peaks that make the wind stumble
they don't care if they crumble,
they don't care if they mould.

Contrast in this case appears between the death-neglecting rocks and the man who fears death.

There is not only a clear structural resemblance between these poems but also a likeness in the subject matter and the philosophical content. Common themes are the metaphysics of mortality and that of the possibility of Being and Nothingness in pieces 14, 27 and 119; and the metamorphosis of becoming another in piece 76 and 99. Simple forms, like these, express a philosophy of profundity and depth. In a comparison of these poems with others within the same cycle, there is reason to believe that the most powerful expression of an ontological content of human existence is reflected just in them. As repeated, the most essential content, like the circle of hermeneutics, turns back to itself. In a poem with the title *A fogak tornáca* 'The Portico of Teeth' (EI II: 9) Weöres writes the following:

Ha pokolra jutsz, legmélyére térj:
az már a menny: Mert minden körbe ér.

If you get to hell, then go to the bottom of it:
that is heaven: For all things move around.

2.1.2.3 Weöres' Philosophy of Poetics

Writing in song-form and in second person singular is a unique way to express one's personality. It can easily remain on the border between the personal and the impersonal. Because song is basically a genre for presenting deep feelings, the presence of the writer is still explicit, though he might have vanished long ago. This is possibly one form of the Empsonian ambiguity.

"I would nearly say, with a little exaggeration maybe, that personality is harmful, that it makes you isolated and narrow. The only way to identify myself with all voices, all kinds of cultures is to get rid of personality. Or to expand it to such a degree that it hardly exists" (Simon 1993:270). This statement of Weöres' is cited from an interview he gave to István Simon in 1976. In another interview with Endre Szekér (1993:322) in 1977 he declares as follows: "I don't want to sweep out personality from poetry, but for my part I don't feel it has any particular importance. There is so much more of universality, of collectivism." He spoke out in this manner from the very beginning of his break-through in Hungarian literature to the end of his career. Eliminating personality manifests itself in various ways in Weöres' poetical work. One unique method he uses for expressing a specific philosophy is speaking in second person singular.

The lyrical genre is essentially the presentation of innermost feelings and moods of the mind in a subjective, open way. Weöres, however, hides himself in his poems and, objectively, cannot be found. He leaves his feelings and moods within the words in order to release himself from them. "The creating of this intellectual freedom in the movement of the intellect, instead of a closed, lyrical Self, was a program for the philosophy of poetics", as Kenyeres (1974:253) puts it.

What are the basic sources of a philosophy of poetry like this? There are certainly many. In the case of the poem starting with the words *A hársfa mind virágzik* 'All the limetrees are in blossom', it could be early experiences in younger days, based on the fact that it was written as early as 1941. Weöres repeatedly declared that the first experiences and impressions of his childhood and youth determined his whole career as a writer. His critics are of the same opinion. There is no development in his philosophy of poetry and, since he was an infant prodigy, no development in form either. There are only variations in the way of expressing them. "I was terribly interested in things unknown and infinite when I was young. For this reason I read the Tao-te Ching and the Vedas. Actually, I am in its power indeed and my poems are woven into it over and over again" (Bertha 1993:151). He said this in 1970, and in 1978 he made the following statement: "The belief I had twenty-five years ago, which was formed by Hindu and Chinese philosophies in the first place, hasn't essentially changed much after all" (Kamocsay 1993:365).

After receiving the Baumgarten prize, which was his first literary prize, he left for the Far East (India and China) and stayed there from 1936 to 1937. The following two years he worked on a translation of the Epic of Gilgamesh, the Sumerian-Babylonian ancient epos, at the request of Nándor Várkonyi, to be used in his work about old civilizations *Sziriát oszlopai* 'The Pillars of Seiris'. Weöres' following works, the *Gilgames* 'Gilgamesh' written in 1937, the *Istar pokoljárása* 'The Wanderings of Ishtar in Hell' and the *Theomachia*, both written in 1938, can all be traced back to these translating experiences. Very strong influences, from primarily Chinese and Hindu philosophies, may definitively be observed within the immanent philosophy of his poetry.

Summing up the most significant components of the topic, I defined four points earlier. These components of theme can also form the basis of the primary structuring principle of contrast. In this principle, the concept of renouncing the world is opposed to the desire for a more substantial, meaningful life. The concept of searching an individual self is also in contradiction with the concept of resignation about not finding the way out of the real self.

There is, however, a balance, a sort of harmony between the positive poles of a world outside and the negative poles of an individual world inside. The diverging motifs run parallel to one another, then converge in the refrain. This unchanged repetition of the first verse comprises an unconditional approval of contradictions as unalterable factors. Thus, there is no struggle between the diverging forces of negative and positive poles. They are balanced from the very beginning. It is much like the principle of *yin and yang, tai-chi* in the philosophy of the Chinese, where *yang* stands for the positive and *yin* for the negative power (Glasenapp 1973:123). Neither the positive nor the negative is evil by nature. Both are equally important, without the intent of subduing each other, but instead with the aim of creating a unity by supplementing each other. The tropes of nature, a world outside, in piece 76 is not on the whole negative, and likewise the tropes of a world inside, describing a wish for contemplation, are not negative either. Like the dynamic forces of *yin and yang* shaping each other all the time, the motifs within the structure influence one another, too. Contradictory, though still fundamentally in mutual need of each other, they create a perfect harmony in the poem.

The self talking in second person singular expresses impersonality. The concept of getting rid of one's own personality is clearly reflected in the motif of undressing vanity in order to wear a monk's habit. What is the origin of the grammatical second person?

Tat twam asi 'this is you' – these Sanskrit words reflect the most fundamental thought of the *Upanishads*: even the smallest living creature comprehends the whole universe and is a manifestation of it; God and the individual soul are substantially identical (Glasenapp 1943:115). The difference between two individuals, the grammatical 'you' and 'me', disappears in this union – 'a spider has spun your pleasure', that is, 'my pleasure' –, the *atman*, the divine substance deeply hidden in all human, dissolves in the universe to become identical with the *brahman*, the absolute spirit. According to Hinduism, life is suffering, and even the beautiful is only painfully beautiful – "The girls open themselves to you" – that's the reason why man strives to abandon suffering in order to unite the *brahman* in a nirvana by means of a total annihilation of the individual self. An endless renewal of the *karmas* is not wanted because every rebirth brings repeated sufferings. For this reason he wishes in some way – "to wear a monk's habit" – to throw off all the desires of both body and soul that could bind him to the ground in a next life.

"A spider has spun your pleasure" – reads the last line of the second verse. One may ask the question: Why a spider? Naturally, one explanation is the end-rhymes in the two lines: *ládikók – pók*. Yet after thoroughly studying the philosophy of the Brahman, and knowing how well-aquainted Weöres was with Hindu philosophy, we can see a certain parallel between this philosophy and this poem of Weöres. "Entsprechend der Theorie, daß jedes Element im Menschen in einem Element des Kosmos seine Entsprechung hat, sah man nun im Atman das letzte Prinzip des Alles. Weil aus diesem alles andere hervorgegangen ist, ist der Atman ein Synonym des Brahma. Er ist die höchste Wirklichkeit aus der alle Lebensfaktoren, alle Welten, alle Wesen, alle Götter hervorgehen, wie Funken aus einem Feuer oder wie der Faden aus einer Spinne". (Glasenapp 1943:115-116). These words originating from the *Brihadaranyakaupanishad* show the context once more in a new light. Is there a God in the spider's web? A God, sought for in the second verse, a God, who can't be found in the third, yet is present, albeit hiding himself, already in the second verse? Within this formal structure of concealed meaning, new contrasts become apparent. There is no need to search for God, when he is present all the time and is not difficult to locate either. His presence is expressed by a short, laconical word that sets the first two and the last two verses apart. He is, then, like the central moving power of everything, in the middle.

2.2 Metamorphosis

(1)   Égen madárhiány eped,
(2)   a nincs-világot sokszorozza.
(3)   Kitárul arcod utcahossza
(4)   a népes elmén átvezet

(5)   átszel minden játszóteret
(6)   végül jelekből kibogozva
(7)   röpíti láb alatt a puszta
(8)   s a végtelenség rámered

(9)   vagy ő nyilall határtalanba
(10) mi kéz nélkül zsong mint a lant
(11) s a kéznek elveszett a lantja –

(12) nincs puszta itt, nincs fönt s alant
(13) hajlék se zár védett világot
(14) de az sincs többé aki fázott.

(1)   Missing birds languish in the sky,
(2)   multiplying the non-existing world.
(3)   The street-length of your face opens out
(4)   and leads through a crowded mind

(5)   it cuts across every playground
(6)   finally figuring out the signs
(7)   the desert lets it fly under its feet
(8)   and infinity stares upon it

(9)   or else he shoots away to the boundless
(10) that handless hums like the lute
(11) yet the lute of the hands is missing –

(12) there is no desert here, no above and no below,
(13) no roof closes in a sheltered world
(14) but not even he exists any more who felt cold.

(*A benső végtelen. Várkonyi Nándornak*; 'The Infinite Inside. To
Nándor Várkonyi'. In: *Átváltozások. 40 szonett* 'Metamorphoses.
40 Sonnets'. In: EI II:340)

2.2.1 The Text

2.2.1.1 The Structure and Shape of the Writing

The poem *A benső végtelen* 'The Infinite Inside' has a regular form, which is in the classical mode of the sonnet. The poem is divided into two parts, the octet, which consists of the first two stanzas, four lines each; and the sestet, containing the last two stanzas of three lines each. All lines are approximately the same length. Only two lines deviate somewhat: the second and the fourth lines of the sestet. The construction of the syntagms is also regular. Each line forms a syntagm, without any regular punctuation. Punctuation marks are regularly used in five cases (lines 1, 2, 11, 12, 14), as compared to seven cases where they are missing (lines 3, 4, 5, 8, 9, 10, 13). The lines, as a rule, do not make complete sentences. Most of the sentences run on to the following lines and even strophes. On account of this, enjambement between the lines and the strophes are frequent. There is only one exception to this consistency in construction: the unity of the first two lines, which together build a sentence. The use of capitals and small letters is in accordance with this pattern. Due to the fact that all the sentences are also some kind of clause, every line begins with small letters, with the only exceptions being in the first sentence and the next monumental sentence beginning in the third line, which both have capitals as initial letters.

2.2.1.2 The Represented Elements of Reality

Unusual associations appearing at right angles to represented reality obviously make an interpretation of the poem difficult. The represented elements of reality appear in the literal sense of the word, when dealing with them separately, but they become abstract, and almost inconceivable, in combination with each other. Thus, a literal interpretation, which seems unmistakably correct at first sight, turns problematical. Behind all concrete substance floats something inexpressible, something unspeakable, perhaps for the simple reason that it is just the unspeakable which is the real essence of the poem. Meaning is realized not only within minor semantical units, but also within the complicated structure that these units build. There are several ways to arrange them. Hence, there are several ways to interpret them.

As the result of its composition, the poem *A benső végtelen* 'The Infinite Inside' takes us from the heavenly heights of the first verse to the *puszta*, the 'desert', of the last. The real-life images, which can be found between these two extreme points and are expressed by the words *utcahossz* 'street-length' and *játszótér* 'playground', seem to portray a town. The syntagm *népes elme* 'crowded mind', can also easily refer to a city. To interpret *jelek* 'signs' as presumptive traffic-symbols in an image of a city may appear to be a remote association. Nevertheless, it might also be a correct one. The concrete pictures of *láb* 'feet' [lit. 'foot] and *puszta* 'desert' meet an inconceivable *végtelen* 'infinity', which is linked by its similarity to the undefinable concept of *határtalan* 'boundless' in the next verse.

The words *kéz-* 'hand-' and *lant* 'lute', looked at as concrete things, might be understood literally. Here, however, emerges a problem of great importance. Neither the hands nor the lute exist. Hands hum without hands and the lute is missing. The same concept of non-existence continues in the last verse, where there is no shelter and not even he, who was looking for it, exists.

Since the title, as a rule, indicates the subject matter, it is of fundamental importance in an analysis of the represented elements of reality. The idea of infinity in the title returns in the last line of the octet: *végtelenség* 'infinity' and in the first line of the sestet: *határtalan* 'boundless'. As a result, there is a triple recurrence of related concepts. Because of this high frequency of the idea, compared with other concepts in the poem, one may conclude that the idea has an exceedingly significant function.

The subtitle is a dedication to Nándor Várkonyi, literary historian and former director of the University Library of Pécs. Because of a presumed correspondence to the grammatical person of the poem which is expressed by the personal pronoun *ő* 'he', this subtitle becomes of primary importance. While the title denotes the wide concept of infinity and for that reason might be conceived as relatively ambiguous, the subtitle is much more definite, naming a real person by a real name.

A similar dichotomy can be observed when considering the poem in its totality. The eight lines of the octet, while they uninterruptedly come closer and closer to the *végtelenség* 'infinity' of the last line, pass through the *népes elme* 'crowded mind', that is, the spiritual life of this unnamed protagonist. In the first line of the sestet, this former logical person, never named by name, is replaced by a grammatical person conveyed by the personal pronoun *ő* 'he': that is, a person, who in his own *határtalan* 'boundless', meets the *végtelenség* 'infinity' of the octet's self. As a result there is a contrast between the logical and the grammatical persons, including the opposition of the first and second person singular.

Another opposition may be found between the concepts of above and below. The bird in the first line, or rather the absence of it, denotes height and is a concept which belongs to an upper sphere, while the shelter, or rather the absence of it, in the last verse, is an expression of an earthly reality. The linear opposition of *fönt s alant* 'above and below' repeats the same contrast.

A third contrast is noticeable on a logical level, including the contradiction of an existing and a non-existing world, and we can find it in the borderland between the octet and the sestet. The self, unnamed in the octet, meets the third person singular in the imaginary sphere of the sestet, expressed by the synonyms *végtelenség* 'infinity' and *határtalan* 'boundless'. These contrasting qualities mentioned above are illustrated in figure 5. Opposition has a decisive

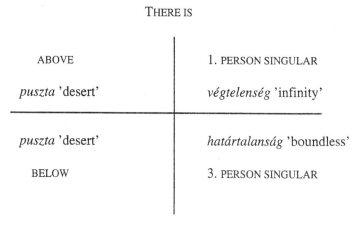

THERE IS

ABOVE	1. PERSON SINGULAR
puszta 'desert'	*végtelenség* 'infinity'
puszta 'desert'	*határtalanság* 'boundless'
BELOW	3. PERSON SINGULAR

Figure 5   THERE IS NOT

influence on structure. It is the principle of contrast, in my opinion, that organizes the text into a complex whole.

The title *A benső végtelen* 'The Infinite Inside' encompasses all the essential elements of form and content that define the style in general. The synonymous *végtelen* 'infinite', *végtelenség* 'infinity' and *határtalan* 'boundless' which occurs three times, is the most common idea in the poem. These terms' central placement in the structure – partly in the title, and partly in the borderland between the octet and the sestet, that is, in the middle of the poem – strengthens the importance of the idea. *Benső* 'inside' as an attribute of *végtelen* 'infinite', although it occurs only in the title, attaches itself to the concept of infinity in a logical sense, looking at the poem as a whole. That is why I consider the title to have a focal quality and a capacity to integrate the represented elements of reality. As both the logical person and the grammatical person are referred to within the title and the subtitle, even infinity exists in a mutual relationship: the first person and the third person singular are united in this joint infinity.

2.2.1.3 The Rhetorical-Stylistic Structure

Of the two sentences building the poem, the second one may be understood as a periodic sentence in its traditional form. Its consecutive clauses, while increasing tension and expectation, unceasingly bring us closer to the decisive infinity in the last line.

Certain words, because of their repetition, require special observation. Content becomes, accumulated in these words, like a surplus of energy. The following words function in this way: *végtelen* 'infinite' (title, line 8), *világ* 'world' (lines 1, 13), *puszta* 'desert' (lines 7 and 12), *kéz* 'hand-', 'hands' (lines 10 and 11), *lant* 'lute' (lines 10 and 11), *nincs* 'non-existing; there is no' [lit. 'there is not'], (line 2 and twice in line 12). The word *nincs* 'non-existing; there is no' is consequently the only phrase that occurs three times and, together with the root-variated form *sincs* [lit.] 'not even he exists' in the last line, it appears four times in the poem. In fact, these negative existence verbs are the most frequently used ones. This circumstance, of course, shows their primary importance. Repetition, as a text-level trope, functions as a means for focusing meaning on adequate keywords.

The only *hapax legomenon*s of the poem occur in the first and the second lines, *madárhiány* 'missing birds' and *nincs-világ* 'non-existing world' are, in a grammatical sense, realizations of the concept of concentration. Their position in the first two lines is characteristic. These lines build one of the two sentences of the poem, the first and shorter one. The concentration in this case is realized within the structure of the words, in contradiction to the periodic sentence that follows this first meaning. There, the concentration involves a repetition of certain keywords, in order to focus meaning on them, and deals with the text as a global category. On the basis of these two contrasts, a further proof of the appearance of a contrasting structuring principle can be established.

The periodic sentence apparently has a rather complex structure. The zeugma in the octet is actually a protozeugma, because the words *arcod utcahossza* 'the street-length of your face' relates both to the first short sentence and the second comprehensive periodic sentence.

There is obviously a certain tension between the different levels of the outside world in the two last lines of the first verse. *Népes elme* 'crowded mind' is not an idiom in daily use. *Népes utca* 'crowded street' is more standard. This compound of the *népes elme* 'crowded mind' is also an enallage, and the *metalepsis arcod utcahossza* 'the street-length of your face', probably based on causal relationships, taken together build a complex trope.

The syntagms within the period are not only connected to each other by the structure of the zeugma, but also by personification. All sub-clauses are related to *arcod utcahossza* 'the street-length of your face'. The word *arcod* 'your face' in the syntagm, as a part of a larger concept, recalls the whole, that is, the third person singular expressed by the personal pronoun *ő* 'he' in the third verse. As a result the trope synecdoche can be recognized.

The tropes, like images in a vision or a revelation, bring us closer, by their increasing intensity, to the *végtelenség* 'infinity' in the last line of the octet. But the images break off in the first line of the sestet, indicating that something new begins here: the *végtelenség* 'infinity' of the first person singular transforms itself into the *határtalan* 'boundless' of the third person singular. After this reversal, the tropes become simpler and clearer. Instead of the complex tropes of the octet, we will find a considerably less complicated simile in the second line of the sestet: *zsong, mint a lant* 'hums like the lute'. Here, the structuring principle of contrast appears as an opposition between the tropes of greater complexity in the octet, and the simpler and thus more comprehensible tropes in the sestet.

The last verse of the sestet may be regarded as a synthesis, which follows the thesis of the octet and the antithesis of the first verse of the sestet. Clauses in a parallel grammatical constuction, parallelism, in other words, can be noticed in the first line of the sestet together with an anafora in the repetition of the word *nincs* 'there is no' as the first words of the syntagms. Together with the word *sincs* [lit. 'not even he exists'] in the last line, these negative existence verbs, as the most frequent verbs in the poem, have a fundamental importance in focusing on the main idea.

There is something inconceivable, unexplainable about this piece of poetry. This sublimity arises from the images expressed as parts of a reality and the difficult conceptual message suggested by them. One may get the impression that the concrete images of reality, as a matter of course, were on a conceptual level from the very beginning, as if there was no contrast between them at all. The mind, however, unceasingly searches for a definite line that separates the real world from a non-real one, all the while oscillating between the two. In this way a piece of poetry becomes a "total metaphor", as Miklós Szentkuthy (1985:143) put it.

2.2.1.4 The Metrical Structure

Indisputably, the sonnet-form is one of the most constrained metrical structures. The number of the lines, the syllables, the arranging of the rhymes, and the rhythm are all factors which define a sonnet. The original pattern of the lines, a Hungarian variant of the Italian *endecasillabo*, is composed of a iambic period of a six foot broken and a five foot iambic line. The number of the lines is always fourteen and the rhymes are arranged regularly, although with several different possible forms.

In *A benső végtelen* 'The Infinite Inside' Weöres follows in Petrarch's footsteps, in terms of the metrical form of the poem. As opposed to the general rhyme-setting in Petrachean sonnets following the pattern *a b b a, a b b a, c d c, d c d*, this sequence is somewhat altered in the sonnet of Weöres, where the rhymes are arranged in the following way: *a b b a, a b b a, b c b, c d d*. A definite distance between the octet and the sestet, created by the different rhymes, is characteristic of Petrarchean sonnets. This distinction cannot be found in the sonnet by Weöres, for the rhymes of the two middle lines in the two strophes of the octet carry over as the rhymes of the first and third lines of the sestet.

The number of syllables in the lines correspond to the rhyme scheme which can be seen as follows: *8 9 9 8, 8 9 9 8, 9 8 9, 8 9 9*. The octet and the sestet become parallel to each other, that is, a rhyme in the pattern marked *a* always occurs in an 8-syllable line, and a rhyme marked *b* always occurs in a 9-syllable line. There is, however, an exception to this rule: the two 9-syllable last lines, which together build a new pair of rhymes.

The dominant metrical foot is the iamb. The stop after the fifth syllable demonstrates the *penthemimeres caesura*:

$$- - \mid \cup - \mid \cup \parallel - \mid \cup \, \overline{\cup}$$
Égen madárhiány eped

$$\cup - \mid \cup - \mid \cup \parallel - \mid \cup - \mid \overline{\cup}$$
a nincs-világot sokszorozza.

$$\cup - \mid \cup - \mid \cup \parallel - \mid \cup - \mid \overline{\cup}$$
Kitárul arcod utcahossza

$$\cup - \mid \cup - \mid - \parallel - \mid \cup \, \overline{\cup}$$
a népes elmén átvezet.

$$- - \mid - - \mid - \parallel - \cup \mid \overline{\cup}$$
átszel minden játszóteret

$$- - \mid \cup - \mid - \parallel \cup \parallel \cup - \mid \overline{\cup}$$
végül jelekből kibogozva

$$\cup - \mid \cup - \mid \cup \parallel - \mid \cup - \mid \overline{\cup}$$
röpíti láb alatt a puszta

$$\cup - \mid \cup - \mid - \parallel - \mid \cup \, \overline{\cup}$$
s a végtelenség rámered

$$- - \mid \cup - \mid \cup \parallel - \mid \cup - \mid \overline{\cup}$$
vagy ő nyilall határtalanba

∪ – | – – | – ‖ – | ∪ –
mi kéz nélkül zsong mint a lant

∪ _ | ∪ – | ∪ ‖ – | ∪ – | ∪̄
s a kéznek elveszett a lantja

– – | ∪ – | – ‖ – | ∪ –
nincs puszta itt nincs fönt s alant

– – | ∪ – | – ‖ – | ∪ – | ∪̄
hajlék se zár védett világot

∪ – | – – | – ‖ ∪ | ∪ – | –
de az sincs többé aki fázott.

When studying this figure, one is likely to observe that the iambs are more regular in the octet than in the sestet. Perhaps as a result of the numerous slow spondées and trochées, we may feel that the iambs break off in the sestet. Contrast, as the primary structuring principle, then asserts itself even in the metrical variation of the octet and the sestet.

There is a more moderate contrast between the octet and the sestet regarding the number of syllables and the rhymes. A certain similarity, shown by an equal number of syllables and identical rhymes in the middle lines of the octet and the first and the third lines of the sestet, has been pointed out earlier. Contrast may only be valued relatively in the case of words that rhyme with each other. The words *puszta* 'desert' and *határtalanba* 'to the boundless' are to be found on the border-line of existence and non-existence. These rhyme-words are emphasized even more by *lantja* 'the lute' [lit. 'his lute'], an object which is contextually both real and unreal. The word *lant* 'lute' at the end of the the second line of the first tercet also rhymes with *alant* 'below' at the end of the first line of the second tercet, and creates an association to the concept of non-existence.

As a synthesis usually does, the concordant rhymes at the end of the two last lines give a summing-up of the poem. The last words of these two last lines rhyme with no other words in the poem except each other. The word *világot* 'world' can be related to both an existing and a non-existing world; and the rhyme-word *fázott* 'who felt cold' [lit. 'he felt cold'] also has this quality, all the more so because the logical person moves absolutely on the ridge between *végtelenség* 'infinity' and *határtalan* 'boundless'.

To sum up, the metrical structure of the sonnet *A benső végtelen* 'The Infinite Inside' is, in accordance with that of the traditional sonnet, a well-ordered form. Weöres accomodates himself to the severe laws of the sonnet-form in a natural way, yet re-shapes them in order to serve his own purposes. The only way, namely, to get through to the infinity inside is while using the most constrained metrical form of poetry.

2.2.1.5 Grammatical Structure

In order to investigate the poem as a whole, the correlation of the title and the poem itself must be examined. By what means does the infinite inside manifest itself? What is of greatest importance is the manifold compound sentence that starts in the third line and actually makes up the poem. The continuous coordinating relation of the clauses and the elimination of punctuation-marks indicates the idea of an endless infinity. Without the strict laws of the sonnet these coordinated clauses would possibly roll along in an unceasing process. Not even the last clause disrupts the structure composed by the coordinated clauses: its' relation to the other clauses is also coordinating. Concerning the lexical elements, a repetition of the word *végtelen* 'infinite' of the title can be observed as the last word of the octet. The fact that this second *végtelenség* 'infinity' may be found between octet and sestet, that is, in the middle of the poem, is crucial. It is an attribute of an infinity one can only meet in the centre, in the core deepest inside, to which every way leads.

The infinity inside is revealed from a bird's-eye view, as the motif of the first sentence suggests. Taking into account the proper role of the title, which is an indication of the theme, the entire poem is an elucidation of the title, and our attention continuously turns back to it. As a result, different elements of the structure interact. The interaction of the title and the first sentence appears as a close semantical relation of two nouns. The concept of *végtelen* 'infinite' is linked to *világ* 'world', which fundamentally is *nincs-világ* a 'non-existing world', and for this reason, due to the conceptual correlation between the words, even *A benső végtelen* 'The Infinite Inside' becomes unlikely and inconceivable. The last word of this first sentence *sokszorozza* 'multiplies' at the same time relates to the periodic sentence that follows: its coordinating clauses multiply the same *nincs-világ* 'non-existing world' with its images.

Like the second sentence, the first sentence is also a compound one. Its clauses, on the other hand, have a more disputable relation to each other than the clauses of the periodic sentence have. Because of a missing conjunction, the expounding of any reliable meaning becomes difficult. The most probable context between the two clauses would be a coordinate relation of copulative sentences with an implicit use of the conjunction *és* 'and'. But one may also see the clauses in a relation of resultative sentences to each other, if one substitutes the conjunctions, *ezért* 'therefore', and *tehát* 'then'. Moreover, there is a possible case of explanatory sentences when using the conjunction *hiszen* 'but, surely, well'. This coordinate pattern of a compound sentence would be analogous, too, and for that reason the most conceivable one, even in the case of the subsequent coordinate relation of the clauses. We may find, however, other possibilities of replacing a missing conjunction. When we look at the first clause as a head clause and the second one as a subordinate clause, the connection between the clauses can be described as a subordinate relation of these two clauses. The conjunction *amint* 'as, while, when', for example, gives a clause of time; the conjunction *mivel* 'because, since, as, for' gives a clause of cause; the conjunction *hogy* 'so that, in order that', gives a clause of purpose; and the conjunction *mely* 'which, that' gives an attributive or relative clause.

The second sentence of the poem is, then, a periodic sentence. If one takes into account the different periodic sentences, it is the romantic type which looks most similar in structure to the periodic sentence of this poem. Within the romantic periodic sentence the logical chain is created by consecutive coordinated clauses, in contradiction to the classical period, where the last clause functions as the main clause for every prior subordinated clause. The structure of the period in Weöres' poem can be diagrammed then as follows:

(A)	Kitárul arcod utcahossza
(A1)	a népes elmén átvezet
(A2)	átszel minden játszóteret
(A3.1)	végül jelekből kibogozva
(A3)	röpíti láb alatt a puszta
(A4)	s a végtelenség rámered
(B)	vagy ő nyilall határtalanba
(B1)	mi kéz nélkül zsong mint a lant
(B2)	s a kéznek elveszett a lantja –
(C) (D)	nincs puszta itt, nincs fönt s alant,
(E)	hajlék se zár védett világot
(F) (F1)	de az sincs többé aki fázott.

(A)	The street-length of your face opens out
(A1)	and leads through a crowded mind

53

(A2)	it cuts across every playground
(A3.1)	finally figuring out the signs
(A3)	the desert lets it fly under its feet
(A4)	and infinity stares upon it

(B)	or else he shoots away to the boundless
(B1)	that handless hums like the lute
(B2)	yet the lute of the hands is missing –

(C) (D)	there is no desert here, no above and no below
(E)	no roof closes in a sheltered world
(F) (F1)	but not even he exists any more who felt cold.

The grammatical structure of this period is illustrated in figure 6. The two clauses of (A) and (B) in the compound sentence are connected as disjunctive sentences; the clauses (B), (C), (D) and (E) are copulative sentences; and the sentences (E) and (F) are adversative. There are mostly coordinate relations between the main clauses. These coordinations are all copulative sentences with three subordinating relations: A3 – A3.1: clause of manner; B – B1: subject clause, F – F1: subject clause (in reference only to the Hungarian version).

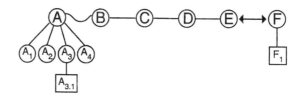

Figure 6

Within the semantical units, the structure described above is linked by the following keywords: *arcod* 'your face' (A), *ő* 'he' (B), *puszta* 'desert' (C), *fönt s alant* 'above and below' (D), *hajlék* 'roof' (E), *az, aki fázott* '[he] who felt cold' (F) (F1). These units are arranged symmetrically: every unit, with an exception of the first and the last sentences, is a copulative sentence in a coordinate relation. The first and the last units – (A) and (F) – are somewhat special, as they are connected to the adjoining clauses in a disjunctive and an adversative relation. Such an arch of a sentence is characteristic of the periodic sentence, where the *protazis*, here the correlation of the parts (A) and (B), as an opening part draws attention to the subject matter; a neutral part, here the units (B), (C), (D) and (E) arouses anticipation; and the *apodosis*, the final expounding part, here the unit (F), creates the synthesis.

As we have now examined the syntactical levels, let us continue with an analysis of the lexical units. From a global structural context it may be instructive to begin with an analysis of the pronouns. When looking at the personal pronouns, one can detect with ease that the first person singular is missing. In other words, it is present only indirectly, that is, not as a grammatical form of an indicated subject, but as a logical form of it. The syntagm *népes elme* 'crowded mind' relates to this logical subject, while at the same time it connects to the title. There is only one personal pronoun which denotes a grammatical subject: the third person singular *ő* 'he' in the first line of the sestet. The pronoun *ő* 'he' refers to *arcod* 'your face' in the third line of the octet, which in turn is related to the subtitle. The personal pronouns of the first, second and third verse, both those of the indicated and the unindicated ones, are followed by two different categories of pronouns in the last line of the fourth verse: *az* 'he', which is a demonstrative pronoun and *aki* 'who', a relative pronoun. Consequently, a certain and determinate proximity of the personal pronouns are succeeded by the more indefinite and indeterminate line of two pronouns that do not exclusively refer to given persons. As a result, one may experience how the named moves smoothly into the nameless, and the close to the remote, the endless and the timeless. The relative pronoun *aki* 'who', which is the last pronoun of the poem, reflects the total vagueness of an unlimited vastness. Whoever the person who felt cold might be depends entirely on who the reader might be. Her exposition may be considerably faciliated by making use of a structural approach. In such an approach one can feel that the title, the subtitle and the last line are harmoniously united, as they would then embrace the poem, like a frame. The personal pronouns of an individual existence fade away and diffuse to a conceptual impersonality, in order to be summed up in *A benső végtelen* 'The Infinite Inside' of the title.

The method of placing impersonality within words can be looked at using other lexical means, too. This can be seen in the *végtelen* 'infinite' composed by the noun *vég* 'end' and the suffix *-telen* '[lit.: 'without'], and the analogous structure of *határtalan* 'boundness' constructed of the noun *határ* 'boundary' and the suffix *-talan*. This can be seen even in the unique locution *madárhiány* 'missing birds' and also the unusual syntagm *nincs-világ* 'nonexisting world' which arises from an extremely uncommon combination of a negative existence-verb and a noun. And this can be seen in the postposition *nélkül* 'without' in the compound of *kéz nélkül* 'handless', in which meaning becomes even more accentuated by a related semantical content of the verb *elveszett* 'is missing' [lit. 'has been lost'] in the next line. This can also be seen in the negative existence-verbs in the last verse: *nincs* 'there is no' and *sincs* 'not even' and the modifying word: *se* 'no' [lit. 'not even'] in the middle line of the last verse.

The significant contextual role that rhymes have on the acoustic level has been mentioned before. The fact that the 'The Infinite Inside' is loaded with tones is not only indicated by the noun *lant* 'lute' which refers to a concrete object but the onomatopoetic verb *zsong* 'hums' too. If one analyzes the sound-spectrum, a frequent use of the consonant *l* becomes apparent. It occurs in such essential words as *végtelenség* 'infinity', *határtalan* 'boundless' and *világ* 'world'. Nouns as *elme* 'mind', *jelek* 'signs', *láb* 'feet' [lit.: 'foot'], *lant* 'lute', *hajlék* 'roof'; verbs as *átszel* 'cuts across', *nyilall* 'shoots away'; the postposition *nélkül* 'without'; the adverb of time *végül* 'finally' and the adverb of place *alant* 'below' all belong to this group. This large-scale presence of a sound may reinforce some level of significance. This musical aspect, in my opinion, emerging through the murmurous sound of a lute, is the most significant.

2.2.2 The World of the Text

2.2.2.1 The Theme

"Il y a donc deux interprétations de l'interprétation, de la structure, du signe et du jeu. L'une cherche à déchiffrer, rêve de déchiffrer une vérité ou une origine échappant au jeu et à l'ordre du signe, et vit comme un exil la nécessité de l'interprétation. L'autre, qui n'est plus tournée vers l'origine, affirme le jeu et tente de passer au-delà de l'homme et de l'humanisme, le nom de l'homme étant le nom de cet être qui, à travers l'histoire de la métaphysique ou de l'onto-théologie, c'est-à-dire du tout de son histoire, a rêvé la présence pleine, le fondement raussant, l'origine et la fin du jeu" (Derrida 1967:427). We presumably all know which one of these two concepts on interpretation Derrida considered to have a fundamental importance. In *Of Grammatology*, one of his major works, he declares the primary role of writing over speaking. Within every spoken language an aboriginal, primary, non-spoken language is hidden: the idea of writing, as he puts it. It doesn't reflect reality as human speech does, in a subjective way, but it comprises the ancient structure of the world which cannot be grasped by languages constructed by human intellect. Derrida denies an organizing activity of the human mind as a central ruling power, and for this reason he replaces this center with the signifier of writing. As a consequence, language takes the author's place, with its substantially open structure in which elements exist equally both within and without a given structure. The arrangment of the elements in a text comes about in the course of the activity of play, when structure functions as possibility and polysemy becomes the essence of language (Bókay 1997:361).

The concept of *différance* is another important characteristic of Derrida's philosophy of language. Unlike Saussure, however, who looks upon *différance* as the basis of identity between two things, for Derrida it always implies the lack of something. Both implications of the French *différer* are comprised in his idea of *différance*, partly denoting the concept of divergence, partly the concept of delaying, of postponement. "Where Derrida breaks new ground, and where the science of grammatology takes its cue, is in the extent to which 'differ' shades into 'defer'. This involves the idea that meaning is always deferred, perhaps to the point of an endless supplementarity, by the play of signification" (Norris 1982:32).

Despite all its impressive abstractness, Derrida and theories of deconstruction may contribute to explaining the "signs" of Weöres' poem. As Bókay also puts it, the deconstruction doesn't intend to break up and disorganize the structure of the text, but to show the text from its very onset, as a matter of course, opened out, and that is why openness and instability are its essential characteristics (Bókay 1997:388).

Instability, however, is not another term for disorganization. By no means can disorganization be said to describe Weöres' poetry. Although deconstruction can reveal disorganization, the interpretation process itself can be exceptionally helpful. Above all, by taking its starting point from the poem itself, guided by the specific nature of the poem, deconstruction thus adopts an appropriate interpretive method. This method is certainly not one for interpreters who work exiled away in a constant search for an explanation somewhere outside the text itself. The only proper means is to engage in play with the author and just maybe, in fascination from the magic spell of playing, the interpreter will at last begin to understand the unchanging evidential facts of human existence. Roland Barthes also underlines the crucial importance of play when he writes as follows: "le texte lui-même *joue* [...] et le lecteur joue, lui, deux fois: il *joue au* Texte [...], il cherche une pratique qui le re-produise; mais pour que cette pratique ne se réduise pas à une *mimésis* passive [...], il *joue le* Texte..." (Barthes 1971:3:231).

The process of becoming conversant with a text is both facilitated and hampered by the text's structural openness. This openness makes entrance into a given text possible from every point. At this point, a question may be raised, namely, does interpretation thus become less difficult? Difficulty, as I see it, lies in the realm of interplay, and that is why it is necessary to find a common denominator to link the work and the interpreter. As a matter of course, it might not unconditionally be found in the work itself. The literal work demonstrates, just because of its structural openness, a way towards the unlimited possibilities of intertextuality.

"Meaning appears not in the relation between a signifier and a signified, but in an independent system of signifiers that is unconsciously kept alive and in motion by the users of the signs" (Bókay 1997:364). If meaning is merely carried by signifiers, namely the words, then there is no connection between the signified, that is, the meaning, and the signifier which places this meaning into words, and that is why *différance* between them emerges. This *différance* is the user's subjective and imaginary sphere which hopes to fill in this gap with meaning. Meaning constructed in this way, however, is deceptive. This is a result of the dynamic and therefore unsteady arrangement of the signifiers within a structure which by its nature is from the very beginning deconstructed. Creating a definition of a stable, unambiguous meaning becomes an unsolvable task. Ambiguity comes to be an essential quality of the text.

If there is no correlation between the signifier, that is, the text, and the signified, that is, the content, then what fills the void of this interval? If the signifier, the text, carries the meaning and its surplus, by what means can we then arrive at an interpretation? This void, I think, is filled in and completed by the act of play. Weöres, the creator of the text, plays when he places the infinity-play within the borders of a well-defined sonnet form and the interpreter plays, too, when she searches in her imagination for a meaning which relates to different possibilities of understanding. After piecing together the signs, she at last comes to a meaning which is in tune with her own personality.

There is no center in the poem *A benső végtelen* 'The Infinite Inside'. The words *infinity* and *boundless* on the border line between the octet and the sestet might be considered a graphic center which is also the theme. The theme, as a matter of course, points beyond itself, not constructing but deconstructing a meaning. Even the existence-verbs deny themselves. All things come to an end in the last verse. The word, the signifier, abolishes itself. It contests its own formal reality and shows the way to the timeless, endless infinity that lies beyond the physical world which, by its nature, is not a formal entity but an abstract idea. Nevertheless, infinity denies itself too, as there is no infinity, either.

The subject in infinity appears in an abstract form, only partially adhering to the words. Thus, the reading of the concrete words is disrupted by a perception of a basic structure, and an independent meaning may come to light, although hidden in the unconscious. This other meaning, concealed on the boundary of existence and non-existence, could also be described as an allegory. There is, however, a difference between allegory in its conventional meaning and this other meaning, as seen in Weöres' poem. In allegory, traditionally, an explicit idea is expressed, principally unaffected by the interpretation of the reader. This idea is at the same time strongly determined by the purposes of the author. Using this concept, the meaning in Weöres' poem is equally formed by both the author's and the reader's intentions.

"... le Texte est toujours *paradoxal*' as Roland Barthes (1971:3:227) puts it. His statement is relevant to this poem of Weöres'. The meaning that manifests itself in the first reading differs from the meaning manifested in the second one, and in any further readings newer and more subtle interpretations are revealed. Starting from a semantic point of view, a first reading brings signifier and signified together. Theme, then, is the contact between the protagonist, represented by the first person singular – presumably the writer – and the grammatical person, expressed by the third person singular – presumably Nándor Várkonyi – and their existence within each other in an endless and timeless infinity.

The deep intellectual contact between Várkonyi and Weöres had its roots in their special interest in mythology and literature and their common view of life in terms of the expansion of the limits of existence. It was to Várkonyi Weöres wrote the often-quoted letter where he tells about the great event of becoming aware of the contextual after a formerly-preferred formal perfection in his poems. "The meaning of the poem is not merely carried by the lines themselves, but also by those associations these lines suggest; the context is not covered by the sequence of significant units but by the thoughts glancing at one another in a spiritual harmony" (Várkonyi 1976:388-389). There, in the intellectual sphere of the infinity inside, contact between two kindred spirits can arise. The logical subject of the octet, that is, the protagonist and the grammatical subject of the sestet, that is, the third person singular and the synonyms on the border of the octet and the sestet, namely *végtelenség* 'infinity' and *határtalan* 'boundless', give validity to this interpretation. When we look at the text as a total and complete structure with a formal center within the last line of the octet and the first line of the sestet, which is also the metamorphosis of the logical and the grammatical subject, this interpretation presents itself.

When the formal center, however, is not considered a center any more, as a result of opening out the text, interpretation becomes much more difficult. Since infinity, as an ontological entity, is omnipresent in the poem and its formal place in the center adjoining the octet and the sestet is only caused by chance, by play, all objects, all individuals become uncertain. And if there is no infinity, either – *nincs puszta itt, nincs fönt s alant* 'there is no desert here, no above and no below' –, because everything vanishes, then even the subjects disappear, both the logical and the grammatical ones: *de az sincs többé aki fázott* 'but not even he exists any more who felt cold'.

The exact and strict structure of the sonnet-form may even suggest an association with the imprisonment of the individual in a biological existence. Because the well-defined frames of the sonnet set clear limits for the outer form, a break-out is possible only when the inner form is dissolved. This happens when the position of the center becomes dynamic. The physical bounds of a biological existence extend beyond being and human experiences move towards a kind of transcendental form of life, in which everything transforms itself in order to be one with this cosmic reality. Metamorphosis can be traced on several levels, supporting the concept of ambiguity. The following examples of metamorphoses may be freely supplemented by other examples seen from other view-points:

1. Logical subject (self) > infinity
2. Grammatical subject (3. person singular) > infinity
3. Grammatical subject (3. person singular) > grammatical subject (Nándor Várkonyi)
4. Logical subject (self) > grammatical subject (3. person singular)
5. Logical subject (self) > grammatical subject (Nándor Várkonyi)
6. Logical and grammatical subject > infinity
7. Biological existence > ontological existence
8. Existence > non-existence

"On the border of understanding one finds the suppressed happenings of non-understanding" (Bókay 1997:427). This non-understanding can be supplemented by other interpretations by other interpreters making use of other strategies, hence expanding the horizon of the different levels of meaning to infinite dimensions.

2.2.2.2 The Poem as Part of Weöres' Lifework

"Which one is my most important work? It is perhaps the sonnet 'The Infinite Inside', published for the first time in the December issue of *Alföld* in 1964" (Weöres 1993c:58). *Önvallomás*, 'Confession' was the title of the article in which these lines were written, from the magazine *Tükör* in 1965. In the three-volume *Egybegyűjtött írások* 'Collected Writings' the sonnet, *A benső végtelen* 'The Infinite Inside' belongs to the sonnet cycle with the title *Átváltozások* 'Metamorphoses'. According to Imre Bata (1979:182, 354), the sonnet cycle was originally published in 1964 in the volume *Tűzkút* 'Well of Fire'. It consisted of merely thirty sonnets. The sonnet *A benső végtelen* 'The Infinite Inside' was not included. In the two-volume *Egybegyűjtött írások* 'Collected Writings', published in 1970, the number of the sonnets increased to forty. *A benső végtelen* 'The Infinite Inside' is number thirty-eight within the cycle. The numerical order is not primarily Weöres' own. It was Bata who first dealt with the sonnets as a sequence of numbers. As a certain relationship between the sonnets is much easier to detect when using his numerical order, I believe that it is the most applicable order for my investigations as well.

Weöres' translations of Mallarmé were published in 1964, the same year as *Tűzkút* 'Well of Fire' came out. Mallarmé had a very strong influence on Weöres' philosophy of poetry. In one interview, for instance, Weöres declares as follows: "It was perhaps the influence of the French symbolists – an indirect and a direct influence of Mallarmé – that sent me away from the individual lyrics" (Liptay 1993:416). As to the grounds for why Mallarmé was such a source of inspiration in his poetry, he responds in the following manner in another interview: "A sonnet in Mallarmeian style is an altogether special matter, as the sentences, like in Latin, become more complicated, more difficult and more compound. The subject matter as well becomes like mist. All these things give the result that the utmost constraints and utmost untyings become combined in such a peculiar way. A sonnet in Mallarmeian style is exceedingly polar; definite, apparently heterogeneous things meet within them. I was interested in this possibility when I began to write sonnets in the Mallarmeian way, although these sonnets are essentially not sonnets, as a matter of fact, but only have the appearance of sonnets" (Cs. Szabó 1993:36).

As Zoltán Kenyeres (1983:248-249) put it, Weöres was not interested in the mysterious issues within the poetry of Mallarmé, but rather in the possibilities of expressing these issues, that is, Mallarmé's special method of connecting distinct levels of ambiguity. The ambition, however, to attain a primal profoundity of poetry by means of language was common to them both. They both aimed towards the realm of a perfectly clean poetry, the Mallarmeian *poesie pure*, released from the magic circle of the things, and which searches for the Absolute beyond all things. Jean-Pierre Richard, in the work titled *L'Univers imagianire de Mallarmé*, attempts to show the provinces of the Mallarmeian fantasy by using Mallarmé's key words and favourite images. Here, Richard points out that in order to establish the theme of a given poem, one must lay stress upon other criteria than the frequency of certain words. The most important matter is the strategical position of the theme, its "qualité topologique". "Le thème nous apparaît alors comme l'élément transitif qui nous permet de parcourir en divers sens toute l'étendue interne de l'œvre..." (Richard 1961:13-38).

When the poet seeks something that lies beyond the represented elements of reality, he eliminates not only those elements but himself as he replaces himself with the words. That is the Mallarmeian way of translating the soul (Espmark 1977:15). "The quest for purity, certainty, became a slow process of self-immolation – a recognition of the truth that perfection is a Nirvana that can only exist in what is a void of human consciousness" (Paul 1966:xvi).

A poetic intonation of the theme of elimination can be seen in a sonnet of Mallarmé beginning with the words: *Ses purs ongles très haut.* When the master, "le Maître", disappears in order to draw up tears from the Styx, the underworld river – *Car le Maître est allé puiser des pleurs au Styx / Avec se seul objet dont le Néamt s'honore* –, it is easy to conjure up Nándor Várkonyi, the mentor of Weöres, in the sonnet, *A benső végtelen.*'The Infinite Inside'. His disappearance into a boundless infinity is a kind of elimination, too, which is the abandonment of individuality that follows after all things have already passed out of sight, similar to Mallarmé's sonnet. The motif of all elimination, whichever form it takes, is to unite the Absolute, akin to Igitur, who achieves the Absolute at the expense of sacrificing himself. There is evidently a similarity between Mallarmé and Weöres not only when they express a related philosophical issue, but when one examines the formal appearance of this issue. Their complex metaphors, which suggest diverse meanings and enigmatic allusions, represent a hidden content.

According to Bata, the deep intellectual relationship between Mallarmé and Weöres originates from the related technique they use in establishing poetic structure: "We must create structures that are able to carry even the inexpressible, [– – –] we must construct compositions that widen the traditional patterns of meaning by means of exposing new connections between the units of the language" (Bata 1979:185). Bata also notices a fundamental disparity in the way the inexpressible is expressed by the two poets. He describes Mallarmé's poetry as being of an inductive nature, in the way "he relies on language", in contrast to the poetry of Weöres, which he describes as being of a deductive nature, because "he turns the physical world of his own into a metaphysical system – an organization of one type of hierarchical knowledge" (Bata 1979:187). The poem with the title *Disszonancia* 'Dissonance' (EI I:53) written in 1931 supports the fact that Weöres initially paid attention to Mallarmé's language style:

Sok hangoknak, kürtökének, imáénak, allarmének
zűr-miséjén fülem dobja visszahallgat Mallarmének

földre ejtett, félig-meddig elfelejtett kínrímére,
ez a vers egy kis levél a múlt századi csín címére.

Within the mess-up-mess of many voices, horns, prayers, allarmes (sic!)
the drums of my ears listen back to Mallarmé

to his make-up rhymes dropped on the ground more or less forgotten,
this poem is a little letter addressed to the last century's neatness.

Weöres, who in 1931 was only eighteen years old, evidently only recognized the dissonance, the make-up rhymes in the poetry of Mallarmé. Nevertheless, he used the same mocking, teasing tone, much to the disadvantage of his own poetry, as he denounced it with the same sarcastic self-criticism:

Mi lesz mostan? Alig használt príma hátultöltő semmi.
Pedig én még most akartam egy igen nagy költő lenni.

And what now? A scarcely used first-class firearm nothing
Still, just now I wanted to be a very famous poet.

(*Disszonancia.* 'Dissonance'. In: EI I:53)

Twenty years later, the very same poems of Mallarmé became such a powerful inspiration to him that he not only undertook a translation of them, but even felt an enormous urge to implement the Mallarmeian style into his own individual style. Influenced by the intellectual emanation of Mallarmé, he wrote the cycle *Átváltozások* 'Metamorphoses'.

The metaphysical system that Bata referred to not only can be grasped in terms of Mallarmé's poetry, but also in that of the cycle *Átváltozások* 'Metamorphoses' of Weöres. Péter Balassa has pointed out the insoluble difficulties of discussing the poems independently from one another, owing to the fact that "every single piece comprehends the entire cycle and [...] every poem proceeds from the previous one, and at the same time is a preparation for the next one, and, at last, beyond this linearity, a net-like system of coherences is formed between elements situated far from each other, by means of agreements based upon either literary coincidences or a similarity between the motifs" (Balassa 1990:369-370). It was Bata who first assumed a certain coherence between the symmetrically arranged pieces. According to him, the forty sonnets of *Átváltozások* 'Metamorphoses' can be classified into four parts, each part consisting of ten units. This arrangement in four parts – marked A, B, C, D – is motivated by the four different topics they deal with. In Bata's opinion all ten pieces of the first part are personifications of the creative spirit or genius; the second ten pieces represent the ontological categories of an existentially conscious life; the third ten pieces describe the epistemological categories of an existentially conscious life; and the fourth ten pieces are a characterization of the Orphic spirit that emerges from history (Bata 1979:183-184). Balassa, in slightly different terms than Bata, also names four groups: "There are four large groups: the archaic-mythical view of existence, the view of history/chaos, the esthetic-artistic view of existence and the substance of two different kinds, and as self-comparing (a Proteus-hermaphrodite component) blocks of the cycle penetrating into each other; they give the same single impression and the same multi-faceted impression" (Balassa 1990:372).

I have no intention of analyzing these four groups identified by Balassa and Bata as a whole. I have not even especially reflected on them as distinct units. However, I am convinced that these divisions of the poems by Bata and Balassa are based on competent analysis. I must also admit that they exercise a very deep influence over my investigation, because I became involved in those possibilities that a demonstration of thinkable parallels between the poems might indicate.

According to Bata's ten-piece units, the poem *A benső végtelen* 'The Infinite Inside' would be assigned the serial number D38. As a result, the poem, as the realization of a fundamental intertextual cohesion, can symmetrically linked with the sonnets A8, B18 and C28. These poems are as follows: A8: *Az ősanya szól az ivadékaihoz* 'The Ancestress Speaks to her Descendants'; B18: *Jelenlét* 'Presence'; C28: *Grammatikai személyek* 'Grammatical Persons'.

What particular circumstances create this structured coherence? In my opinion, it is the specific style by which a measurable time is transformed into timelessness and the topographical limits of space are replaced by limitlessness. The person who absolves herself from the bounds of time and space is capable of any kind of metamorphosis.

The ancestress moves through time when she speaks to her descendants, that is, humankind:

Ösvénytelen csönd és homály legyen,
árnyék-párta símuljon sírotokra,
tovább-lengő fények mögött vigyen
pályátok a teljes csöndbe vissza.

Lámpa lámpát érint az asztalon,
sok göndör fénylugas egymásba olvad,
közéjük mégis árny karéja horpad,
ott a vakon-látó bogár oson.
sugárban én ezer makacs szülöttem,
sok meggyalázott, úgy igyál-egyél,
mint légbe sarat öntő sűrű ködben,

hol görcs kérgekből pillog a veszély,
míg rádlel ködöt-tépő gyors körökben
a legvégső, feloldó, korom éj.

Let there be a pathless silence and obscurity,
let shadow-diadems nestle in your grave,

behind lights that sway along
let your course take you back to total darkness.

Lamp touches lamp on the table,
many curly arbours of light melt in each other,
yet the lobe of shade dots dented amongst them,
there a blind-sighted beetle sneaks.

In glory, a thousand stubborn children of mine
many dishonoured, let you drink and eat,
like in a dense fog pouring mud into sky,

where danger peeps from gnarled bark,
till in fog-tearing quick circles
the final, releasing, coal-black night will find you.

> (*Átváltozások. Az ősanya szól az ivadékaihoz.* 'Metamorphoses.
> The Ancestress Speaks to her Descendants'. In: EI II:310)

These words echo from the remoteness of a mystical obscurity, with no path
leading out of it – for one must find the way by one's self. They symbolize an
absolution of the present arising from the past and foreshadowing "the final,
releasing, coal black night". The poem *Jelenlét* 'Presence' also relates to past,
present and future at the same time:

A megkövült pokol már nem mér bajra bajt,
csak asszonyom sürög, tükörben jár a hulla,
munkál, szerez, díszít, emelkedve-lehullva,
pokoli szélmalom kit lég hiánya hajt.

Ő egyhelyben szalad, én bensőmben szököm meg
zúzmarás ágyamról s tárul az ősvilág
hol fiú-fog között ropogtak az atyák
nem várva meg élve jöttét a förtelemnek,

vagy torony-erkélyről szétnézek a jövőben
hol elmúlt ártalom halk habot habra sző.
A térben csapdos ő. Én ázom az időben.

Fölöttünk dermesztő dülledt Medusa-fő.
Szól: "Segíts magadon! Egy ajtót nyitva hagytam:
már les rád a titok. Hát nézd meg, jobb-e ottan."

This petrified hell doesn't strike me as evil any more,
just my wife is bustling about, the corps walk in the mirror,
she works hard, raises riches, decorates; rising and falling,
a hellish windmill who is driven by lack of air.

She is running in place, I do my escape within me
from this rimy bed of mine and an ancient world opens up
where the forefathers were cracked in the teeth of the sons
not waiting for the monstrosity to come alive,

or from a tower-balcony I look around in the future
where past harm weaves low foam to foam.
He beats about in space. I get wet in time.

Above us there is a stunning Medusa-head.
She speaks: "Help yourself! I left a door open:
the secret already watches you. Then go and see, if over there is better to be."

> (*Átváltozások. Jelenlét* 'Metamorphoses. Presence'. In: EI
> II:320)

In a literal translation of this poem, difficulties arise in expressing the gender. There is, namely, only one single form in Hungarian for the third person singular personal pronoun: *ő*. In most cases gender becomes clear within the context. This is, however, not the case in *Jelenlét* 'Presence'. I think this ambiguity is intentional. The main point is, as a matter of fact, not to create an absolute elucidation of whether this third person singular is female or masculine, because that would only be a meaningless expression of worldliness. And it is not what this poem is about.

In *Grammatikai személyek* 'Grammatical Persons' the three phases of time show an even stronger connection. Past, present and future are connected in the images of a present hunger and a future foreboding of death, through hardly explained signs:

Perceket érleltél magadban
omló kévéket éjszakát
értük megölt a rádtalált
szép szem víg fogsor álmaidban

csak engem hagysz meggyilkolatlan

nekem jelet egyik sem ád
féltitek tőlem a halált
mert hízlaljátok őt titokban

kiárasztván sok kedvese
nyájára (birkát sohase
látva mind oroszlánnak érzi)

egymásra titkot nem bízunk
ki-ki maga árnyát bevérzi
az éhkoppon így osztozunk.

Minutes you made ripe in yourself
sheaves that tumble down night
for their sake you were killed in your dreams
by the beautiful eyes the merry row of teeth that found you

only me you don't let die
no one gives me a sign
you fear death from me
because you fatten it in secret

while pouring forth to the flock
of her many lovers (never seen a sheep
she thinks they are all lions)

we don't share a secret
each bleeds his own shadow down
thus we share our starvation.

> (*Átváltozások. Grammatikai személyek* 'Metamorphoses.
> Grammatical Persons'. In: EI II:330)

The poem *A benső végtelen* 'The Infinite Inside' that, similar to the above-mentioned three poems of the cycle, brings together past, present and future, in one respect, however, differs from them: *A benső végtelen* 'The Infinite Inside' moves not only in time but also in space. The motifs expressed by the words: *A térben csapdos ő. Én ázom az időben* 'He beats about in space. I get wet in time' and: *én bensőmben szököm meg* 'I do my escape within me' in the poem *Jelenlét* 'Presence' take place specifically in time. Still, the Medusa-head in the last line opens the imaginary door towards the space where the secret lies hidden. This self of *Jelenlét* 'Presence', however, doesn't enter the door. It is the self of *A benső végtelen* 'The Infinite Inside' who does. Here, in this poem, a total fulfillment comes about, which is the same thing as total annihilation, where everything comes to an end. The person in *Jelenlét* 'Presence' from whose rimy bed an ancient world is flung open, no longer exists in *A benső végtelen* 'The Infinite Inside': *az sincs többé, aki fázott* 'but not even he exists any more who felt cold'.

As a result the sonnet *A benső végtelen* 'The Infinite Inside' can be considered a synthesis of the three previous sonnets – A8, B18, C28 – combined in a dynamic structural interaction. And as a result of a horizontal movement of time–phases turning into a vertical movement of a more accentuated phase of space between height and depth, new dimensions of existence open up. In its own right, it is a change, too, and can be termed the metamorphosis of time and space. It is in the poem *A benső végtelen* 'The Infinite Inside' where the secret is discovered. In opposition to a word-for-word representation of *titok* 'secret' in the sonnets *Jelenlét* 'Presence' and *Grammatikai személyek* 'Grammatical Persons', where the word occurs in the last verse in both cases – *már les rád a titok* 'the secret already watches you'; *egymásra titkot nem bízunk* 'we don't share a secret' –, in the sonnet *A benső végtelen* 'The Infinite Inside' there is no *titok* 'secret' at all. It disappears into an inner infinity. One can already feel the same infinity in the image of the *a legvégső, feloldó, korom éj* 'the final, releasing, coal-black night' in the poem *Az ősanya szól az ivadékaihoz* 'The Ancestress Speaks to her Descendants', but only as a vague expectation projected into the future. *Korom éj* 'coal-black night', furthermore, may be a reference to the lines in the poem *Ses purs ongles très haut* of Mallarmé, where the Phoenix, the mythological bird, burns the dreams to coal, not allowing them to rest in an ampora: *"Maint rêve vesperal brule par le Phénix / Que ne recueille pas de cinéraire amphore"*. In a *legvégső, feloldó, korom éj* 'the final, releasing, coal-black night' there is no need for dreams. *Korom* 'coal' in this light reflects both the color of the night and the dreams that turned to ashes. The fire burns down at last and no longer gives warmth. But there is no need for the fire either, for as expressed in *A benső végtelen* 'The Infinite Inside': *az sincs többé, aki fázott* 'but not even he exists any more who felt cold'.

As pointed out above, this fourth poem, marked D38, is a synthesis of the three previous ones, that is, of the poems marked A8, B18 and C28. Their relation then must consequently be that of thesis to antithesis. If we regard A8 and B18 as the thesis, C28 as the antithesis and D 38 as the synthesis, we will find a structure comparable to the sonnets.

Mythical motifs are the primary connection between the poems *Az ősanya szól az ivadékaihoz* 'The Ancestress Speaks to her Descendants' and the *Jelenlét* 'Presence'. It is as if Gaia, the ancestress of the world and the titans who took revenge on their fathers and Medusa, the human Gorgon in the mythology of the Greeks have awakened in these poems. The ancestress in the cycle *Átváltozások* 'Metamorphoses' also alludes to another character of Weöres named Gaia, the mother of the titans, in his oratorio-drama with the title *Theomachia*, written in 1941. *Medusa* was the title of his next work, published in 1944. The frightful monster, Medusa, who changes all living beings into stone with a glance, also symbolizes liberation in Hellenic mythology: namely, it is with her head that Perseus liberates his country. After this, the Medusa-head embellishes the shield of the goddess of justice, Pallas Athéne.

After the thesis, represented by the two poems *Az ősanya szól az ivadékaihoz* 'The Ancestress Speaks to her Descendants' and *Jelenlét* 'Presence', the antithesis follows, represented by the poem *Grammatikai személyek* 'Grammatical Persons'. The word *titok* 'secret' in the last verse of *Jelenlét* 'Presence' and in the last verse of *Grammatikai személyek* 'Grammatical Persons' connects the two poems. But it is also this *titok* 'secret' that separates them, as it carries the opposition between thesis and antithesis. In the poem *Jelenlét* 'Presence' *titok*, 'secret' is a possibility for self-deliverance – *Egy ajtót nyitva hagytam: / már les rád a titok. Hát nézd meg jobb-e ottan* 'I left a door open: / the secret already watches you. Then go and see if over there is better to be' – but this possibility is not realized in the poem *Grammatikai személyek* 'Grammatical Persons', as *egymásra titkot nem bízunk* 'we don't share a secret'. The image of satiety in *Az ősanya szól az ivadékaihoz* 'The Ancestress Speaks to her Descendants' expressed by *igyál-egyél,* 'drink and eat' contrasts to the image of hunger denoted by the word *éhkopp* 'starvation' in the *Grammatikai személyek* 'Grammatical Persons'. But satiety and hunger are in opposing positions within this poem, that is, the image of a fattened death and the image of hunger. The secret which is hidden within the relation of death and the desire for it, however, has not been unveiled, as the *jelek* 'signs' necessary for revealing it are still missing: *nekem jelet egyik sem ád* 'no one gives me a sign'.

It is the word *jel* 'sign' that connects this third poem of antithesis to the synthesis of *A benső végtelen* 'The Infinite Inside'. There is no *titok* 'secret' here any more, as the vertical move in space has dissolved it, but there are *jelek* 'signs': *végül jelekből kibogozva* 'finally figuring out the signs'. There is no time either, it perhaps extinguished itself. The line *ki-ki maga árnyát bevérzi* 'each bleeds his own shadow down' may even have suicide in view. But it is not certain, either. The secret, entangled in the signs, may show itself differently when it shines through a particular infinity within the individual. That is why there is no absolute interpretation which excludes other and even contradictory ones. My analysis is only one of many possibilities.

2.2.2.3 Weöres' Philosophy of Poetics

"Like a fly running to and fro on the outside of a glass ball, wanting at any price to get inside to the secret, but merely hesitating, searching about, in the way the soul of Gilgamesh circled, and ran about on the wall of the impenetrable other world. He returned time and time again to the same place where he had started. And an endless space dilating in all directions surrounded him and this space had no center. An endless path carried him away and it had no aim, meaning or opening. An endless world lay beneath him, always beneath him and there was no way to come into it, to probe deeply into its center, to uncover its secrets. Or, yet, was there a way? O, yes, there was! Gilgamesh, who gained possession of a magic power from his master, Samas-sum-iddin and who once even raised Annunaki from the underworld, why would he not raise the soul of Enkidu from the realm of Nergal? Only once, one single time, only now!" This piece is cited from a novel of János Kodolányi (1958:629) with the title *Új ég, új föld* 'New Sky, New Earth'. Gilgamesh, the hero of the Sumer-Babilonian legend, two-thirds god and one-third human, lost his true friend, the human Enkidu. In his unbearable sorrow, he calls the soul of Enkidu. Suddenly, it gets cold around him and Gilgamesh begins to feel cold when Enkidu shows himself. When Gilgamesh asks him, Enkidu begins to talk about the underworld and the last doom of the mortal human beings. And then suddenly, exactly like he came, he disappears, and Gilgamesh discovers, while shivering, that not a single grain of sand has fallen in the sand-glass. Time stopped. Gilgamesh gets frightened at the thought of death. He doesn't want to die as Enkidu did. In his fear, at first without any plans, then later, when his destination in a flash becomes clear to him, he flees the world. He runs to his immortal father, Utnapishtim in order to receive the tree of life from him – it is a blue flower according to the version of Kodolányi –, which has the power to wake Enkidu from his death and can also give eternal life to Gilgamesh himself. After wandering across seven worlds, he finds the blue flower at last, but during the time that he bathes in a cistern, a snake crawls away with it. Immortality is gone forever. Or, maybe not, and Gilgamesh might learn that "the ever changing world dies in every birth, is born again in every dying, but being is everlasting?" (Kodolányi 1958:678).

Like Gilgamesh conjures the spirit of Enkidu, Weöres calls Nándor Várkonyi to mind in the poem *A benső végtelen* 'The Infinite Inside'. The characters Gilgamesh and Enkidu were very familiar to both of them. It was in fact Weöres who translated parts of the *Epic of Gilgamesh* to be used in Várkonyi's work titled *A Sziriat oszlopai* 'The Pillars of Seiris'. János Kodolányi made use of the same Weöres translations in his novels about Gilghamesh (Várkonyi 1976:356). Consequently, it was the influences of three writers – Kodolányi, Várkonyi and Weöres – that were combined in a single character of the Sumer-Babilonian hero.

Immortality and time which ends are the topics both for the Epic of Gilgamesh and the Weöres' poem. In *A benső végtelen* 'The Infinite Inside' this theme is shown through the motifs of a close friendship and the timelessness and the boundlessness in the meeting of two kindred spirits. It is Várkonyi himself, in his biographical work titled *Pergő évek* 'Running Years', who gives the facts about the background from which the poem originated. In 1964, while working on the *Sziriat oszlopai* 'The Pillars of Seiris', Várkonyi sent his related thoughts about the universe, myths and an everlasting human longing for an universal harmony, to Weöres, his friend, in whom he recognized a cosmic mind, similar to his own. "I only have to seek if he is able to carry out the impossible, express the inexpressible, if he can suggest, make absurdity sensible" (Várkonyi 1976:393-394). It was a test indeed, a test of understanding, as to whether these thoughts of Várkonyi had a natural place in Weöres' poetical spheres. Weöres' answer was, apart from an appreciative letter, also the poem *A benső végtelen* 'The Infinite Inside' with a dedication to Nándor Várkonyi. Várkonyi writes as follows about the poem: "It is a sonnet consisting of four strophes all in all, and whereas it is about the infinite inside of the title, there is a whole, immense infinity in it, in the same way as I would like to see it. I also called it the sonnet of the universe, I put it in a frame and hung it on the wall. This is my diploma" (Várkonyi 1976:394).

Nevertheless, the parallel I draw between the *Epic of Gilgamesh* and this poem of Weöres does not emphasize the motif of deprivation in the first place but the motif of meeting someone while still living, a meeting that shines through the limits of existence, a meeting of two immortal spirits in the limitlessness. There is no time here, because infinity doesn't shape its structure within time but within space and likewise dissolves in space, too. In an endless room there is no center, according to the cited lines of Kodolányi. "There are moments sometimes that are hung out from time" as Weöres wrote already in 1935 in the poem *Örök pillanat* 'Eternal Moment'. These moments cannot be caught in time for they are timeless, they are the moments of eternity. "And you taste eternity this side of death" as he wrote in the same poem. Similar to Gilgamesh, the lines of Weöres' sonnet break up the boundaries of time, in order to meet the former master within the highest spheres of the human spirit. And, like Gilgamesh, Weöres is also in need of some magic power. His magic power is formed by the words of poetry. A meeting within the highest spheres is possible only by this method. Gilgamesh still feels cold when he meets the mortal Enkidu who comes up from the underworld and disappears later (Kodolányi 1958:630), but in Weöres' sonnet, however, even the person who was cold disappears. That is, the meeting of Gilgamesh and Enkidu doesn't take place in eternity, only on the boundary to it; the meeting of the logical and grammatical persons of the poem *A benső végtelen* 'The Infinite

Inside', however, does takes place indeed in eternity, which abolishes them both.

The philosophy that these thoughts are based upon is for the most part from the ancient Greeks. When Plato in Phaedo declares that the ideas are constant, unchanging components that independent of time or space always exist, and which cannot be comprehended by our senses; and when he clarifies that the ideas are implied in the human soul, which for this reason becomes immortal – we are then not far from Weöres' manifestations of the same thoughts through the means of poetics. When we study the main ideas of the work of Gorgias with the title *Peri tou me ontos e peri physeos* 'On that which is not or on Nature', we may, together with Weöres, find that nothing really exists, neither the existing nor the non-existing. And when Plotinus (1984:63) writes about the origin and order of things and declares that "...but Intellect is still more emphatically not in space, so that neither is this [higher] soul. Since therefore it is nowhere but in that which is nowhere, it is in this way also everywhere, but if, as it proceeds upwards it stops in the middle before completely reaching the highest, it has a medium life and stays in that [middle] part of itself", then we once more are reminded of the ideas expressed in *A benső végtelen* 'The Infinite Inside'.

What is this quality that can raise us from an existing world to a world beyond the senses? What kind of a supernatural aptitude is required? Béla Hamvas called this talent a kind of mystical intuition and defines the concept as follows: "A mystical intuition is the capacity that removes the human soul from life and transfers it to existence. It is the *epopteia*, or ecstasy to use another Greek word, the dream or the rapture, the prediction or the prophecy, the vision or the trance, the inspiration or the enthusiasm. [– – –] The mystical intuition removes you from a circle of an enclosed self and frees you, and in the circle of the ancient images of realities it opens the eyes of the soul" (Hamvas 1995a:96).

Hamvas' mystical intuition is attached to the mystery religion of Orphicism. According to the theory of Orphicism, the human soul, because it keeps God himself inside, is immortal, but because it is imprisoned in the body, it is excluded from immortality. For that reason man must try to set the immortal soul free by means of the use of a pure outer and inner form. That is the *poesie pure* in poetry in true Mallarmeian fashion. The only way to get to the ancient images of reality is by means of a purification of formal elements. This is the oldest, original form of poetry, the poetry of Orpheus. There are certain features of this poetry which are common to that of Weöres'. Like Orpheus going down to the nether world in order to meet the companion of his soul and the meaning of his life, Eurydiké, Mallarmé and Weöres strive to reach the sources of human existence. "This is the very essence of the Orphic mystery. He who is able to release his own soul from the realm of Hades, he who can defeat the power of the night, the darkness, the evil and the blemish with a passionate desire for the light, may be apt to lead other stray persons to the way of light" (Hamvas 1992:480).

Magyar Orpheus 'Hungarian Orpheus' is the title of a book, published in 1990, in the memory of Sándor Weöres. There is a poem in this volume with the title *Orpheus* written by János Parancs (1990:392) The subtitle is *Weöres Sándor köszöntése* 'Greeting to Sándor Weöres'. A detail from this poem illustrates the Orphic essence:

a csontváz összeroskad zuhan az alvilágba
ő mégis itt maradt birodalmának nincs határa
magányos vackán a bölcs csillagok komája
nem köti idő s tér: a kettős börtönajtó
nincs vágya kezében citera szól és énekel
halálról feltámadásról

the skeleton breaks down crashes into the nether world
he remains here all the same his empire has no borders
companion of sage stars on his lonely bed
time and space don't bind him: the double doors of imprisonment
he has no desires a zither is playing in his hand and he is singing
about death about resurrection

There is no time, no place in Orphic poetry. The body vanishes, but the soul is immortal, since it broke through the limits between time and the timeless. The poet in the poem of János Parancs, who plays the zither and sings, and he who listens to the silent voices from the boundless in Weöres' poem *A benső végtelen* 'The Infinite Inside', is the immortal self. It is Orpheus, who personifies an individual inner infinity, our real and innermost face, the hiding place of eternal truths. The first verse of a poem of Weöres' with the title *Orpheus* 'Orpheus' (EI II:275) reads as follows:

Íme a vándor, porlepte énekes, akinek garast hajítsz,
az idegen, a másféle, akit rettegve keresztre vonsz,
önnön benső, igazi arcod, akit nem ismersz,
nélküle tested akollá sötétül, eszméleted ura.
See! The wanderer, the dusty singer, to whom you throw a penny,
the foreigner, the different, who you, terrified, crucify,
your own inner true face, who you don't know,
without him your body darkens to a sheep-fold, the lord of your consciousness.

The fourth part of *Orpheus* 'Orpheus' with the title *Lebegés a határtalanban* 'Floating in the Infinite' is, as Bata (1979:174) put it, pure poetry, that is, the Mallarmeian *poesie pure*. "This is the dimension of the vision and the dream, nothing else but floating, rushing within the lack of life. Here Weöres and Orpheus meet". Orpheus is the symbol of an ancient poetry deeply absorbed in the mind, which is the very last point of all descent. Orphic poetry is the most original and pure of all literary compositions.

Egyszerre két este van
Mindkettő csak festve van
harmadik az igazi
koldusként áll odaki

At once there are two evenings
Both are only painted
the third is the real one
like a beggar he stands outside

(*Tapéta és árnyék*. 'Wall-papper and Shadow' In: EI II:454)

Whether intentionally or unintentionally, these lines of Weöres' take the reader to the remote world of Orpheus. The binary opposition between the concepts of *there is* and *there is not* organizes the poem, where contrasts emerge not only within the structure as a whole, but also within their own context, as they deny what they actually mean. The idea of *there is* here means both the idea of *there is* and *there is not* at the same time and vice versa. It is Orpheus indeed, who "like a beggar stands outside" and to whom "you throw a penny", and though he is the defrauded, the cheated, still he is the only one who exists. He is real. He is difficult to find when he stands like a beggar outside. He has nothing and that is the reason why nobody wants him to be inside. For most people, he, the real, hardly exists. The logical and the grammatical persons of the poem *A benső végtelen* 'The Infinite Inside' stand outside too, for this third person, the real, can only be found outside its structure. Namely, "the real" can be found in the title, the sentence with focal quality. As a result, one could refer to an inner form of the poem because the deepest content is expressed by just this infinity. When studying the characteristics of the outer form, however, this infinity can be found in the synthesis after the thesis and the antithesis. The third person, the real, the homeless one who feels cold stands outside, but only in an aspect of the outer form. The infinity of the profound inner form, by means of turning everything to nothing, eliminates all finite, exact substance and becomes an absolute, pure form in itself.

2.3 Becoming Another in Different Form

(1)

Dzsá gulbe rár kicsere
áj ni musztasz emo
áj ni mankütvantasz emo
adde ni maruva bato! jaman!

(2)

Ole dzsuro nanni he
ole csilambo ábábi he
ole buglo iningi he
lünjel dáji he! jaman!

(3)

Vá pudd shukomo ikede
vá jimla gulmo buglavi ele
vá leli gulmo ni dede
vá odda dzsárumo he! jaman!

(1)

Szél völgye farkas fészke
mért nem őriztél engem
mért nem segítettél engem
most nem nyomna kő! ajaj!

(2)

Könnyemmel mosdattalak
hajammal törölgettelek
véremmel itattalak
mindig szerettelek! ajaj!

(3)

Földed tüskét teremjen
tehened véres tejet adjon
asszonyod fiat ne adjon

édesapád eltemessen! ajaj!

(1)

Valley of winds den of wolf
why didn't you take care of me
why didn't you help me
then stone wouldn't press me! woe is me!

(2)

I washed you with my tears
I wiped you with my hair
I gave you my blood to drink
I always loved you! woe is me!

(3)

May your land raise thorns
may your cow give bloody milk
may your wife never give you a son
may your father bury you! woe is me!

> (*Barbár dal. Képzelt eredeti és képzelt fordítás* 'Barbarian Song.
> Imagined Original and Imagined Translation'. EI I:725)

2.3.1 The Text

2.3.1.1 The Structure and Shape of the Writing

The poem *Barbár dal* 'Barbarian Song', as indicated in the subtitle, consists of
two parts: an imagined original and an imagined translation. When one first
looks at the outer form, the imagined original is in harmony with the imagined
translation, as both are constructed of three strophes, each consisting of four
lines. Every strophe begins with capital letters and ends with punctuation
marks. The lines are of comparatively similar length, the only exception being
the last lines of the first and the third strophes, which are somewhat longer

than the other lines. Each strophe is a sentence and each line is a regular clause, except the first and the second lines in both versions, which taken together build a syntagm. The exclamation mark is the only punctuation mark in the poem. There are no commas between the clauses, only the two exclamation marks of the last lines. The poem displays a regular shape in the arrangement of its language-units, even when looking at the correspondence between the two versions in orthographics and interpunction.

2.3.1.2 The Represented Elements of Reality

The represented images of reality are non-real in the version of the imagined original. It is very obvious, as the language itself is imaginary. It gives a sense of some ancient, and for that reason now incomprehensible language being revived by these words. This sense of unintelligibility can, however, also be explained by the fact that the magic words of the Hungarian ancient rituals were from the very onset incomprehensible. There are many examples of these magic words, preserved in counting games, nursery rhymes and folksongs. We cannot decode the words of the following counting game, either:

An tan ténusz
szóraka ténusz,
szóraka tiki taka
bim bam bum.

This is the very essence of magic. It aims at transforming the real into the unreal in order to re-shape the world. Language might act as a means for this change, as a form that reflects reality in its now-altered condition. For this reason, language takes on a new symbolic form, in which understanding no longer depends on logical rules, but on ancient ritualistic patterns.

In terms of understanding this imagined original we expect to get some help from the imagined translation. Due to their fictitious character, however, both the original and the translation take place in an unreal sphere and as a result are types of interpretations. The question as to whether the imagined original or the imagined translation was composed first must be left open for the time being. Nevertheless, the only way of studying the represented elements of reality on a conceptual level is to start from the version of the imagined translation.

Similar to the oldest lyrical songs of man, the first line conjures up supernatural forces. The first man asked for the protection of natural powers mightier than himself, such as the wind or the wild animals, such as the wolf. Supposedly, it is these powers which are called upon in the next lines of the first strophe. Nevertheless, other interpretations are possible within the context of the two next strophes. The stone that lies heavy on the protagonist is in all probability a gravestone. He is then buried and it is too late for help.

In the next strophe normal daily acts are connected to objects basically irrelevant within that given context. These unusual associations create a mystical atmosphere. The last line, however, puts the deepest human feelings into words.

The last verse is a kind of a conclusion, in which all complaints from the prior verses seek solutions. Images from everyday life appear again, but similar to the second strophe, these scenes, originally of a positive nature, turn out to be the opposite, as each one of them foreshadows the final dissolution. Indeed, each line is a curse, which step by step prepares the reader for the last line. Here we have arrived at the heaviest curse of all: similar to the one who already is dead, he who is responsible for all distress and sorrow is also doomed to die.

The principle that predominantly organizes the text is a recognizable parallel grammatical sentence structure, that is, the principle of parallelism. This primary structuring principle is reinforced by a successive intensification of the consecutive lines, that is, by the marching figure of the *climax* or *gradatio*.

According to Elemér Hankiss (1970:132), the focal point of a poem is usually one single word or one single trope. In the poem *A barbár dal* 'Barbarian Song', the focus is one single word. This word, however, when looking at the two different versions, is manifested as two separate words: *jaman* and *ajaj* 'woe is me'. The essentially emotional meaning of the poem has been converged and concentrated in these words. Obviously, it would be difficult to give preference to any conceptual meaning in the case of a poem which is not only a fictitious translation but a fictitious original. A contingent conceptual meaning is namely altered by the imaginary form to become some kind of an illusory reality based on emotions. This emotional meaning, expressed by the imaginary interjections *jaman* and *ajaj* 'woe is me' is the only real meaning, because the non-real forms are validated by a real emotional content. For these reasons I find the words *jaman* and *ajaj* 'woe is me' to possess both focal quality and an integrating capacity.

2.3.1.3 The Rhetorical-Stylistic Structure

A study of the rhetorical-stylistic structures in the version of the imagined original is likely to meet with some difficulties. Having no knowledge of the meaning of the words, any interpretation of this version must be focused on its form. The symmetrical arrangement of identical words, *áj, emo, ole, he, vá* which noticeably begin and end the lines, indicate a parallel construction of the sentences. The primary structuring principle of parallelism and the related principle of *gradatio* will be further demonstrated by the number of repetitions of the above mentioned words: *aj* and *emo* occurs twice in the first strophe, *ole* and *he* can be found three times in the second strophe and *vá* turns up four times in the third strophe. As these figures are repetitions of the same words at the beginning or at the end of successive clauses, they are also examples of the rhetorical figures of *anaphora* and *epiphora*. These two figures taken together build the figure of *complexio*. We can find two examples of this figure in the connection of the words *áj* and *emo* in the first strophe and three examples in the connection of the words *ole* and *he* in the second strophe. In contrast to this frequency, there are no examples of the figure in the third strophe.

Refrain is a special form of parallelism. The word *jaman* must be considered a dominant structural unit as a result of its placement as the last word in all three strophes. This word ends the three strophes no less than three times.

This symmetrical arrangement of the rhetorical-stylistic elements creates a balanced structure. The lack of conceptual meaning reflected in this structure inevitably calls attention to the emotional meaning, which must be considered in any interpretation. As Weöres put it: "Many masterpieces can only be understood with the aid of commentaries and what is more, there are even some which have no content expressible in prose at all and are seemingly senseless and incomprehensible. The strength of these lies in the atmosphere, the structure, the dynamics and the sound: its meaning, significance, the things it has to say are inconceivable, yet it exists in the same way as music exists: we don't know what it means, yet it heightens and changes us" (Weöres 1993a:43).

The fictitious translation, as opposed to the fictitious original, can be studied not only as a manifestation of formal units of a language-structure, but also on the conceptual level. First, however, the formal units will be examined in close connection with the fictitious original. Obviously, the structuring principle of parallelism and the connecting principle of gradation have a leading part in the fictitious translation as well. In this version, however, the *gradatio* is not based on quantitative factors, as we have seen in the fictitious original, but on qualitative factors. In the successive lines, which incessantly bring us closer to the final point of the last curse, the action becomes more and more intense from a semantic point of view.

We can also find examples of the figures of *anaphora*, *epiphora* and *complexio*, but these are not as frequent as in the version of the fictitious original. While a complete coherence with this former version can be recognized in the first strophe – the words *mért* 'why' and *engem* 'me' show a structural coherence with the words *áj* and *emo* –, these figures cannot be found in the second strophe and there is only one *epiphora* in the third strophe, represented by the word *adjon* 'may [...] give'. The three-time recurrence of the interjection *ajaj* 'woe is me' is structurally analogous to the word *jaman* in the fictitious original.

Given full knowledge of the words, several more figures and tropes can be traced. This is characteristic of the pragmatical figure of the *apostrophe* or *aversio*, which, in the same manner as the Homeric invocation, turns away from the reader and instead turns to supernatural forces for support. We must emphasize this interpretation of the first line, because a different interpretation with a syntactic emphasis would indisputably lead to another, essentially different conclusion.

Both the lack of punctuation-marks and the conjunctions between the syntagms are significant to the whole structure of the poem, which circumstantially illustrates the figure of *asyndeton*.

We ought to make mention also of the figures of the sounds in this version of the fictitious translation. In the word *ajaj* 'woe is me' we recognize the figure of *prosthesis*. As the usual form of the word is *jaj*, then the form *ajaj* is an amplification of this. It may even be assumed that this two-syllable variant is some kind of an adjustment to the version of the imagined original. In a case like this, we must prove that the version of the imagined original is á prior to the translation.

Summing up the results of these investigations of the rhetorical-stylistical structures in the poem *A barbár dal* 'Barbarian Song', we may note that there are frequent congruencies between the two versions. The fact that the complex structures of the figures of speech, like the metaphor or the simile, are missing is also common to both versions. The subject-matter, substantially unreal, is reflected by several forms of repetitive structures. This is also the most prominent feature of folk-poetry and all ancient forms of lyrical representations.

2.3.1.3 The Metrical Structure

As an introduction I will quote from two statements. One of these comes from Ildikó A. Molnár (1977:32), who had the unique opportunity of listening to Weöres' own recitation of the poem at hand. Referring to the dissimilarity between the written text and that recitation she writes as follows: "Owing to difficulties of typographical reproduction, the poet jotted down the fictitious text with the standard letters used in Hungarian ortography, but the acoustics of the poem put down this way and recited according to the laws of pronunciation in Hungarian is a long ways from the acoustics of the imagined poem. There is only one long vowel in the written text, namely the vowel *á*, but there are other long vowels in the recited version, namely the vowels *a* and *e*. The sound marked by the letter *ü* is not of full value, that is, it is a palatal, indistinct derived vowel. The fictitious text – particularly the version recited by the poet – as a result of its acoustical patterns in the first place, reminds us of the gypsy language".

The other pronouncement comes from László Lator (1990:534): "[...] as this ancient voice from the beginning was settled in him, as the archetypal ideas in fact were thronged and crowded in him. [– – –] But in any case, it is still astounding how genuine this rude-forced funeral-song, this imagined original of the poem 'Barbarian Song', written in 1944, felt. He spoke it on the record with a wild, strong, sing-song voice. In comparison to the translation, the translation seems more gentle, more European and more civilized. When I first heard this twin-poem interpreted by Sándor Weöres, I thought for the first time in my life that in fact those people who believe that poems ought to be read in original must be right".

I believe it is important to refer to these statements for the single reason that we are reduced to using the only available written version of the poem. Whatever version we start with, we will in all certainty find the poem pulsating, and whirling along when we read it. We may even get the feeling of almost memorizing it, without caring about what the words mean. The stream, which with every single line uninterruptedly carries us nearer and nearer to the wail of the last lines, seems much more significant. What keeps this stream rolling along? Surely the parallel repetitive structures of language, which are manifested in several ways.

Obviously, parallelism was a substantial feature of ancient poetry. In his studies on Russian and Polish folk-poetry, Roman Jakobson (1974) took the different cases of grammatical parallel structures into special consideration. Already in 1934, however, Wolfgang Steinitz in his pioneer work on Finnish-Karelian folk-poetry, with the title *Der Parallelismus in der finnish-karelischen Volksdichtung*, underlined the necessity of an analysis based on the grammatical structure of language when investigating this phenomenon of language. Robert Austerlitz, too, in his work the *Ob-Ugric Meters*, written in 1958, demonstrated the essential role of parallelism in the folk-poetry in the Finno-Ugric language territory. András Kecskés wrote about parallelism in language as follows: "If we should try to systematize these primary coherences, these first, initial manifestations of the poetical form in some way, then we will demonstrate that poetry in all likelihood commenced with a reiteration of certain sentences: somebody found a state or exclamation was of such great importance and connected to so many things that he felt that he must repeat it. By repetition – not consciously, of course – without adding anything to the actual meaning of the text, he intensified it, inbued it in the emotional sense of the word, and he placed it in a new light and shaped his thought, mood and message to a specific subject-matter separable from his own person" (Kecskés 1984:37).

In a parallel sentence-structure, rhythm arises from regular intervals of repetition of sentences with congruent grammatical construction. In early poetry, then, rhythm springs up from the repetition of parallel grammatical structures independent of both the length of the syllables and of certain stress-factors. These very same features of parallel sentence-structure are essential for old Hungarian poetry, too. "Presumably, the only certain thing is that the ancient types of working songs and ritual songs also existed in the Hungarian population, and these poems were improvisational and had no knowledge of either settled rhythm or rhyme" (MIT I:24). Lajos Vargyas (1966:131) also emphasizes the fact that regular metrical units and rhymes were not found in the old Hungarian minstrel-songs and nursery rhymes.

As pointed out earlier, the principle of parallelism is of primary impor-tance to the structure of the poem *Barbár dal* 'Barbarian Song', too. It is the main principle that organizes this text. Lines with identical grammatical construction follow each other without any constraint concerning the number of the syllables and the metrical pattern. There are mostly seven syllables in each line but we can find lines with eight, nine and ten syllables. Each concep-tual unit builds a line of its own which never transgresses to the next line. Rhymes, if any, are very rudimentary: as identical rhymes, they repeat the very same word; as *homoioteleuton*, it is the inflectional ending which is repeated.

Regarding the number of syllables in the lines and the arrangement of the rhymes we probably cannot find any similarity between the two versions. Regarding intonation, however, we may detect certain parallel structures between them. András Kecskés (1984:46) pointed to the fact that in ancient poetry verse and melody were inseparable. The poem *Barbár dal* 'Barbarian Song', in my opinion, may be looked upon as feasible evidence of this state-ment. Stress and cadence, which together define the intonation-line of the poem, are strikingly similar in the two versions. In the following outline of a comparative demonstration of the intonation-lines in the versions of the imag-ined original and the imagined translation, I will use the symbols denoting the degrees of accentuation created by Kecskés (1984:123):

╪ = main stress, also when beginning a sentence
╪ = main stress
+ = half stressed syllable
| = absent stress

Using these signs we can see correspondences between the two verses accord-ing to figures 7, 8, and 9.

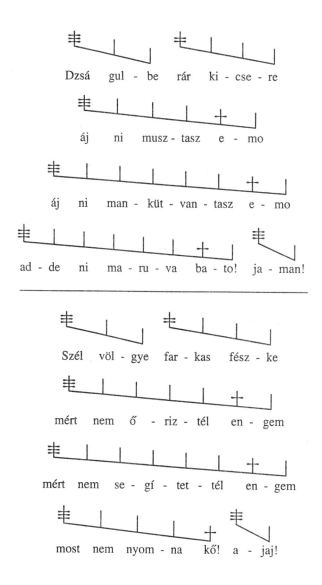

Dzsá gul - be rár ki - cse - re
áj ni musz - tasz e - mo
áj ni man - küt - van - tasz e - mo
ad - de ni ma - ru - va ba - to! ja - man!

Szél völ - gye far - kas fész - ke
mért nem ő - riz - tél en - gem
mért nem se - gí - tet - tél en - gem
most nem nyom - na kő! a - jaj!

Figure 7

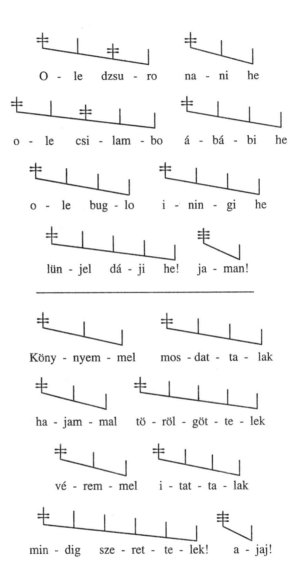

Figure 8

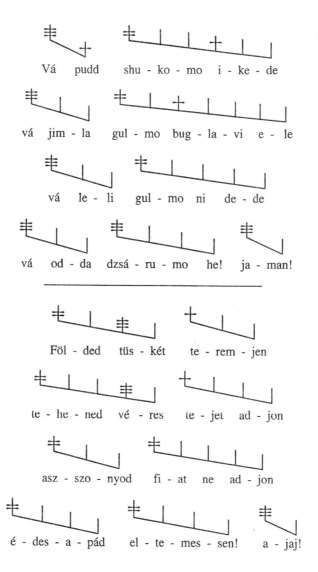

Vá pudd shu - ko - mo i - ke - de

vá jim - la gul - mo bug - la - vi e - le

vá le - li gul - mo ni de - de

vá od - da dzsá - ru - mo he! ja - man!

Föl - ded tüs - két te - rem - jen

te - he - ned vé - res te - jet ad - jon

asz - szo - nyod fi - at ne ad - jon

é - des - a - pád el - te - mes - sen! a - jaj!

Figure 9

As the occurence of parallel grammatical structures in the version of the imagined original is not merely an assumed base for the emotional stress but also for a conceptual base when adapting factual grammatical rules, this twofold imagined text occupies a place in a realistic context and is then reshaped as an authentic one.

2.3.1.5 Grammatical Structure

An investigation of the grammatical structures of the two versions of the poem *Barbár dal* 'Barbarian Song' must begin with the imagined translation, since it is the version construed of words with significant meaning, which allows for an analysis of grammatical structure. Beginning this way makes also the study of the imagined original feasible, particularly as the imagined character is common to them both.

The complaint, expressed in the first verse, obviously calls for the help of supernatural forces. There are two possessive relations in the first line which consist of two words each and form a coordinate relation with each other. Without any punctuation mark at the end of this first line, these presumed supernatural forces become hardly identifiable and may also compromise the entire structure by a possible allusion to some real, but unnamed or unnamable person.

All three strophes of the poem seem to be imperative sentences because of the exclamation point after them. The interjection *ajaj* 'woe is me' as the last word of each strophe, which is also followed by an exclamation point, creates an even stronger emotive charge. When studying the two first strophes more closely, however, we may recognize that these are in fact not imperative sentences. All the predicates of the sentences are in indicative mood, indicating declarative sentences. In contrast to these two verses, the exclamation point at the end of the third verse is quite appropriate to use, as the predicates are in the imperative mood. The fact that the only punctuation marks of the poem are the exclamation points in the last lines may be explained by the primarily "barbarian" nature of the poem. This profusion of emotional content is very characteristic of early lyrics when the lines appeal to supernatural forces. This places the words in a magical context. Nevertheless, by means of a consecutive use of exclamation points, the main structuring principle of parallelism that modifies the sentences to imperative is reinforced even further.

The chain of the subsequent coordinate clauses also shows an analogous grammatical structure. These are related to each other as copulative sentences with the only possible conjunction *és* 'and' between them.

The parts of the sentences also build a parallel structure. The same kind of word is to be found in exactly the same place in two sentences contiguous to each other. The dissimilar word-order of the last lines of the first and second verse are the only exceptions.

In the case of phonetical occurences, we may observe the near-total absence of alliterations and onomatopoetic words. Rhymes, if any, are only concerned with identical flectional endings.

When turning to the version of the imagined original, our investigation of the vocabulary must be based on the version of the imagined translation. Weöres himself gives some help when he declares as follows: "The text in the imagined language of the 'Barbarian Song' is, as a matter of fact, overflowing with gypsy-like accents. East-European, Balkan, Moldavian flavours are mixed with an almost European stock of words. The word *odda*, for example, comes from the German origin 'addar, fater', other words reveal a Gypsy and a Rumanian origin" (Czigány 1993a:74). Ildikó A. Molnár (1977:32) in analyzing the phonetical patterns of the poem, also befriends the decoding of the vocabulary. She shows that the fictititous *ni* corresponds to the Hungarian negative particle *nem*, that the suffix for the imperative is -*o*, that the second person singular possessive suffix is -*vá* and the flexional suffix for the Hungarian instrumental adverb, -*val*, -*vel* corresponds to *ole* in the fictitious language. These observations are undoubtedly correct but can also be supplemented with further ones:

Strophe 1:
Line 1: *dzsá* = szél 'winds' [lit. 'wind']; *gulb|e* = völgye (*e* = possessive suffix, 3. person singularis) 'valley'; *rár* = farkas 'wolf'; *kicser|e* = fészke 'den' [lit. 'nest']
Line 2: *áj* = mért 'why'; *ni* = nem 'didn't you' [lit. 'no']; *muszta|sz* = őriztél (*sz* = personal suffix., 2. person singular, past tense, indicative mood) 'take care of me [lit. 'took care of me']; *emo* = engem 'me'
Line 3: *mankütvanta|sz* = segítettél 'help me' [lit. 'helped me']
Line 4: *adde* = most 'now'; *maru|va* = nyomna (personal suffix, 1. person singular, present tense, conditional mood) 'shouldn't press me'; *bato* = kő 'stone'; *jaman* = ajaj 'woe is me'

Strophe 2:
Line 1: *ole* = -val, -vel (flexional suffix of the instrumental case); *dzsuro* = könny 'tears' [lit. tear]; *nann|i* = mosdattalak (personal suffix, 1. person singularis, past tense, indicative mood) 'I washed you'; *he* = téged 'you'
Line 2: *csilambo* = haj 'hair'; *ábáb|i* = törölgettelek 'I wiped you'
Line 3: *buglo* = vér 'blood'; *ining|i* = itattalak 'I gave you to drink'
Line 4: *lünjel* = mindig 'always'; *dáj|i* = szerettelek 'I loved you'

Strophe 3:
Line 1: *vá* = -d (possessive suffix, 2. person singularis) 'your'; *pudd* = földed [lit. föld] 'land'; *shukom/o* = teremjen (personal suffix, 3. person singularis, imperative mood) 'let rise', *iked|e*= tüskét (*e* = flexional suffix of the object) 'thorn'
Line 2: *jimla* = tehened [lit. tehén] 'cow'; *gulm/o* = adjon 'let give'; *buglavi* = véres 'bloody', *el/e* = tejet 'milk'
Line 3: *leli* = asszonyod [lit. asszony] 'wife'; *ded/e* = fiat 'son'
Line 4: *odda* = édesapád [lit. édesapa] 'father'; *dzsárum/o* = eltemessen 'let bury you'

As can be seen from the semantic approach suggested above, there is a correspondence in the parallel arrangement of the parts of the sentences in the version of the imagined original, too. In regard to phonetics, there are, however, more significant discrepancies between the two versions. Similar to Weöres, Molnár also (1977:32) refers to the fact that the acoustics of the fictitious text reflects the Romany-language. The results of her investigations of the phonetical patterns may be summarized as follows:

a/ A quantitative analysis of the vowels and the consonants in the two versions shows patterns considerably different from one other: there are 48% vowels in the imagined original, compared to 43,5% in the imagined translation; 52% consonants in the imagined original, compared to 56,5% in the imagined translation. It can be seen from this comparison that the version of the imagined original has more sonority than the imagined translation.

b/ The palatal and velar vowels also differ in proportion: there are 58,7% back vowels in the imagined original, compared to 33,3% in the imagined translation; and 41,3% front vowels in the imagined original, compared to 66,7% in the imagined translation. An obvious prevalence of velar vowels in the imagined original makes this version much more soft-toned than the imagined translation.

c/ There are many more voiced consonants in the imagined original than in the imagined translation. Voiced consonants placed together with vowels add up to 90,1% in the imagined original, which makes this version exceedingly melodious.

By arguing for the prominence of the vowels and the voiced consonants in the version of the imagined original compared to the imagined translation, Molnár wishes to demonstrate its primal tunefullness, its melodiousness. She emphasizes the irregularity in accentuation and intonation, too (Molnár 1977:32). In my opinion as well, the imagined original is more melodious than the imagined translation, but not exclusively due to the circumstances indicated by Molnár. I don't think that this quality of melodiousness of the poem *Barbár dal* 'Barbarian Song' can be compared to that of the pieces of *Rongyszőnyeg* 'Rag-carpet' or *Magyar etüdök* 'Hungarian Etudes'. The significantly constrained metrical pattern which gives those pieces their unique melodious quality cannot be seen in the version of the imagined original of the poem *Barbár dal* 'Barbarian Song'.

2.3.2 The World of the Text

2.3.2.1 The Theme

Analogous to the study of the text and its inner context, this discussion about the theme of the poem *A barbár dal* 'Barbarian Song' will also begin with the version of the imagined translation. Without any doubt, the poem places a curse on somebody. The reader, however, is not given any explanatory notes about the curse's victim. Nevertheless, the third line in the third verse: *asszonyod fiat ne adjon* 'may your wife never give you a son', points to a masculine character afflicted by the curse. Probable grounds for that are offered in the lines of the first strophe: not giving support to somebody who needed it, and leaving somebody in the lurch. This conclusion can be drawn by using the meaning of the words as the basis of an interpretation. All other collateral and underlying meanings belong to the spheres of imagination, intuition and the spirit (Réz 1993:52). In order to interpret these spheres, a synchronical study must inevitably be completed alongside a diachronical one.

The title itself, *Barbár dal* 'Barbarian Song', indicates the sources of inspiration: these must be found in ancient poetry or at least in the oldest forms of lyrical representations. Traces of prehistoric religious beliefs can be discerned in the lamentation of the protagonist. The four words of the first line, which raise supernatural forces severely forbidden to name by their real name, become filled with magical content and the complaint changes to a bewitchment.

The funeral-song and the shaman-song are two main categories of Hungarian ancient poetry. The funeral song, as a form of the ritual song (MIT I:22) can be traced back to the days of matriarchy. It has always been a genre utilized by women and its form hasn't changed through the course of time. It is characterized by momentariness, improvisation and the repetition of certain words and word-groups essential to emotional efficacy (Dugántsy 1991:51), for instance the interjection *jaj* 'woe is me'. The shaman-song has bearing on the shaman-belief of the ancient Hungarians. These songs were also improvisations, words which held magical power in relation to supernatural forces. The incantations and enchantment prayers of the 15th and 16th centuries may be seen to originate in the shaman-song (MIT I:23). These prayers, striving get rid of evil or trying to bewitch the enemy with magical words, reflected some kind of a superstitious belief.

The poem *Barbár dal* 'Barbarian Song' is in many ways similar to those first representations of poetry. As to the form, it is a combination of the funeral-song and the shaman-song. However, it differs from them both. It is dissimilar to the funeral-song, as here it is the deceased who weeps over himself, and it is dissimilar to the shaman-song, too, for here it is not the shaman but the deceased who calls down the the curses. These circumstances might help in the attempt at unraveling the theme of this poem. In spite of the words which are comprehensible at least in the case of the imagined translation, we cannot find any distinct course of events, a circumstance that definitely motivates some individual paths of interpretation. An image of the abandoned girl is likely to appear, the girl who takes her own life, and when in death she curses the seducer with the words of depravation, she becomes like him.

An investigation of only the imagined translation is, however, not sufficient. In order to explain the more concealed dimensions of meaning, we must also take the imagined original into consideration. Is it possible to penetrate a seemingly meaningless text with music in such a way that it ultimately obtains a meaning? This question, put to Weöres, was answered by him in the following way: "'Ange amban ulanoje balanga janégol', or 'Panyigai kudora kudora'. These words have no meaning that can be found or inserted into a vocabulary, their only meaning is comprised by the sounds, the dynamics and the structure" (Hornyik 1993:92). We can assume a meaning similar to this in the imagined original version of the *Barbár dal* 'Barbarian Song'. Such fields of meaning were discussed in the chapter dealing with the context within. Meaning is part of the inner context in these seemingly meaningless poems and is thus independent from a context outside the structure. In the inner context, however, meaning is absorbed by the sign. The field of semantics is replaced by that of semiotics.

According to Jurij Lotman (1974:54, 62), each level of poetry is an independent bearer of meaning and each integral part of a language-structure might obtain the semantic level. In the imagined original version of the poem *Barbár dal* 'Barbarian song' the signs by themselves are the bearers of meaning. This meaning mingled in the signs cannot be grasped by everybody, much like the shaman, whose magic words addressed to supernatural forces are deliberately incomprehensible to people outside the magic circle. Whilst calling these supernatural forces, the shaman falls into a trance. Entrancement takes place in an ecstasy, that is "in a state of unconsciousness lasting for a certain time" (Diószegi 1983:103). It was Pál Hunfalvy who first pointed out the correspondences based on etymological relations between the words *révül* 'falls into trance' and *rejt, rejtőzik* 'hide, conceal [himself]' (Diószegi 1983:102). Judging from the common origin of these words, there is a fundamental interdependence between the entrancement of the shaman and the act of hiding himself. It is the phenomenon when the soul of the shaman moves off to remote and mysterious dimensions where it hides itself. This is his only way to get in contact with the supernatural forces.

István Szerdahelyi (1996:114) wrote as follows about the abstruse passages of ritualistic worship: "In magic texts, however, we perceive this same lack of meaning 'with a holy shiver' and as a sign for a chance of freedom of a sublimity far beyond us, because these rites are altogether secret, incomprehensible to the uninitiated". When Weöres (1964) explains the poem with the title *Rejtelem* 'Mystery', he expresses himself as follows: "I don't write for myself but for others. This is why I strive for suggestiveness. It doesn't matter if they understand it, but the nerves should shiver like the stroked string in the wind". This "holy shiver" leads the way to the innermost dimensions of meaning. It is the place of the shaman.

2.3.2.2 The Poem as Part of Weöres' Lifework

The poem *Barbár dal* 'Barbarian song' was written in 1944. It was first published in the volume titled *Elysium* in 1946 and later in the volume titled *A hallgatás tornya* 'The Tower of Silence' in 1956. In this burdensome period of Hungarian history, definitely unfavourable to a free development of poetry, charges of being apolitical and antisocial and caring very little for the building of a communist society were brought against Weöres, as well as many other outstanding Hungarian writers. To what extent should we rely on this charge? Many poems of Weöres written in the year 1944, by all accounts, repudiate this impeachment. The poem with the title *A reménytelenség könyve* 'The Book of Hopelessness' (EI I:700-707), which Attila Tamás (1978:55) calls "a document against Fascism", was written in 1944. According to its message, there is only one hope in total hopelessness and that is to recognize the fact of this hopelessness. In Imre Batas' (1979:113) opinion, "this is the point where Weöres consorts with the philosophy of existentialism":

A sötétség pohara ez,
a reménytelenség könyve.

Íme a reménytelenség: az utolsó remény!
Görnyedj le, vessz el:

átoknak hangzik, és íme az utolsó áldás!

Boldog, aki nem vár javulásra:
tudja, mi rejlik mögötte.
Boldog, aki nem vár élvezetre:
tudja, mi rejlik mögötte.
Boldog, aki nem vár törvényre:
tudja, mi rejlik mögötte.
Boldog, aki nem vár semmit
és a teljes sötétséget magára ölti.

This is the tumbler of darkness,
the book of hopelessness.

See, the hopelessness: the last hope!
Break down, perish:
it sounds like a curse, and see, the last blessing!

He, who doesn't want any betterment, is happy:
he knows, what is hidden behind.
He, who doesn't wish any delight, is happy:
he knows, what is hidden behind.
He, who doesn't expect any law, is happy:
he knows, what is hidden behind.
He, who doesn't expect anything, is happy
and he puts on a total darkness.

The outspokenly political subject-matter is clearly indicated in such titles as
Elesett katonák 'Fallen Soldiers', *Szirénák légitámadáskor* 'Sirens at Air-raid'
or *Háborús jegyzetek* 'War Notes', from poems also written in 1944. The
poem *A magyar tanulság* 'The Hungarian Lesson' (EI I:698) has an unmistakable political conviction and sensibility:

Ne azt a nemzetet csodáld,
mely hadonászva, kiabálva
egy új téboly jelszavát kitalálja
s fejére gyűjti a halált –

ó, azt csodáld nagyon,
mely ki tud maradni a táncból!
mert századunk harsogó tébolyából

nincs más menekvés, mint bölcs nyugalom.

Do not admire that nation
which while gesticulating, shouting
concocts the slogan of a new frenzy
and hoards death to itself –

o!, admire most that one
which can stay away from the dance!
because from the roaring frenzy of our century
there is no other escape, than a wise tranquillity.

As early as 1933 Weöres published a poem with the significant title *Hitler* (EI I:79):

A dermedt Föld
figyelme
jégcsapként lóg a bajuszán.

The attention of the
frozen Earth
hangs like an icicle on his moustache.

In the poem titled *Ijedtség* 'Fear' (EI I:708), also written in 1944, he writes about his own worries:

Költő voltam, szálltam isteni magasban,
magyar szó előttem oda nem hatolt még.
Most szavam botorkál: mert nappal zaklatnak,
s nincs lámpám, gyertyám, hogy éjjel verselhetnék.

Amit én a mezőn elvégezni bírok,
tízszer jobban végzi akármelyik béres,
de amit a papír-mezőn elmulasztok,
az Isten sem viszi énnélkülem véghez.
I was a poet, I flew to heavenly heights,
words in Hungarian had never made their way there before me.
Now my words stumble along: for they disturb me by day,
and I have no lamp or candle for writing in the night.

The work I can do in the fields,
any day-worker can do ten times better,
but the work I leave undone on the paper-field,
not even God carries out without me.

These poems cited above might be understood without difficulty, but there are
also poems written in the same year which are not so easy to explain. The
poem with the title *Az áramlás szobra* 'The Statue of the Stream' (EI I:613),
with the former title *Eidolon* is one such poem. When it was published for the
first time in 1947, it took the readers aback. This was partly because its use of
grammatical rules in a completely arbitrary way, and partly for the reason that
Kenyeres (1983:116) expressed as follows: "He tested the philosophical possibilities of a concentrated poetical way of phrasing, wondering whether the
very substance of movement is possible to catch with words which by nature
are immobile, and if an adequate lingual copy, an eidolon can be made from
movement, as an 'ideal reality'":

> éj kert hold pad
> üres szívdobogás
> dobéjdob dobkertdob dobholddob dobpaddob
> föld homok kavics
>
> lámpás madarak ablaksora
> folyton távozik
>
> night garden moon bench
> empty heart-beating
> drumnightdrum drumgardendrum drummoondrum drumbenchdrum
> earth sand pebble
>
> window-row of birds with lamp
> it always moves off.

Weöres calls the poem an experimentation "in order to try out if by means of
a totally loosened line of thoughts, a breaking of the grammatical rules and an
irregular twisting up of the words, some kind of aesthetic value, that is, a beautiful poem can possibly arise" (Eidolon:26). Certainly, the avantgarde, especially the Surrealist movement in literature and Dadaism exercised a very
strong influence on Weöres' poetry during this time, and he also made several experimentations with poetical form. The poem *Az áramlás szobra* 'The
Statue of the Stream' was very likely a trying-out of automatic writing. Other

poems that experiment with words are poems like *A megmozdult szótár* 'The Dictionary that Made a Move', *Dob és tánc* 'Drum and Dance', *Ablak az éjbe* 'Window to the Night'. In the finale of the poem *A kilencedik szimfónia* 'Night Symphony' every tenth word originates in a novel with the title *Elnémult harangok* 'The Bells which Became Silent' by Viktor Rákosi, and is an example of objective automatic writing. The other form of automatic writing is the subjective one, which can also appear as so-called psychodelic art, the creation of the state of inspiration by drugs. Nevertheless, this other form has nothing to do with the poetry of Weöres.

Another group of poems which are difficult to explain are those which are absolutely unintelligible. They are unintelligible because in these poems the language itself is incompehensible. The poem *Táncdal* 'Dancing Song' (EI I:613), written in 1942, hints at meaning only through the intensively pulsating rhythm:

panyigai panyigai panyigai
ü panyigai ü
panyigai panyigai panyigai
ü panyigai panyigai

The motto of Weöres' dissertation with the title *A vers születése* 'The Birth of the Poem' (EI I:217) is a magic formula uttered by the aborigines when asking for the rain:

Dád a-da-da
dád a-da-da
dád a-da-da
da kata káj!

Déd o-de-do
déd o-de-do
déd o-de-do
da kata káj!

In the poem betitled *A képzelt város* 'The Imagined Town' (EI II:33), written in 1947 the priests sing like this:

Juhova huluma jeniva
emora homeja kullo
tepale meluva...
Jeniva homeja juhoa
kullo tepale...

The essential question we now may propose is probably as follows: how did these poems come into being? Using the poem with the title *A csillagok* 'The Stars', originally *A sorsangyalok* 'The Angels of Destiny' as an example, we can refer to Weöres' (WW:128) own information about its course of writing: "The first phase is, when certain meaningless words suddenly appear in the mind (naur glainre iki..). From these the rough text emerges, giving the words several meanings". About the phases following this first phase, Kenyeres (1983:108) writes as follows: "The poem advances towards the meaning and the subject matter as if on a 'turn-bench of a metrical moulding'. It is not accidental that the poems composed according to some method of automatic writing are always in prose, and that they have no experience of settled rhymes or metrics, because obligations and restrictions belong to the *faber* (hand-wrought) charasteristics of poetry. From a meaningless, shapeless row of sounds, in a metrical-structural manner, the well-shaped, well-sounding poem developed conforming to the taste of Weöres, and the actual marks of automatic writing faded away and then the poem suddenly became connected with the electrical circuit of a strange philosophical content".

Did the poem *A barbár dal* 'Barbarian Song' originate in the same way? Most likely, it did. In his dissertation Weöres goes into particulars about how to compose a poem. One of the feasible ways is when "the bud of the poem is metrical form, which only later becomes attached to content" (EI I:245). The metrical form, however, is inclined to develop such great importance that it crushes everything else, even the words. The rhythm then becomes the only thing which exists. The poem *A barbár dal* 'Barbarian Song' also has this characteristic of pulsating rhythm in its lines. But neither the rhymes nor the metrical form display any constrained pattern. Still, the *faber* character does not disappear, for there is a conscious detail present: the logic of the grammar.

The epic poem entitled *Mahruh veszése* 'The Loss of Mahruh', written in 1952, descibes a long-vanished primaeval world. It tells about the last days of the ancient star, Mahruh, in the time before the deluge. All the strange names of the work are fictitious and the title mentioned in the preface as the original one is in a reconstructed ancient language, according to Weöres: *Kana vuanh athetan jargelih*, or in Weöres' translation: 'Gyászdob száz lerogyó világért Jargeh városában'; 'Mourning drum for hundred falling worlds in the town of Jargeh'. Neither the ancient world nor the ancient language is real. Nevertheless, a certain sense of verisimilitude suggests to the reader that they could have been real once. This is because of imagination, which when realized in poetical form is capable of breathing life even into the non-real. This is similar to the authentic-like language of the poem *Barbár dal* 'Barbarian Song', in which the fictitious language is equipped with grammatical rules.

In terms of the meaning of the meaningless poem, Weöres, in an interview to Mátyás Domokos (1982:548), made a statement as follows: "it often stands against our own age and criticizes or denies the validity of it". And to the question, what type of nostalgia is in evidence in the meaningless poem, Weöres answered: "A nostalgia for a more well-ordered, more intelligible, more perspicuous world". The poems in broken languages discussed above came into being during a time when trust in a better future was also broken. Many writers were sentenced to silence by a dogmatic political climate. Weöres was one of them. He could not publish a new volume until 1956, which had the title: *A hallgatás tornya* 'The Tower of Silence'. We can perhaps presume that it was just this atmosphere of crisis which helped shape these meaningless poems. A further investigation on issues connecting to the philosophical matters may, however, shed light upon other contributory causes.

2.3.2.3 Weöres' Philosophy of Poetics

Olvass verseket oly nyelveken is, amelyeket nem értesz. Ne sokat, mindig csak néhány sort, de többször egymásután. Jelentésükkel ne törődj, de lehetőleg ismerd az eredeti kiejtésmódjukat, hangzásukat. Így megismered a nyelvek zenéjét, s az alkotó lelkek belső zenéjét. S eljuthatsz oda, hogy anyanyelved szövegeit is olvasni tudod a tartalomtól függetlenül is; a vers belső, igazi szépségét, testtelen táncát csak így élheted át.

Also read poems in languages which you don't understand. Not much, only a few lines every time, but then do it several times. Don't care about what they mean, but if possible, learn the right pronunciation, the acoustics. You then become acquainted with the music of the language and the inner music of the creating spirits. And you may get to the point that you can read the texts of your own language independent of the content, and this is the only way to experience the innermost real beauty, the incorporeal dance of the poem.

> (*A teljesség felé. A versről.* 'Towards the Absolute. About the Poem'. In: EI I:671)

The prose-sketches of the work *A teljesség felé* 'Towards the Absolute' were published in 1945, a year after the poem *Barbár dal* 'Barbarian Song'. The undeniably moderate enthusiasm with which Weöres welcomed the new era of socialism is easy to recognize in the poems written during this time. They express a primary disillusionment arising from the belief in the "complete hopelessness of redemption by society" (Kenyeres 1983:122). We might be aware of some kind of passive resistance and also of a firm conviction which in general rejects all progress. For Weöres progress is of no significance: "I believe in movement accomplished by people, but I don't believe in progress. [– – –] When the mechanical, technical civilization develops, it happens at the cost of the spiritual refinement. [– – –] Something happens all the time, but nothing really substantial ever happens" (Bertha 1993:152). When Ferenc Karinthy (1990:276) sprang the question on Weöres in Rome – the journey supported by a scholarship –, as to why Weöres refused the idea of progress, when today it takes only two hours to fly to Rome, in contrast to the time of Traianus, when it could take two weeks between Aquincum and Rome, Weöres retorted as follows: "What do you say? Two hours? [...] I waited for my passport for six months!"

Without doubt, such an insubordinate philosophy has an effect on private life, too, especially during that historical period when it would have been more remunerative to show some enthusiasm. The reason why Weöres didn't act in this way can be explained by his spontaneity and straightfor-wardness. He was, as a matter of fact, not a public poet before 1945, but the disregard he suffered after this year completely spoiled his interest in politics. That freedom, which in society is an illusion, becomes rearranged in a unique individual freedom, followed by a virtuostic moulding of the language. Weöres catches and masters "the nothingness of a shattered world" with his art (Németh 1992:244). It is perhaps not accidental that a shattered world is mirrored by shattered words.

Dadaism was also an intellectual product of a crisis. The untranslatable poems of Harry Ball are very similar those by Weöres and to the imagined original of the *Barbár dal* 'Barbarian Song'. In order to find a way out of the crisis, the poet searched for the original, magical and mystical in the words, the most primary strata, which are exempt from every evil use (Jonsson 1971:176). It is a fact that Weöres, particularly at the beginning of his carrier as a poet, was open to various poetic experimentations. As a consequence of this, we may also notice a kind of universal nihilism in his poetry, presumably traceable to the Dadaist influences.

Russian Formalism appeared at roughly the same time as Dadaism. The deliverance of words from intellectual restrictions was also a main task for the representatives of the Formalist movement. It was Viktor Shklovsky who first gave voice to the conjecture that, similar to objects which get worn away, words become automatized when used too often. This is a completely uncon-scious process, but has the ultimate result of objects and events losing their significance and words losing their meaning. According to Shklovsky, the main task for art is to re-establish the lost balance betwen the objects, the events and the way they are expressed for the sake of proper understanding. This happens through alienation of the object, *priem ostranenija*, by expression of a deliberately obstructed form, *priem zatrudnennoj formy*. This deliberate-ly obstructed form at the same time necessitates the abstraction of language, the process of the words being arranged into figures, metaphors and tropes or when existing words are replaced by imagined words.

This "language beyond reason" was called *zaum* by the formalists. It is characterized by the fact that words are devoid of meaning, yet they are still words, because they possess the formal distinctive features of words (Lotman 1974:92). "The zaum is a language which completely lost its connection with meaning, its relation to something and turned into a pure form, to music" (Bókay 1997:162). Without meaning, there is only the shape of the word left and this form reflects the inexpressible, secret, transcendental essence, or as Weöres put it:

A szavak különlévők és gyöngysor-szerüek, a dolgok összefüggők és halom-szerüek. Ezért a szavak és a dolgok csak súrolják egymást.

A gondolat összetett és kimondható, az igazság egyszerű és kimond-hatatlan. Igazságot csak beszéd nélkül tudhatsz meg, tehát csak önmagadtól. Tedd alkalmassá lelkedet arra, hogy az igazságot tudhasd benne.

The words are separate and are like a necklace of pearls, the things are connected with one another and are like a heap. That is why words and things merely brush against each other.

Thought is complex and expressible, truth is simple and inexpressible. You become aware of a truth without speech, that is, from within yourself. Make your spirit able to know the truth.

> (*A teljesség felé. Az igazságról.* 'Towards the Absolute. About the Truth'. In: EI I:689)

Concerning "modernity that broke up" Ernő Kulcsár Szabó (1992:24) wrote as follows: "In the modality of the poetic language the unconscious forms of existence and self-interpretation of the individual also manifest themselves". Roman Jacobson (1974:216-226) examines subconscious forms in Russian poetry and he particularly stresses the importance of these patterns in folk-poetry. According to Imre Bori (1984:462), Weöres portrays the "sublogical moments" in his short poems. All these reflections have the very same idea: beneath the surface of the personality there is something incomprehensible and unfathomable, which is the genuine, primary form.

The stages in development of language as Béla Hamvas (1995b:157-174) made clear are as follows: primary language, idea-language, symbol-language, myth-language, poetic language, everyday language and conceptual language. Paradoxically, it is conceptual language which is the most undevel-oped aspect. Concepts are namely devoid of content in this language, because it doesn't reflect things in their real shape, and as a result things lose their real sense of meaning. Everyday language is not constant. It changes for different reasons. In poetic language everything is subordinated to the individual who expresses herself. Its biggest mistake, according to Hamvas, is the trope simile, which "confuses the external with the internal and believes that it ought to illuminate the figure, and looks at the figure as an outer thing, though it is the inner figure, and just that figure, which must be illuminated". This mistake has been resolved in the language of myth and symbol-language which "conceals what it says and says what it conceals". Idea-language is the momentary manifestation of "an understanding beyond reason" intelligible by only a few. The most advanced stage is primary language, which is completely incomprehensible for the human intellect. However, it might arise in some people during special ecstatic moments, as a very remote surmize. "We can recognize primary language by the way it phrases the words in their original meaning, in their original intensity, in their original tension of the creating-act and in their shining power". In primary language there is an analogy between things, that is, each thing is identical with every other thing. Every single thing can be seen in another, for in oneness every thing is the same thing. Individual character has vanished, or, as Hamvas put it, the "soul is not like a butterfly, but the soul is the butterfly itself".

Weöres strived to entrap this primary language, wishing to revive the ancient unity of things, events and words (Mórocz 1996:107). The innate units of this unity are the voices and the melodies (Kecskés 1984:46). The version of the imagined original of the poem *Barbár dal* 'Barbarian Song' is composed only of voices and melodies. Its words exist only in a formal sense, yet we perceive the poem as if it had a concrete, definite meaning. The reason for this is the method with which Weöres is able to raise the intuitively emerging words of a non-existing reality to a conscious level. This happens when using a real, researcher-compiled and thorough, non-fictitious grammar. This non-fictitious grammar of a fictitious language infuses life into the non-existing words and the unintelligible becomes conceivable. The compilation of rules for a grammar, even if it is for a non-existing language, is in any case a conscious activity, in the same way as play is when it uses toys to imitate real life. In the same way Weöres, too, plays, using the words as toys.

Bori (1984:459) calls certain poems of Weöres "hypocritical poems". The most essential characteristic of these poems is that the poet, in the same way as a child plays, becomes another character, and appears in another role. According to Bori, the poem *Barbár dal* 'Barbarian Song' belongs to this group and he also points out its significance in the following way: "[...] with this poem, after all, he exposed his workshop: the double mask not only reinforces the sense of play, but at the same time it also denies it and calls attention to the fact that at the bottom of poetic play there is an earnest poetic ambition" (Bori 1984:459).

Kenyeres (1974:293) refers to these "hypocritical", impersonal poems as some kind of "play-poem", using his own term for the concept. A characteristic of the play-poem is that it doesn't associate with play in the formal sense, as for example counting-games do, but associates with play in subject-matter, which is, as a matter of fact, a metamorphosis, a transformation to another character in a fantasy. This form of the exchange of roles is easy to prove in works like *Psyché*, where the poet transforms himself into a poetess who lived in the 17th century; nevertheless, it becomes much more difficult in the poem *Barbár dal* 'Barbarian Song'. In my opinion, the poem also belongs to the group of the play-poems and the hypocritical poems. As a play-poem, I think that both the form and the subject-matter are attached to play. Its form, similar to counting-games, represents an imagined language. In terms of the subject-matter, it is the exchange of roles which is its motivational force, not only in a sense of the form, as Bori seems to indicate by the relation of the imagined original and the imagined translation, but also within the context of the imagined original. For when the poet gets to the bottom of the meaningless words and fills them with secret meaning springing from the rules of grammar, he also becomes transformed. He turns into the first poet of the first poem, who speaks in a different time, with a different voice and in a different language. As absolute meaninglessness is expressed in that only existing form in which the facts of reality disappear, the identity of the poet also evanesces in this form and becomes identical to language, the only conceivable quality.

3 Without a home

(1)

Sebzett szarvas tiszta érre,
menyasszony a vőlegényre,
égő erdő fuldokolva
a lángfojtó hűs záporra,
éji mécs a kihúnyásra
hogy a vak rendet ne bántsa:
sose vágyik hevesebben
mint halálra testem-lelkem.

(2)

E világot feleségül
az ész hozománya nélkül
minek vettem? Alma-forma
fara perdül jobbra-balra,
simul minden kelme rajta,
hizelegve körülnyalja
hullámozva, örvényt ontva,
préme, selyme, vászna, rongya,

főz, varr, hímez, zongorázik,
táncol, szeretkezve játszik,
de nézz közelről szemébe:
nincs nézése, köd a mélye,
és mint megkoccantott lárva
szinte kong a butasága.

(3)

Olykor édes-szenvedélyes,
máskor haragos-szeszélyes,
körültombol vörös hajjal
mint egy bosszúálló angyal,
hozzám-vagdos órát, tányért,
nem enyémet, a magáét,
csak ruhámat óvja féltve
irtózatos gyengédsége.

(4)

Dühöng s békémet nem érti,
ekkor lepleit letépi,
pőre testét földhöz csapja
zokogva és sikongatva.
Nem kell nékem főztje, ágya,
szemfényvesztő sok ruhája,
doktor-látta pőresége,
csak engedjen haza végre.

(5)

Az ő otthonába honnan,
mikor, miért vándoroltam?
Tán az anyából tudatlan
s akaratlan fölfakadtam;
vagy csábított durva kéje
és mohón buktam beléje;
vagy mint elkorhadt halottat
elevenek ide dobtak;
vagy sírván a szenvedőkért
alázattal jöttem önként;
bárhogy: itt sülök a máglyán
mint egy nyársra húzott fácán.

(6)

Bármennyi a gondja, kínja,
bírom, noha nyögve, ríva,
nem mártírként énekelve,
csak pólyásként berezelve;
de a gyönyör zabálását
utálom mint mézes-kását,
mégis bajban elepedve
kapaszkodom élvezetbe.

(7)

Mindazt ami hol-nincs hol-van,
most fölbukkan, meg elillan,
bujócskázó dőreséget

úgy unom, hogy szinte éget.
Higyjem-e: csak meg kell halnom
s vele többé semmi dolgom?
A halott, ha léte nincsen,
oly szabad, mint maga Isten.

(8)

Hogyha semmivé nem égek,
tudom, folyton visszatérek
nyomorúság legmélyére,
mindig sűrűbb süppedékbe.
Mert aki bolondház rabja,
ha meggyógyul, odahagyja,
de aki bolondot ápol,
ott lakik és el nem pártol.

(1)

Wounded deer to clear stream,
bride on the bridegroom,
burning forest gasping
for the fresh shower to choke the flame,
night-light to go down
not to disturb the blind order:
never longed more
as my body and soul long to die.

(2)

Why did I marry this world
without the dowry of
common sense? Her apple-like
back-side turns to the left and to the right,
all her clothes fit her,
flattering, swelling, pouring whirlpool
lick her around
her furs, silk, linen, rags,

she cooks, sews, embroiders, plays the piano,
dances, plays when making love,

104

but look in her eyes closely:
she has no look, there is fog in the deep,
and like a grub that knocked against
her dumbness nearly resounds.

(3)

Sometimes she is sweet and passionate,
another time she is wrathful and whimsical,
she raves around me with sandy hair
like a revenging angel,
she slams at me watches and plates,
not mine, but her own,
only my clothes are anxiously saved
by her horrible tenderness.

(4)

She fumes and cannot understand my peace,
then she tears off her covers,
casts her disrobed body to the floor
sobbing and screaming.
I don't want her cooking, her bed,
her delusive many clothes,
her disrobed body watched by the doctor,
only she would let me go home at last.

(5)

From where, when and why did I come
wandering to her home?
Unconsciously and involuntarily maybe
from the mother I arose;
or I was tempted by her rough delight
and eagerly I fell in her;
or like a rotten corpse
I was cast here by the quick;
or crying over those who suffer
humbly I came by myself;
anyhow: now I'm roasted here on the bonfire
like a pheasant on a spit.

(6)

No matter how much her worry and pain may be
I bear it, though groaning and weeping,
not while singing like a martyr,
only like a babe in a funk;
but the devour of the delight
I hate like honey mash,
still, wasted away in grief
I hold on to the pleasure.

(7)

Everything exists now and then,
suddenly appearing and getting away,
folly that plays hide-and-seek
I am so bored by, that it nearly burns.
Shall I believe that I only must die
and then I won't be concerned with her any more?
The dead losing her existence,
is as free as God himself.

(8)

If I don't burn to nothing,
I know, I always return
to the very depth of misery,
every time to an ever thicker sinking.
For he, inprisoned in a madhouse
if recovered, may depart
but he who takes care of a madman,
is living there and doesn't turn away.

(*Magna Meretrix*. In: EI II:451-453)

3.1 The Text

3.1.1 The Structure and Shape of the Writing

The poem in fact consists of nine strophes, an arrangement that isn't in concord with our grouping into eight units above. This altered ordering of the parts of the strophes is mainly determined by decisive contextual factors. An obvious imbalance in the shape of the writing is created by the different number of the lines in the strophes. Each verse, except the third and the sixth, consists of eight lines. The third strophe is made up of six lines, in contrast to the sixth verse, which contains twelve lines. The length of the lines is comparatively the same, but without any regular alternation of the longer and shorter lines. Many lines build a syntagm of their own, but there are many enjambements, too. Punctuation marks are regularly used, and each strophe, with the exception of the center of the two-part second strophe, is closed by a full stop.

3.1.2 The Represented Elements of Reality

The title *Magna Meretrix* comes from the Latin, roughly meaning: the great lecherous one. The attribute *magna* defines the gender as feminine. As the title predominantly determines the subject-matter, an inescapable starting-point in a study of the elements of represented reality must be to disclose the identity of this *Magna Meretrix*. The description of the actions of a wife is related to that of the world, as demonstrated already in the second strophe. The character of the wife is a personification of the concept of the world. We have the following actors: the main character, indicated by the first person singular and the *Magna Meretrix* of the title, indicated by the third person singular, meaning both the character of the wife and the concept of the world.

The first and the last verse function as a frame in the poem. This enclosure is not a result of formal reasons but for the most part because of the subject-matter. Both strophes deal with the main character in the first person singular. In the seven medial strophes a certain structural balance between the first and the third person singular can be seen. Examining the two parts of the second strophe as a unit, where the two parts together build a single strophe, we find that the three first strophes portray the wife or the world and the three last strophes portray the main character. A contraction of the two parts of the second strophe can be motivated in many ways. One reason is the enjambement, which reflects an unity in content and another reason is the fact that the unit of three strophes dealing with the protagonist also contains a longer strophe. The two longer strophes are symmetrically arranged: the two-pieced second strophe corresponds to the longer fifth strophe, and both are followed by two regular length strophes which are related to the same semantical context (fig. 10).

Strophes:	1	2	3	4	5	6	7	8
Persons:	1. p. sing.	2. p. sing.	3. p. sing.	4. p. sing.	1. p. sing.	1. p. sing.	1. p. sing.	1. p. sing.

Figure 10

The analysis of the represented elements of reality is based on this structure of the eight strophes illustrated above. This arrangement of the strophes draws attention to another structural characteristic, that of the dominating role that the number eight signifies. The eight strophes of the poem, except for the second and the fifth strophes each consist of eight lines and the eight lines of the strophes are each made of eight syllables. The diverging second and fifth strophes, however, both phrasing a question in their first sentences, show a distinct parallelism within their grammar.

Elements of the outer world appear predominantly in connection with the character of the wife. This tendency is shown by the image of diverse material objects, such as furs, silk, linen and rags and also actual human activites, such as cooking, sewing, embroidering and playing the piano. The character of the wife reflects the external world with all its material objects. In contrast to this extroversion is the inner world of the self, where the images of material objects are replaced by concepts and ideas, such as death, delight and pleasure. Here the verbs don't refer to actions, as seen in the strophes relating to the wife, but instead, in most cases, are reflections on the nature of the world.

The represented elements of reality function as counterparts of a contradiction at the semantic level. The contrasting points which define the global structure of the poem are sketched out in figure 11. In addition to these oppositions we can observe the opposition of the two strophes which form the frame-like structure. There is a longing for death expressed in the first verse

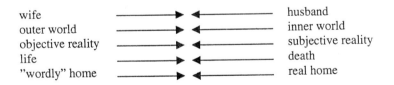

Figure 11

108

and a resignation over the fact that this longing cannot be realized. A further contrast is revealed in the relation of the title to the subject-matter. The title, denoting the feminine and also personifying the world, is opposed to the underlying context, that of the masculine protagonist, whose character symbolizes an alienation from the vanity of the world.

However, this contrasting principle can be proved not only on a global level, but by looking at the minor elements of represented reality. Citing oppositions of words based on their semantic content would create a long list. Some examples are the opposition of the words *menyasszony* 'bride' and *vőlegény* 'bridegoom'; *égő erdő* 'burning forest' and *hűs zápor* 'fresh shower'; and *testem* 'my body' and *lelkem* '[my] soul' in the first strophe.

As the contrasting principle works within both the global structure and the minor elements of it, and as it can also be revealed in terms of the subject-matter, I consider it to be the primary structuring principle of the text.

A sentence with focal quality and an integrating capacity is a statement which comprises all the spheres of meaning at once. These spheres of meaning are developed and expanded by the other sentences in the given text (Szabó 1988:102). In the poem *Magna Meretrix*, as I see it, it is the first question, *E világot feleségül / az ész hozománya nélkül / minek vettem?* 'Why did I marry this world / without the dowry of / common sense?' which meets these expectations. All the other sentences in the poem search for a feasible answer to this question. This question is repeated as the first sentence of the fifth strophe in another form, but in the same semantic context: *Az ő otthonába honnan, / mikor, miért vándoroltam?* 'From where, when and why did I come / wandering to her home?' This second question is, however, an almost unvaried repetition of the first one, in addition to the fact that here the relation between the signifier, the wife, and the signified, the world, explicitly indicated in the first question, is much more indistinct. Because of this, it lacks the requirements of a sentence with focal quality.

The concentration on all the spheres of meaning at the same time, as expressed by the sentence with focal quality, is illustrated in figure 12.

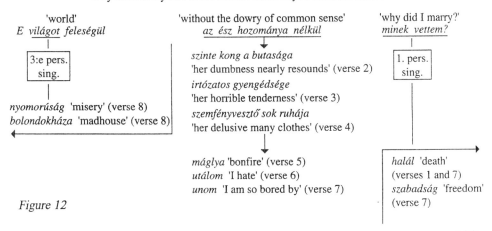

'Why did I marry this world without the dowry of common sense?'

Figure 12

109

3.1.3. The Rhetorical-Stylistic Structure

The personification of the world through the character of the wife is also an allegory. The title *Magna Meretrix* determines both the figurative level, expressed by the character of the wife, and the conceptual level, expressed by the concept of the world, since the common features for both are brought together in it.

The three poetic questions in the second, fifth and seventh strophes form the structural basis of the poem. While the questions of the second and fifth strophes are discursive by nature and are followed by the long passages of three strophes each, the third question in the seventh strophes is a simple yes or no question, which, however, receives no definitive answer.

Enumerations or *denumeratio* have a fundamental role in the poem. The parallel grammatical structures in the first strophe are also examples of this figure. Enumerations are generally a means for increasing the tension, which can also be intensified by an unusual word-order. The first strophe is composed of an eight line full simile, where the conjunction *mint* 'as', opposed to its usual initial position, according to the grammatical pattern: *Mint a sebzett szarvas* 'As / Like the wounded deer', appears in the last line of the strophe. This unusual and unexpected word-order is apt to encourage several interpretations. Looking at the grammatical structure shown in the text at hand, we may regard the inversion as a form of the figures *anacoluchton* and *zeugma*. As there is a common verb for all the syntagms, namely: *vágyik* 'long' [lit. 'it longs'], the figure *adjunctio* can also be shown. In any case, the conjunction *mint* 'as' has a double function: partly, it is undenoted in an initial position referring to the first six lines of the strophe, and partly, it is denoted in the last line, also referring to its context.

After the first question in the second strophe comes the three strophes long passage of the presentation of the wife, or the world in a figurative sense as one kind of *denumeratio*. The figures of *anticlimax* and *climax* in the middle of the strophe are further proof of the coherence between the two lines and also of the unity of the strophe. This relation is illustrated in figure 13.

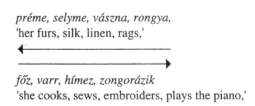

préme, selyme, vászna, rongya,
'her furs, silk, linen, rags,'

főz, varr, hímez, zongorázik
'she cooks, sews, embroiders, plays the piano,'

Figure 13

There are many examples of the figure *denumeratio*, too, often as parallelism in the next two strophes. The similes of the second and third strophes: *mint megkoccantott lárva* 'like a grub that knocked against' and *mint egy bosszúálló angyal* 'like a revenging angel' are both incomplete and implicit, as they omit the element of comparison, the primary image of the wife. This primary image draws attention to the other part of the personification, the world.

The real impact of the locution *irtózatos gyengédsége* 'her horrible tenderness' is quite ironic because of the two contrasting words. This ironic effect increases in the next verse: *pőre testét földhöz csapja* '[she] casts her disrobed body to the floor'. The last four lines of the fourth verse are a summary of the encounters with this anthropomorphous world and as it is also a judgement of it, it can also be studied as the figure *sententia*.

The presentation of the inner world of the self begins with a question in the fifth strophe: *Az ő otthonába honnan, / mikor, miért vándoroltam?* 'From where, when and why did I come / wandering to her home?' There is, however, similar to the first question, not any clear answer to this question. Only proposals of the possible reasons are lined up in the form of the different figures. These are the figure *divisio*, which expounds the contradictory choices and the *polysyndeton*, seen when using the conjunction *vagy* 'or' between the sentences. The strophe is closed by a simile, in which the compared, as seen by the use of the first person singular, is distinctly present, which illustrates the full simile.

Comparing these similes of the poem, we can trace some striking parallels between them. There are three similes in the unit of the first four strophes, which occur in the first three strophes. The unit of the next four strophes mirrors this arrangement of the questions, as these also occur in the first three strophes of this second unit. Futhermore, the first three similes are all somewhat indefinite, either when shaded by the complex structure of the inversion or as they are incomplete and implicit. In contrast to these three similes of the first unit, the three similes of the second unit are definite when all are full similes. As a result, the contrasting principle as the main organizing rule of the poem is further supported.

The two *amplificatios* in the sixth strophe, as the two last words of the two first lines *gondja, kínja* 'worry and pain' and *nyögve, ríva* 'groaning and weeping', are symmetrically arranged. The two first lines of the seventh verse have a similar grouping, contrasting the word-groups *hol-nincs hol van* 'exists now and then', where the explicit use of the *anaphora* can be seen, and the syntagms *most fölbukkan, meg elillan* 'suddenly appearing and getting away'. This strophe contains the third question of the poem: *Higyjem-e: csak meg kell halnom / s vele többé semmi dolgom?* 'Shall I believe that I only must die / and then I won't be concerned with her any more?', which – similar to the two preceeding ones – is waiting for an answer. The two last lines comprise a *sententia*: *A halott, ha léte nincsen, / oly szabad, mint maga Isten.* 'The dead losing her existence / is as free, as God himself'. This *sententia* is a simile, too, which, as it contains all the elements of a simile, is the most complete of all the similes of the poem, and for God the only righteous one.

As seen in figure 14, which shows the conceptual relation of the

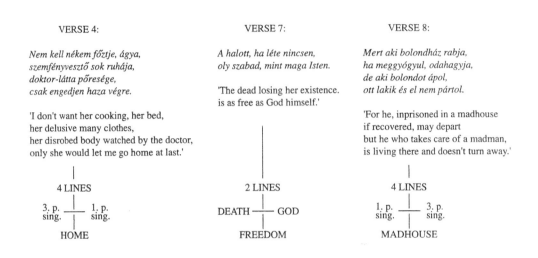

Figure 14

three sententias, there is a discernible symmetry and balance in the connection of the three sentencias, when both the form and the subject-matter are concerned.

When dealing with the acoustical figures, we may observe alliterations in certain places, which in most cases don't indicate any semantic cohesion between the words. Feasible exceptions, in regard to the global structure, are the words *utálom* 'I hate' in the sixth strophe corresponding to *unom*, 'I am so bored' in the seventh strophe and *semmi dolgom* 'I won't be concerned' [lit. 'I have nothing to do with'] in the seventh strophe, correlated to both *semmivé* 'to nothing' and *sűrűbb süppedékbe* 'to an ever thicker sinking' in the eighth strophe.

It can be ascertained that units constructed by three elements are of primary importance for the rhetorical-stylistic structure of the poem *Magna Meretrix*. These units are the three poetic questions, the three sentences and the three similes in the two separate parts.

112

3.1.4 The Metrical Structure

Looking at the rhymes, we see that they are mostly assonant rhymes. There are very few perfect rhymes and many of them are rhymes due to identical endings. A common feature of the rhymes is that they are all descending, two syllable rhymes, i.e. feminine rhymes.

Despite an apparently similar arrangement of the rhymes, we cannot point out any regular pattern. It is to be noted, however, that irregular patterns are also consistently used and not important to the rhyme scheme. Divergences emerge in the middle of the strophes, in the arrangement of the couplet rhymes:

aa bb bb cc: in the 1. and 4. strophes
aa bb cc dd: in the 3., 6., 7. and 8. strophes
aa bb bb bb cc dd ee: in the 2. strophe
aa bb bb cc dd ee: in the 5. strophe

Consequently, there is a certain dissonance in the rhyme scheme, a circumstance which is not characteristic of the poetry of Weöres in other cases. Therefore the question will immediately arise: what is the reason for this divergent pattern in the rhyme scheme? There may be some metrical reasons, and that is why we must first analyze the metrical structure.

The whole poem is characterized by a regular rhythm. All the lines are eight syllables each, which can be divided into two equal parts of four syllables, according to the pattern: 4+4. This is the pattern of the ancient Hungarian *felező nyolcas*, i.e. an eight feet bisector metre with the most outstanding example being the poem *Nemzeti dal* 'National Song' by Sándor Petőfi: *Talpra magyar, hí a haza! Itt az idő, most vagy soha!* 'Magyars, rise, your country calls you! / Meet this hour, whae'er befalls you!' (transl. Watson Kirkconnell). It is characteristic of many Hungarian folk-songs and also of the so-called *kuruc* songs, songs of the Hungarian refugees in the time of Ferenc Rákóczi's war of independence. In our example of a *kuruc* song above, an allusion to the poem *Magna Meretrix* can be experienced not only in the sense of the form but also that of subject-matter:

Elindultam szép hazámból:
híres kis Magyarországból.
Visszanéztem félutamból,
szememből a könny kicsordult.

Bú ebédem, bú vacsorám;
boldogtalan minden órám.

Nézem a csillagos eget,
Sírok alatta eleget.

Jaj istenem, rendelj szállást,
mert meguntam a bujdosást:
Idegen földön a lakást,
éjjel-nappal a sok sírást.

I left my beautiful country:
my famous little Hungary.
I looked back half-way,
tears came to my eyes.

Sorrow is my lunch, sorrow is my dinner;
unhappy are all my hours.
I look at the starry heaven,
I cry under it quite often.

O, my God, give me a shelter,
for I got tired of emigration:
of living in a foreign land
of crying so much day and night.

Poems with the metrical pattern of this eight-feet bisector metre have only one thing in common: the metrical pattern. In most cases there are four lines in the strophes, but we can find poems with more lines than that. The rhymes are most often couplet rhymes, but there are also other variants. In this respect, the poem *Magna Meretrix* is not different from other poems which have this ancient metrical pattern, because the divergent pattern of the rhymes can be explained by the metrical structure. As a result, we cannot speak about dissonance, either.

Erika Szepes (1996:248), in writing about the force of expression possessed by the *felező nyolcas* said that a popular manner, simplicity and pureness are common characteristics of poems using this metrical pattern. I think that this important aspect of simplicity, of clear thoughts and deep feelings reflected by a pure form, is seen in the poem *Magna Meretrix*, too.

3.1.5 The Grammatical Structure

Every strophe forms a separate unit, indicated by the periods at the end of the

114

sentences. Enjambements are frequent between the lines, but there is only a single one between two strophes. This particular case is the two-piece unit of the second verse. In examining the grammatical structures of this second strophe, we can also observe the unity of the two parts of it, as the coordinated clauses of the first part are interruptedly carried on in the second one. The period closing the sentence reinforces the unity, too.

The majority of the sentences are lengthy, compound sentences. The first, second and sixth strophes, for example, consist of one single sentence. There are only two simple sentences: the interrogative sentences in the second and the fifth strophes. As pointed out before, the question in the second verse is of focal quality, while the question in the fifth one is essentially a repetition of its content. The third question in the seventh strophe, while also forming a different semantical unit, is not of focal quality and not a simple sentence either.

The large sentences of the first four strophes are mostly compound sentences in a coordinating relation, without any conjunctions between the clauses. The same parts of the sentences, similar to the coordinating sentences, often follow each other, as the enjambement in the middle of the second strophe containing the set of two parallel lines of four nouns and four verbs shows. The only adversative sentence of the unit of the first four strophes, which as an antipole follows the powerful deluge of the coordinating sentences, is a part of a compound sentence: *de nézz közelebbről a szemébe* 'but look in her eyes closely'. Complex clauses such as the two comparative clauses of the first unit: *mint megkoccantott lárva* 'like a grub that knocked against' and *mint egy bosszúálló angyal* 'like a revenging angel' appear within the compound structures. In the four last lines of the unit, the same parts of the sentences are subsequent to each other.

The dominant grammatical constructions of the four strophes of the first unit are compound sentences. These structures are the best at putting into words the real subject, which is the recounting of all the charges constituting the basis for a feasible divorce from the wife or the world personified.

To shed light on the first strophe may, however, involve some difficulties. This is not an impeachment yet, only a sort of a complaint which also introduces the essential topic. The main components of this complaint are reflected by coordinating clauses and the connecting comparative clause of the last line: *mint halálra testem-lelkem* 'as my body and soul long to die'. As pointed out earlier, the conjunction *mint* 'as' has a double function. As denoted, it refers to the last line, and as undenoted, it refers to the whole strophe. This function when undenoted is also motivated by an obvious allusion to the texts of old Hungarian psalms: *Mint szarvasgím a források vízére* 'As much as / Like the deer for the water of the springs' (Hozsanna: 500); *Mint a gímszarvas vágyik a források hűsére* 'As much as / Like the deer craves for the coolness of the springs' (Hozsanna: 501); *Mint szarvas ér vizéhez* 'As much as / Like the deer to the water of the stream' (Hozsanna: 186); *Mint az szomjú szarvas, kit vadász rettentett* 'As much as / Like a thirsty deer frightened by a hunter' (Balassi 1994:88).

Undoubtedly, the poem *Magna Meretrix* is a paraphrase of these psalms. And this is the reason that grammatical interpretation is somewhat difficult. The associations to the first lines of well-known Hungarian psalms sets a kind of an oscillation in motion between the syntagms of this first strophe, which makes the logical place of the conjunction *mint* 'as' contestable. Thus, if the sentence is started with the conjunction, the relation between the head-clauses and the sub-clauses changes. The formerly main-clauses of a compound relation turn to sub-clauses in a complex sentence, at the same time as the last line becomes a main-clause with an altered focus on the body and the soul.

The fifth strophe starting the other large unit of three strophes, now dealing with the protagonist, parallel to the part dealing with the wife, or rather the world, begins with an interrogative sentence: *Az ő otthonába honnan, / mikor, miért vándoroltam?* 'From where, when and why did I come / wandering to her home?' This repetition of the same parts of the sentence is represented by the three adverbs following each other. This question is followed by a compound sentence, containing a series of alternative sentences and a coordinating one which is connected to a subordinated clause of comparison.

Consequently, we find some clear syntagmatic correspondences between the second and the fifth strophe, the factual axis of the poem, which can be summarized as follows:

1. The first sentences are interrogative in both cases.
2. There are predominantly compound sentences in both strophes.
3. The last clauses in both strophes are subordinated clauses of comparison.

The grammatical structure of the sixth, seventh and eighth verses, however, shows a dissimilar pattern. This divergence is indicated by the shift of dominance from the former compound sentences to complex ones. Two examples may illustrate this conversion.

The first example is the syntactical structure of the second sentence in the fifth strophe:

(A)	Tán az anyából tudatlan
	s akaratlan fölfakadtam;
(B)	vagy csábított durva kéje
(C)	és mohón buktam beléje;
(D1)	vagy mint elkorhadt halottat
(D)	elevenek ide dobtak;

(E1)	vagy sírván a szenvedőkért
(E)	alázattal jöttem önként;
(F) (G)	bárhogy: itt sülök a máglyán
(G1)	mint egy nyársra húzott fácán.

(A)	Unconsciously and involuntary maybe
	from the mother I arose;
(B)	or I was tempted by her rough delight
(C)	and eagerly I fell in her;
(D1)	or like a rotten corpse
(D)	I was cast here by the quick;
(E1)	or crying over those who suffer
(E)	humbly I came by myself;
(F) (G)	anyhow: now I'm roasted here on the bonfire
(G1)	like a pheasant on a spit.

This relation between the clauses is according to figure 15.

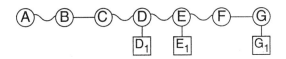

Figure 15

The five alternative sentences (A), (B), (D), (E), (F) and the intermediate coordinating sentence (C) are followed by a coordinating clause (G). A subordinated clause of comparison (D1), an attributive clause (E1) and another clause of comparison (G1) connect to these main clauses.

The second example is the syntactical structure of the second sentence in the sixth strophe:

(A1)	Bármennyi a gondja, kínja,
(A) (A2)	bírom, noha nyögve, ríva,
(A3)	nem mártírként énekelve,
(A4)	csak pólyásként berezelve;
(B1)	de a gyönyör zabálását
(B) (B2)	utálom, mint mézes-kását,
(C1)	mégis bajban elepedve
(C)	kapaszkodom élvezetbe.

(A1)	No matter how much her worry and pain may be
(A) (A2)	I bear it, though groaning and weeping,
(A3)	not while singing like a martyr,
(A4)	only like a babe in a funk;
(B1)	but the devour of the delight
(B) (B2)	I hate like honey mash,
(C1)	still, wasted away in grief
(C)	I hold on to the pleasure.

This relation between the clauses is according to figure 16.

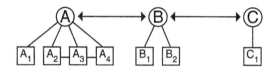

Figure 16

There are seemingly more subordinated clauses in this example of the sixth strophe. The three main clauses (A), (B), (C) are related as adversative sentences. Connected to these different kinds of subordinate clauses are: an object clause (A1), a clause of concession (A2), an adverbial clause (A3), another adverbial clause (A4), an object clause (B1), a comparative clause (B2), and an adverbial clause (C1).

In the seventh and eighth strophes the bulk of subordinating constructions can also be noticed. In these strophes, however, a different type comes in sight: the conditional clause. There are three of them: *ha léte nincsen* 'if losing her existence' in the seventh strophe; *Hogyha semmivé nem égek* 'If I don't burn to nothing' and *ha meggyógyul* 'if recovered' in the eighth strophe. These three conditional causes might be compared to the number of the syntagms using the conjunction *mint* 'like' and that of using the conjunction *de* 'but'. There are three clauses containing the conjunction *mint* 'like' in each of the two large units and there are also three clauses with the conjunction *de* 'but' in the poem as a whole.

3.2 The World of the Text

3.2.1 The Theme

The global structure of the concrete formal elements is the most essential factor in dealing with the theme. The analysis concerning the inner context of the poem *Magna Meretrix* showed that it also has a regular, balanced structure. The primary structuring principle of contrast has an distinctive influence on the connecting structural units. No less than the theme is defined by it: the vanity of the world, expressed by the image of the wife, is opposed to the idea of a lost world. In addition, the disgust with wordly vanity is opposed to the hope for return to the real home.

This world of endless suffering is not the real home. The real home did exist once and the image of it still sometimes appears, but vaguely. The desire to run away from this unendurable world is focused on the imaginary world, which is named only once as *haza* 'home' in the fourth verse. There are, however, many allusions to the world, such as the personification of it in the character of the wife, represented by various means of expression, as well as the *figura etymologica* of two related concepts in the last verse: *bolondház* 'madhouse' and *bolond* 'madman'.

There is only one way out of a distorted world and that is death in its most definitive form, which implies a total annihilation of human existence in order to put an end to the pain caused by enduring the world in vain.

This main concept is reflected in the two parallel poetic questions in the second and fifth verse. Their message could briefly be expressed in the following way: why be born at all? Similar to the third question in the seventh strophe, however, there is no answer. Nevertheless, the shift of the mood from former indicative to conditional indicates the only solution: burning everything to ashes, total annihilation, is the rescue from the perils of reincarnation.

The conjunction *ha* 'if', repeated three times, is followed by the conjunction *de* 'but' in the adversative sentence in the two last lines: *de aki bolondot ápol, / ott lakik és el nem pártol* 'but he who takes care of a madman, is living there and doesn't turn away'. These conclusive lines shed light upon another aspect of the theme: the walls we raise around us are only illusions of a home, for the real home is somewhere else. Our hopes and desires are not in accordance with this existing world. We cannot identify ourselves with it, because living with the idea of another, now lost world, changes us.

3.2.2 The Poem as a Part of Weöres' Lifework

The poem *Magna Meretrix* was published for the first time in 1964 in the volume with the title *Tűzkút* 'Well of Fire'. Imre Bori (1984:476) wrote as follows about this volume: "The collection of the poems in the volume 'Well of Fire' is then of a synthetic nature, a summing up of his poetic themes and ideas on a higher level, it is a finale in which the melodies and the themes of the former volumes resound one after the other". Bori also calls the volume the volume of synthesis and Kenyeres (1983:211) is of the same opinion: "The 'Well of Fire' is the volume of synthesis of the romantic-aesthetic approach, and is Weöres' most well-considered and most systematically compiled book of poetry".

The well is one of the motifs most frequently used by Weöres. Already in a poem written in 1935, entitled *Levél Füst Milánnak* 'Letter to Milán Füst' (EI I:122), it appears: *Akár mély kútba, hulltam önmagamba és senkise húzhat ki onnan* 'Like into a deep well, I fell into myself and nobody can pull me out from here'. Piece 68 in the *Rongyszőnyeg* 'Rag-carpet' cycle (EI I:406) says as follows: *Akár kútba ugorhatnám, / önmagamba fulladok* 'Even when jumping into a well, / I will drown in myself'. In the poem *Harmadik szimfónia* 'Third Symphony' (EI I:352) the well is a picture of a heavenly, archetypical image of a lost world:

Odafönn villámló kútnál
remegő gyöngy közt aludtál –
remegő gyöngy közt a kútnál
tán már aludni se tudnál.

Above there at the shining well
amongst trembling pearls you slept –
amongst trembling pearls at the well
maybe you could not sleep any more.

In the piece 21 of the *Rongyszőnyeg* 'Rag-carpet' (EI I:358) cycle the "heavenly child" is also related to the image of the well:

Idők elején álmodtalak én
világ-ölü mennyei kútnál,
fény sávjai közt, tűz ágai közt,
féltő szívemen aludtál.

I dreamed of you at the beginning of time
at the well with the world on its lap,
amongst the streaks of light, amongst the branches of fire,
you slept on my caring heart.

In the prose poems of *Teljesség felé* 'Towards the Absolute' (EI I:641) the only way to completeness is through the well: *Szállj le önmagad mélyére, mint egy kútba; s ahogy a határolt kút mélyén megtalálod a határtalan talajvizet; változó egyéniséged alatt megtalálod a változatlan létezést.* 'Go down to the bottom of yourself, like you would go down into a well; and as you find the unlimited underground water on the bottom of the limited well; so will you also find the unchangeable existence beneath your changeable personality'.

How deliberate the use of this motif was is further demonstrated by the choice of title for his next-to-last book, published in 1987: *Kútbanéző* 'He who Looks into the Well'. One poem in this volume, with the title *A kútba néz valaki* 'Somebody looks into the well' using the first person singular, surely sheds light upon the identity of the person who looks into the well. Because the well mirrors the inner world, it is also a source for truly experiencing it.

The volume *Tűzkút* 'Well of Fire' also contains the cycles with the titles *Graduale*, later *A grádicsok éneke* 'The Song of the Stairs', *A hang vonulása* 'The Moving of the Sound', *Átváltozások* 'Metamorphoses' and many major poems as *Nyolcadik szimfónia* 'Eighth Symphony', *Fairy Spring, Salve Regina, Kilencedik szimfónia* 'Nighth Symphony', *Tizedik szimfónia* 'Tenth Symphony' and *Harminc bagatell* 'Thirty Bagatells'. Bori called the cycle *A grádicsok éneke* 'The Song of the Stairs' (EI II: 395-407) the plan of the volume *Tűzkút* 'Well of Fire', and "a confession of the synthesis Weöres reached, a signaling of the most important stations of the journey between earth and heaven, from the human to the world, the plan of travel colored by the long-range play between the micro- and macrocosmos" (Bori 1984:478). Both the discernible motifs and the atmosphere of the tenth piece of the cycle recall that of the poem *Magna Meretrix*:

Nem gyarapodni többre,
  nem élni, oda vágyom
honnan hűségesen kísér szerelmem,
  izzón olvadni benne,
  legyen szabadulásom
attól, mi én, s nem az ő tükre bennem.

  Vagy azért kell-e élnem,
  hogy haldokolva, kedvét
messziről sóvárogjam kiszakadtan,

örvényben ingva nézzem,
mily diadalmenetként
vonúl, nem nőve-fogyva, mozdulatlan!

Not to grow richer,
not to live, that I wish for
where my love faithfully escorts me,
to melt in her while glowing,
let me be released
from what is mine and not have her mirror in me.

Or must I live for the reason,
that while dying, from a distance, broken away,
I would yearn for her desire,
while wobbling in a whirlpool I would watch
as she moves like a triumphal march
without growing and decreasing and without moving!

The poem *Magna Meretrix* belongs to the cycle *A hang vonulása* 'The Moving of Sound', together with many other poems dealing with cosmic perspectives of the macrocosmos of a world outside reflected in the microcosmos of the inner world of the individual. The poem with the title *A benső végtelenből* (EI II: 447) 'From the Infinite Inside' demonstrates this:

A benső végtelenből néhanap
még kitekintek arcomon keresztül:
felhőt látok, vagy csillag fénye rezdül.
Romlik szemem, már ez is elmarad,
s külvilág rám-zárja kapumat
s ott maradok, hol nincsen föld, csak ég;
nincs esemény meg tünemény varázsa,
se felszín, látszat, habzó semmiség,
csak a valóság békés ragyogása,
mérettelen, számtalan, névtelen,
vágytalan, változatlan szerelem.

Kapumnál a lázas világ megáll:
"Őrült! Önző! Áruló! – kiabál.
Várjatok, pékműhely van odabenn,
majd táplál most még forró kenyerem.

From the infinite inside, sometimes
I still watch out through my face:
I see a cloud or is it a star that vibrates.
My sight is failing, this too falls behind,
the outside world locks my door on me
and I remain where there is no earth, but heaven;
there are no happenings and no magic of miracles,
no surface, no show, no lathering nothingness,
only the pieceful brightness of the truth exists,
the unmeasured, countless, nameless
love without desire, without change.

The fevered world stops at my door.
"Idiot! Egoist! Traitor!" it shouts.
Wait! There is a bakery inside,
my bread, still hot, will feed you once.

The individual sphere here is extended to a social sphere of the calling and the
responsibility of the poet. The last piece with the title *Nehéz óra* 'Heavy Hour'
of the prose poems *Tizedik szimfónia* 'Tenth Symphony' (EI II:471) suggests
a possible nuclear war as it visualizes the breakdown and degeneration of
humankind:

Az ember, tagjaiban öngyilkos hatalommal, vérében méreggel, fejében őrület-
tel, mint a veszettkutya; nem tudni míly végzetre jut. Ha új pusztító-eszközei-
vel végigboronál népein: eljut a kerék és a tűz elvesztéig, a beszéd elfeledtéig,
a négykézlábig.

We cannot know what destiny the man with suicidal-power in his limbs, with
poison in his blood, with the madness of a rabid dog in his head, ever achieves.
If, with his new, destructive instruments, he harrows through his people: he
then attains the loss of the wheel and fire, the forgetting of speech, and returns
to the stage of those who walked on all fours.

Only the improvement of the individual inner world can stop this process
towards death:

A megismert és rendezett bensők túlnőnek egyéni mohóságaikon, egymással
összeférnek, külső világukat is harmonikussá alakítják.

The recognized and well-ordered inner worlds outgrow their individual eagerness, they get on well with each other, and also shape their outer worlds harmoniously.

The voices of the poem *Tizedik szimfónia* 'Tenth Symphony' are imbued with a confidence and hope that is not easily found in the poem *Magna Meretrix*.

In looking at this volume, called the volume of synthesis, where the themes and motifs are reappearances of familiar forms, intertextual analysis will not be difficult. It is a well-known fact that Weöres' philosophy of poetics did not change significantly over the years; those philosophies he learned when he was young structured his thoughts throughout his work. The theme of the homeless wanderer turns up very early in his oeuvre. The original wording of the first line of the poem *De profundis* (EI I: 302-303) was as follows: *Földön élek, a mennyből kiűzve* 'I live on earth, expelled from heaven'. In the three-volume *Egybegyűjtött írások* 'Collected Writings' there is another version of the first line, although the other lines remain unchanged:

Bárhonnan is lettem, földre űzve
ruhámból e lenti akol bűze
nem múlik soha.
Itt Istennek barma és virága
tolong egymás elevenét rágva,
szörnyü lakoma.

No matter where I came from, chased to earth
the stink of this lower sheep-fold
never leaves my clothes.
Here the cattle and the flowers of the Lord
elbow each other as they nag each other alive,
a horrible feast.

In the 21st piece of the *Rongyszőnyeg* 'Rag-carpet' cycle (EI I: 385), the motif of the "ever-thicker sinking" as it is worded in *Magna Meretrix*, takes shape as follows:

Te égi gyerek, te angyali jó,
mért jöttél szökve utánam?
óvd lépteimet, mert sűlyedek, ó
sűlyedek az éjszakában.

124

You heavenly child, you angel-like good
why did you in fight come after me?
Guard my steps, for I am sinking now,
I am sinking in the night.

The subject-matter is clearly indicated by the title of the poem: *Egy másik világ* 'An other world' (EI I: 355):

Egy másik világ küldött engem,
hogy milyen volt, már nem tudom,
de tört sejtése visszafénylik
színek nélküli fátyolon.

An other world sent me,
how it was, I don't know any more,
but its broken image shines back
onto the colorless veil.

The 144th piece of the *Rongyszőnyeg* 'Rag-carpet' cycle (EI I: 443) is a clear allusion to the fifth verse of the poem *Magna Meretrix*:

Mikor anyából földre tettek,
hová keverték röptömet?
Embernek többé ne szülessek,
szárny nélkül élni nem lehet.

When they put me on the earth from the mother,
where did they mix up my flight?
I will not be born to a man any more,
one can not live without wings.

The lines of the *Harmadik szimfónia* 'Third Symphony' (EI I: 348-354) voice the same sense of not belonging and homelessness, too:

Ki merne súgni neked
arról, hogy mi lett veled?
melyik ég rejti helyed?
őrzi-e gyöngyeidet?

Ki egét elhagyta, lássa:

habos örvény a lakása,
fedelének éj az ácsa,
sötétség a kalapácsa.

Who would whisper to you
about what happened to you?
which heaven hides your place?
does it care for your pearls?

He, who his heaven abandoned, may see:
his home is a lathering whirlpool,
the night is the carpenter of his roof,
the darkness is his hammer.

Reminiscences are also easy to find in the poems of other Hungarian poets. The poem with the title *Ahogy Júliára talála* 'As he found Julia' by Bálint Balassi, serves as an example. The first lines of this poem bring the other strophe of *Magna Meretrix* to mind: *Ez világ sem kell már nékem / Nálad nélkül szép szerelmem* 'I don't want this world either, / Without you, my beautiful love'. The basis of this allusion is obviously similar rhytmical patterns to the *felező nyolcas*, that is, an eight feet bisector metre, but coincidences regarding the subject-matter may also be noticed: If the most essential thing in one's life is missing, then life is not worth living.

On the Margaret Island János Arany wrote down his autumn-thoughts in a book he called *Kapcsos könyv* [lit.] 'Book with a Clip'. He gave the title *Őszikék* [lit.] 'Small Autumn Things' to the poems. These are the poems of an old man, seasoned and mature, for whom, because of the necessary work of living, the much longed-for freedom of writing is forever unattainable. Similar to the main character of the poem *Magna Meretrix*, the man who by his sense of responsibility has sentenced himself to a distressed existence, Arany cannot turn away from his obligations. Even if he would ultimately be released from them, it would be too late, or, as Arany put it in the poem with the title *Epilógus* 'Epilogue':

    Mert hogy' szálljon,
Bár kalitja már kinyitva,
Rab madár is szegett szárnyon!

    For how could he fly,
Though his case is open,

A captive bird with broken wings!

3.2.3 Weöres' Philosophy of Poetics

"The only expedient move is the search of how to adapt himself to what has passed... . Until one has not reached this state, he is dying. This dying is the existence within historical time" (Kabdebó 1980:212). This quotation, in my opinion, describes Weöres' Weltanschaung. The main character of the poem *Magna Meretrix*, placed on the bonfire, is dying too. Nevertheless, this is not a death of the body, but of the soul. If we cannot identify with the world around us, if its laws are not consistent with the laws inside us, but instead are fundamentally alien to our personality, then we are thrown into a strange world where we cannot find our real home. "The man who is left alone moves towards the inner infinity" (Kabdebó 1980:206). We have the choice of throwing away the burden of endurance and searching for the real meaning within the boundaries of our own existence, that is, in our own inner infinity. This is the freedom of choice between the state of an "ever thicker sinking" and remaining in the "madhouse" or the possibility of becoming "as free as God himself".

Alienation, choice, freedom – these concepts are all significant within existentialism. They also can refer to the concept of *Angst*, the state of the *csak pólyásként berezelve* "only like a babe when in a funk", as Weöres formulated it, a circumstance which is brought about by the sense of consciousness in terms of the responsibility of choice. That is, we are not only involved in freedom of choice, but also in the consequences of it. We surrender to our own decisions, particularly when we cannot even find a God in a material universe. This is similar to Mersault, the main character in Camus' novel, *Indifference*, who is so alienated that, totally indifferent to the gravity of the deed, he commits a murder. He has no confidence in Providence, either, and his only hope is that there will be many onlookers at his execution so for once in his life he does not feel alone.

Is it the same freedom seen in the poem *Magna Meretrix*? Is it the freedom of a God-rejecting atheist, or a God-seeking transcendental-teleological man? The two last lines of the seventh verse *A halott, ha léte nincsen, / oly szabad, mint maga Isten* 'The dead losing her existence / is as free as God himself', are significant in terms of analyzing the text's meaning. First, we must note that this is the only place in the poem where God is named. Using a capital as the first letter and also as part of a simile, he becomes transferred into the real sphere of existence. But the two rhyme-words: *nincsen – Isten* 'there is no' – 'God', cast doubt on this existence. In other words, the same existence which is asserted by the inner context is simultaneously contradicted by the formal category of the rhymes, which then becomes a category for the subject-matter.

Though God is only named in one single place, there are other parts of the poem clearly referring to some religious concept, such as the image of the wounded deer, a feasible simile originating from well-known psalms; the simile of the revenging angel in the third strophe; the two lines in the fifth verse explicitly pointing to God, the Redeemer; and the motif of being burnt on a bonfire in the fifth verse, which may allude to Purgatory or the first Christian victims, and to which the word *mártir* 'martyr' in the sixth verse could also refer.

Consequently, this existentialism is closely connected to a religious belief: the ambition of all existence should be to try to be like God as much as possible. Or, as Weöres put it: "I think that there is only one man who exists and this man is Jesus Christ. Other people exist or don't exist to such a degree that they are identical to him. Here I don't think of some Christianity of course or something like that, that is, if they have spread some consecrated oil on him, or something like that, then he becomes identical to Jesus Christ" (Cs. Szabó 1993:40). This unmistakable scepticism is obviously not related to an absence of religious belief, but instead refers to the establishment and its institutionized forms. Weöres' scepticism at the same time has an openness towards other religious beliefs and philosophies which fit his own general view of life. This creates a unique juxtaposition between religious existentialism and individual religious beliefs.

"The fight against religion and a detachment from religion is a duty for the philosophical faith" (Hamvas 1941:29). Further on, citing Karl Jasper, Hamvas writes as follows: "The common thing in religion and philosophy: 'the profound existence must be opened in order to recognize the hardship of the task. Real existence, no matter what, cannot be gained without questioning itself'". Weöres, as a matter of fact, also extends the concept of existence. It becomes united with a religious faith, but not exclusively to Christian forms of faith. From the last verse of *Magna Meretrix* and especially the first four lines of it, new juxtapositions come into view. As pointed out above, the motif of burning may relate to Purgatory. To go through the purifying fire, however, does not mean the possibility of total annihilation, for then there would be no resurrection. Burning like a pheasant on the bonfire is, however, only a special sort of prolonging suffering and for this reason is not desirable. This pheasant of the poem, as opposed to the mythical phoenix, doesn't burn to ashes in order to re-create himself, but is instead submitted to continual burning, and to eternal suffering.

Nirvana in Hinduism means not only extinguishing the fire, but also extinguishing the individual life when the Atman, that is, the super-individual of the human, unites with the Brahman, the absolute spirit. In the philosophy of Buddhism nirvana stands for a complete extinction of individual life, too. The fire in Buddhist writings is represented as an undesired constraint, as the fire of hate, sensual delights and fraudulent illusions. The only way to let the fire die out is by not feeding it any more (Humphreys 1962:77). Or, as we can read in the *Fire Sermon of the Buddha*: "All things, O Priests, are on fire [– – –] And with what are these on fire? With the fire of passion, say I, with the fire of hatred, with the fire of infatuation [– – –] Perceiving this, O priests, the learned and noble disciple conceives an aversion [– – –] And in conceiving this aversion, he becomes divested in passion, and by the absence of passion he becomes free, and when he is free he becomes aware that he is free; and he knows that rebirth is exhausted, that he has lived the holy life" (Warren 1972:352-353).

The idea of life as a chain of sufferings and rebirth for this reason is a frightening perspective. This is common to Hinduism and Buddhism. According to the *Benares Sermon of Buddha*, sufferings are caused by the thirst for life. To satisfy desires is not enough to put an end to suffering, because these are uninterruptedly followed by new desires. Nevertheless, in Buddhism there is a way to cease suffering, by means of the *Eightfold Path*. Can this have some relevance to the poem *Magna Meretrix*? Many aspects of the subject matter can be seen to have similarities to Buddhist thought. In addition to these correspondences, the thesis of the *Eightfold Path* reveals some other connections. These connections are not related to the subject matter of the poem, but are reflected by its formal disposition. As said before, the structure of the poem is largely influenced by the number eight. There are eight strophes in the poem with eight lines in each and the lines consist of eight syllables. On the basis of such correspondences, we may even locate a philosophy reflected in an analogous form.

According to Hamvas (1941:19-20) the common primary experience for Kant, Jung and Kierkegaard was Hindu, especially Samkhya philosophy. Weöres was also influenced by these philosophies. In the poem *Magna Meretrix* the philosophies of Hinduism, Buddhism and existentialism have merged with the images of a Christian belief and the influence of his mentor, Béla Hamvas, into a peculiar and most individual poetic form.

How may the lonely and homeless protagonist of *Magna Meretrix*, thrown into an undesired state of existence, find a way out of this melting pot of philosophies? How may he become aware of the meaning of his existence? Most likely, I think, through that form that Jaspers represents within the philosophy of existentialism, that is, the God-related, transcentental form of it. Or, as Jaspers (1950:21; 22) put it in the work Einführung in die Philosophie: "Machen wir unsere menschliche Lage auf andere Weise deutlich als die Unzuverlässigkeit allen Weltseins. Die Fraglosigkeit in uns nimmt die Welt als das Sein schlechthin. [– – –] Jederzeit muß der Mensch im Blick auf sie aus eigenem Ursprung finden, was ihm Gewißheit, Sein, Verläßlichkeit ist. Aber in der Unverläßlichkeit allen Weltseins ist der Zeiger aufgerichtet. Er verbietet, in der Welt Genüge zu finden; er weist auf ein anderes". In most religions this other thing is the promise of redemption. Philosophy gives no redemption, but according to Jasper, it also transgresses the world. Religion and philosophy are then related through the transcendental idea.

In addition to the concept of redemption, certainly represented in very disparate forms, there is also another common concept within Hinduism, Buddhism and the philosophy of existentialism: the concept of freedom. There is, however, a fundamental divergence in the definition of the concept in these philosophies. In Hinduism and Buddhism, it stands for a total elimination of the individual in order to be dissolved in an eternal substance, whereas for the philosophy of existentialism, it concerns freedom of choice. Regarding Weöres, both of these definitions are included in his view of freedom. In order to achieve freedom, suffering, which is the basis of all existence in Hindu and Buddhist philosophy, interwines with the anguish of responsibility caused by freedom. The desire of uniting the Absolute also means a chance of abandoning the world. Nevertheless, these are only possibilities. For he who is "imprisoned in a madhouse" will not be cured and cannot be "as free as God himself". There is only suffering and anguish in a world where we don't belong. The poem *Magna Meretrix* is one of Weöres' most pessimistic poems.

4 Chaos and Harmony

1

(1) Tüzes csőrű madarakat láttam és
(2) fojtottan parázsló zenét hallottam
(3) nem magamnak: neked, világos...

(4) Ki tudná elmondani, mi van a kárpitra festve!
(5) és mily tompaságot rejt a csarnok mélye,
(6) szemnek, fülnek – minden nevezhetőnek!

(7) Névtelen vagy te, világos,
(8) ki lány képében heversz az ajtó mellett
(9) s ki emlékemben fekszel, mint kemény ágyban

(10) s ki a történésekben sétálsz, vagy elnyugszol,
(11) gyors macska, vagy áldozati csésze, vagy csak árnyéka valaminek
(12) s kiről azt se tudom: más vagy-e? vagy én vagyok?

(13) Benn, mélyen, a csarnok mélyén.
(14) a király! Tán szórakozik, tán munkálkodik.
(15) Így kell lenni. Vagy kié a sok zene, a sok madár?

2

(1) Mikor a termeken végigmentem.
(2) hatalmas arcát mutatta a fény,
(3) szél volt, függönyök lobogtak,
(4) mikor a termeken végigmentem,
(5) hadseregként jött a kinti világ,
(6) erősen, az oszlopok közt.

(7) Sokszor mentem végig a termeken,
(8) én lelkem, mégis először,
(9) szemem száraz volt, belül sírtam,
(10) sokszor mentem végig a termeken,
(11) a függöny fényt ragadott, én lelkem,
(12) könnyem nem volt, mint a száraz fa, sírtam.

(13) Többé nem tudok végigmenni a termeken,
(14) ó vakító, tudd meg, ürességben járok,

(15)   mert minden belém temette arcát,
(16)   többé nem tudok végigmenni a termeken,
(17)   szememből kiesett a tekintet, ó vakító,
(18)   föl-le jár emlékemben a fény, a szél.

3

(1)   Két kő-szörnyeteg közt
(2)   – fekete, sötétkék és arany –
(3)   libeg a hűs esti levegő.
(4)   Nézz rám, te hajlós testű
(5)   elnyujtózol a kerti füvön,
(6)   benned gyümölcsöző
(7)   a káprázat és a szerencse.

(8)   Nézz messze, nézz messze,
(9)   az est ég sárgája fölött
(10)   egy csillag buzog pirosan.
(11)   Dalolj, eleven kút,
(12)   homályból előfehérlő:
(13)   belőled isznak
(14)   a legdúsabb pillanatok.

(15)   Szikrázik egy csillag:
(16)   "Fény vagyok, fény vagyok,
(17)   ezért tudsz szeretni engem."
(18)   Táncolj, kereplő derekú,
(19)   a gyöngyös, sötét füvön.
(20)   Dalomra forog a táncod,
(21)   ezért tudsz szeretni engem.

4

(1)   ... bozót vagy, ember vagy, angyal vagy, megmondom neked,
(2)   a csonkaság fénye vidám, a teltség fénye szomorú,
(3)   a csonkaság sötétje szomorú, a teltség sötétje vidám,
(4)   aki tud, csituljon, bozóthoz, emberhez, angyalhoz könyörögjünk,
(5)   mert a bozót angyalt fordít a földtömeg sötétsége felé,
(6)   mert az angyal bozótként fordul a teljesség felé,
(7)   mert az ember köztük bolyong, pótolva bozótot, angyalt...

1

(1)   I have seen birds with flame-colored beaks and
(2)   I have heard glowing music suppressed
(3)   not for me: for you, clear...

(4)   Who could tell what is painted on the curtain!
(5)   and what hollow is covered in the deep of the hall,
(6)   for the eyes, for the ears – for all nameable things!

(7)   You are nameless, clear,
(8)   who, in the image of a girl, rests beside the door
(9)   and who lies in my memories, like on a hard bed

(10)   and who walks in the happenings, or takes a rest,
(11)   swift cat, or offering cup, or only the shadow of something
(12)   and of whom I do not know either: are you somebody else? or are you myself?

(13)   Deep inside, in the deep of the hall,
(14)   there is the king! Maybe he enjoys himself, maybe he works hard.
(15)   It must be that way. Or whose is this music and these many birds?

2

(1)   When I wandered through the halls,
(2)   the light showed its mighty face,
(3)   the wind was blowing, the curtains waved,
(4)   when I wandered through the halls,
(5)   like an army the outside world came,
(6)   heavy, amongst the columns.

(7)   Often I wandered through the halls,
(8)   my soul, still for the first time,
(9)   my eyes were dry, I wept inside,
(10)   often I wandered through the halls,
(11)   the curtain was caught by the light, my soul,
(12)   I had no tears, I wept like a dead tree.

(13)   I cannot wander through the halls anymore,
(14)   o, glare, I want you to know, I walk in emptiness,
(15)   for everything buried its face in me,

(16) I cannot wander through the halls any more,
(17) the gaze dropped out from my eyes, o, glare,
(18) the light, the wind walks up and down in my memories.

3

(1)   Between two stone-monstrosities
(2)   – black, dark-blue and gold –
(3)   the fresh evening breeze floats.
(4)   Look at me, you, nimble-bodied,
(5)   you stretch yourself out on the garden grass,
(6)   in you is fruitful
(7)   the mirage and the fortune.

(8)   Look far, look far,
(9)   above the yellow evening sky
(10) a star bubbles reddening.
(11)   Sing, living well,
(12)   white emerging from the dusk:
(13)   the wealthiest moments
(14)   drink from you.

(15) A star glitters:
(16) "I am light, I am light,
(17) that is why you can love me."
(18)   Dance, rattle-waisted,
(19)   on the pearly, dark grass.
(20)   Your dance goes round to my song,
(21)   that is why you can love me.

4

(1)   ... you are brushwood, you are human, you are angel, I will tell you,
(2)   the light of the broken is merry, the light of the whole is sad,
(3)   the dark of the broken is sad, the dark of the whole is merry,
(4)   he, who can may quieten, let us pray to the brushwood, the human, the
      angel,
(5)   for the brushwood turns the angel towards the darkness of the Earth,
(6)   for the angel like the brushwood turns towards the Absolute,
(7)   for the human roams amongst them while substituting the brushwood,
      the angel...

(*Atlantis*. EI I: 595-597)

4.1 The Text

4.1.1 The Structure and Shape of the Writing

The four parts of the poem *Atlantis* are clearly indicated by four Arabic numerals. The first three parts are somewhat longer than the fourth part. The strophes of the four parts consist of varying numbers of lines in each, which creates a certain imbalance in structure at first glance. When, however, one looks closely at these larger formal units of the poem, we can also detect the well-ordered structure concealed behind the visible imbalance.

The first part is composed of fifteen lines, compared to eighteen lines in the second part, twenty-one lines in the third part and seven lines in the fourth part. This proportioning of the number of the lines in the consecutive parts is of primary importance. The second part consists of three more lines than the first one, and the third part is three lines longer than the second one. The fourth part consists of only seven lines. In the last part then, the clear structural analogy connected to the numeral unit of three suddenly and unexpectedly breaks off. In addition to this, there are other structural inconsistencies taking shape in a more subtle way. The twenty-one lines of the third part divided by three, the common denominator of the first three parts, equals seven, which is exactly the number of lines in the fourth part of the poem.

The main structuring principle, where the numerical units three and seven dominate, manifests itself more inexplicitly. The three lines of the strophes in the first part correspond to the three strophes of the second part. The symmetrical progression of the three times three and four line units of the third part, where the number of the lines equals seven, is analogous to the seven lines of the fourth part. This manner of creating harmonic unity from discordant elements is, in my opinion, relevant in terms of the Aristotelian principle of *concordia discors*.

4.1.2 The Represented Elements of Reality

In this investigation of the represented elements of reality our starting point is the title, *Atlantis*. When it is mentioned for the first time in Plato's *Dialogues*, Atlantis is described as a blissful island that existed in ancient times and because of the sinful life of its inhabitants was sunk into the sea by the mighty gods. Many studies of the origin of the Atlantis-myth try to prove its real existence. This known wavering between real and unreal indicates that the title of Weöres' poem *Atlantis* is likely to be experienced as enigmatic and ambiguous, which suggests two different ways of interpretation: a literary one, that is, the *census litteraris* and an allegorical one, that is, the *sensus spiritualis*. The poetic question of the first part: *Ki tudná elmondani, mi van a kárpitra festve!* 'Who could tell, what is painted on the curtain!', as a possible projection of Plato's doctrine of ideas, offers further grounds for these two different methods of interpretation. Things painted on the curtain are not real. They are only reconstructions of a reality that is impossible to perceive with the eyes, or to be named by a real name.

A literal interpretation has the level of occurrences in view. These occurrences, as part of a course of events, are to be examined within the global structure of the poem. Spatial or linear coherences can be explained by means of often repeated words or word groups denoting place, which in the poem *Atlantis* are as follows: *a csarnok mélyén* 'in the deep of the hall' in the first part; *termeken* 'through the halls' in the second part; *kerti füvön* 'on the garden grass' in the third part; and an undefinable sphere somewhere between *a földtömeg sötétsége* 'the darkness of the Earth' and the *angyal* 'angel' in the fourth part. Based on the semantical intimation of the verbs, we may perhaps see the plot as follows: the first part concerns the dreams of the poet, in which the image of the mythical island Atlantis emerges, and an unnamed girl and a king living in a palace appear. The second part concentrates on the main character wandering through the halls of the palace, who in the last verse cannot walk there anymore for there is only emptiness, created by the lost Atlantis. The image of the girl appears again in the third part, depicted in a very sensual way: she is the *hajlós testű* 'nimble-bodied', the *eleven kút* 'living well' and the *kereplő derekú* 'rattle-waisted' and these appearances of the girl are followed by the mythical intercourse beneath the stars. The fruit of this union is the *ember* 'the human', first revealed in the last part, who in his nameable uniqueness unites all unnameable and unnamed.

An allegoric interpretation then develops on the basis of the represented elements of reality. In this sense the title, which is the word *Atlantis* written on the paper, is just as real as the pictures are that are painted on the curtain. *Atlantis* then becomes a symbol with another meaning, the symbol of a golden age when there was no history but occurrences – *ki a történésekben sétálsz* 'who walks in the happenings' – and when the state of oneness also meant the unity of the female and the male nature of the human – *más vagy-e? vagy én vagyok?* 'are you somebody else? or are you myself?' When, however, this blessed island passed out of sight, then the original oneness within the well-ordered cosmos also smashed to pieces and turned to chaos, which also caused the definite separation of the female and the male. The Greek word *chaos* denotes an abyss, an empty room, the lack of something, that is, a well-ordered state existing in *cosmos* (Filosofilexikonet 1988:305). In a state of chaos the most substantial other part of the human is missing: *minden belém temette arcát* 'everything buried its face in me'. The human, conceived in chaos, can only perceive the ancient oneness through his individual existence. Substituting the *bozót* 'brushwood', a symbol for chaos, and the *angyal* 'angel', a symbol for the wholeness or cosmos, the ancient oneness, or the macrocosmos, is then reflected in his own individual microcosmos.

Kenyeres (1974:291) wrote as follows about the structure of the myth: "The myth is a thematic structure, its logic depends on the arrangement of the motifs in the text; this was one of the main issues in Weöres' poetry already from the beginning, and it remained". But in what way are these motifs arranged? Lévy-Strauss declares in the preface of the analysis of Baudleaire's poem *Les Chats* that the foundations of semantics must be taken into consideration when analyzing a myth. Concerning the most essential aspect of the structure of the myth, he wrote as follows: "The function of repetition is to render the structure of the myth apparent. [– – –] Thus, a myth exhibits a 'slated' structure, which comes to the surface, so to speak, through the process of repetition" (Lévy-Strauss 1968:229). Or as also Bata (1979:150) put it: "The most fundamental aspect of the myth is its repetititive structures".

In the poem *Atlantis* this structuring principle of repetition is possible to follow in two ways: one way is to carry out an investigation of the four parts one by one, the other way is to carry out a study looking at the four parts as a whole. An analysis of the separate parts sheds light upon the following major repeated patterns:

Part 1: Repetition of words with or without suffixes: *madarakat* 'birds', *madár* 'birds' [lit.'bird']; *zenét* 'music', *zene* 'music'; *világos* 'clear', *világos* 'clear'; *csarnok mélye* 'deep of the hall', *mélyen* 'deep inside', *csarnok mélyén* 'in the deep of the hall'

Part 2: Repetition of certain parts of sentences: *Mikor a termeken végigmentem* 'When I wandered through the halls'; *Sokszor mentem végig a termeken* 'Often I wandered through the halls'; *Többé nem tudok végigmenni a termeken* 'I cannot wander through the halls any more'

Part 3: Repetition of sentences: *Nézz messze* 'Look far'; *Fény vagyok* 'I am light'; *ezért tudsz szeretni engem* 'that is why you can love me'

Part 4: Repetition of words with or without suffixes: *bozót* 'brushwood', *bozóthoz* 'to the brushwood', *bozót* 'bruswood', *bozótként* 'like the brushwood', *bozótot* 'the brushwood'; *ember* 'human', *emberhez* 'to the human, *ember* 'the human'; *angyal* 'angel', *angyalhoz* 'to the angel', *angyalt* 'the angel', *angyal* 'the angel', *angyalt* 'the angel'.
Complex or mixed repetitions: *a csonkaság fénye vidám* 'the light of the broken is merry'; *a teltség fénye szomorú* 'the light of the whole is sad'; *a csonkaság sötétje szomorú* 'the dark of the broken is sad'; *a teltség sötétje*

vidám 'the dark of the whole is merry'.

One of the main functions of repetition is to emphasize the most important elements of subject matter. The repeated words within a repetitive structure are the most significant in understanding the occurrences. These occurrences are, however, only parts of a surface structure, using the generative grammar term, and as a result are not sufficient in defining the meaning. It is the deep structure which brings meaning within reach, but its patterns are much more difficult to find. Weöres' own terms of horizontalism and verticalism in all probability are related to the definitions of these generative grammar terms. Horizontalism, to Weöres, is connected to the surface structure and verticalism to the deep structure. Nevertheless, Weöres reckons himself among the verticalists and comments: "I am a verticalist. I explore the depth and the height, not the level which can immediately be perceived. In other words, the profundity of an instinctual world and the altitudes of the spiritual spheres" (Weöres 1993c:59). Consequently, an analysis which follows this vertical way of thinking must be based on the whole text and use a deductive method, as opposed to the former investigation of the repetitive patterns of the four separate parts of the poem.

Teun van Dijk (1972:77) called the power which keeps the textual elements together macro-cohesion or global cohesion. This power can be created by the repetition of certain words or sentences in which the main content is concentrated. At this point, the question arises: can we find any word, probably one which is often-repeated, which coheres the whole text in the poem *Atlantis*? According to my calculations, there is a word which could create global cohesion. The word *fény* 'light' occurs three times in the three strophes of the second part; twice in the third part and twice in the fourth part. Taken as a whole, this totals seven times, equal to the number of the lines of the fourth part of the synthesis. In my opinion, this numeric coincidence has a certain repercussion within the subject matter.

The primary structuring principle of the poem *Atlantis* is then the principle of repetition, both in view of its surface structure and its deep structure. The focal point or focus of the poem, as it appears to me, is the single word *fény* 'light', which is also connected to this main structuring principle. Klára Széles (1996:102) asserted that "focus is characterized by an inner contradiction and is dialectic in itself" and she based on this discusses the bipolaric nature of focus. In the poem *Atlantis* this bipolarity is represented by the concept of darkness, expressed contextually as: *tompaságot* 'hollow', *árnyéka valaminek* 'shadow of something', *ürességben* 'in emptiness', *homályból* 'from the dusk'.

4.1.3 The Rhetorical-Stylistic Structure

In terms of the rhetorical-stylistic structure of the poem *Atlantis*, the primary structuring principle is explicitly seen to be repetition. The several repetition-patterns define both the surface structure and the deep structure, acting as rhetorical figures which intensify certain elements.

Using the surface structure as our starting-point, we may distinguish between two forms of repetitions: repetition of words and repetition of sentences. The figure *polyptoton* belongs to the first form, involving identical words which appear in different places of the text. Examples of this figure were given in the previous chapter. In the case of *geminatio*, the elements of the repetitive structure are most closely connected to each other, with only a word or locution between the repeated words, as the following examples show: *Benn, mélyen, a csarnok mélyén* 'Deep inside, in the deep of the hall', *Tán szórakozik, tán munkálkodik* 'Maybe he enjoys himself, maybe he works hard', in the first part; *Nézz messze, nézz messze* 'Look far, look far', *Fény vagyok, fény vagyok* 'I am light, I am light', as it is worded in the third part; and *bozót vagy, ember vagy, angyal vagy* 'you are brushwood, you are human, you are angel' in the fourth part. The two first lines of the fourth strophe, including the figure *divisio,* can be studied as repetitive structures, as well as the contrasts of the second and the third lines of the fourth part where antonyms are opposed to each other: *a csonkaság fénye vidám, a teltség fénye szomorú, / a csonkaság sötétje szomorú, a teltség fénye vidám* 'the light of the broken is merry, the light of the whole is sad, the dark of the broken is sad, the dark of the whole is merry'. The enumeration and the *congeries* of the next line can also be noted: *bozóthoz, emberhez, angyalhoz könyörögjünk* 'let us pray to the brushwood, the human, the angel'.

The refrains of the second and the third parts of the poem are the most obvious demonstrations of sentence repetition: *mikor a termeken végig-mentem* 'When I wandered through the halls', *Sokszor mentem végig a termeken* 'Often I wandered through the halls', *Többé nem tudok végigmenni a termeken* 'I cannot wander through the halls any more'; *Nézz messze* 'Look far', *Fény vagyok* 'I am light', *ezért tudsz szeretni engem* 'that is why you can love me'. Sentences with parallel grammatical structure are also included in this form of repetitive structure, which, occurring as they do throughout the poem, serve to reinforce the main structuring principle.

A discussion concerning the numerous metaphors essentially means a discussion concerning the poem as a whole. Because of this, I confine myself to those metaphors in which the nameless of the first part appears. The following metaphors belong to this group: *gyors macska* 'swift cat', *áldozati csésze* 'offering cup', and *árnyéka valaminek* 'shadow of something' in the first part; *hajlós testű* 'nimble-bodied', *eleven kút* 'living well', and *kereplő derekú* 'rattle-waisted' in the third part.

Repetition-patterns operating within the deep structure, however, much more than those discovered in the surface structure, are essential in attempting to reveal dimensions of the meaning. Those patterns which integrate several elements very often shed light on new contexts of meaning. The word *fény* 'light', as mentioned before, is the word with focal quality and an integrating capacity. The contrasting concept of darkness, expressed with words belonging to the same contextual sphere, draws even more attention to the focal point of 'light'. If both appear equally within the surface structure and deep structure, the images of light and darkness are also symbols, the meaning of which is difficult to explain. Peter Hallberg (1975:83-84) writes as follows about this ancient trope: "The symbol on the other hand is likely to be connected with the more profound and original layer of our consciousness or subconsciousness. That is why there is no definitive explanation for it. To all appearances much depends on its influence of this feature of something irrational and evanescent". Owing to the fact that the factual image from which the symbol originated in the course of time lost its significance, this primary meaning has disappeared in most cases. However, as Beáta Thomka (1992:113-114) put it: "... some figures and tropes originally belonging to lower language levels can also transgress their original competence: the simile, the metaphor, the symbol, even the enjambement, the several kinds of repetitions, parallels, ellipses can attain a formal level, which means that they can be interpreted as the main organization principle of the entire poem". This occurs, as I see it, in the case of the symbols of light and darkness, as the light, as focal point, enlightens and outlines every single element of the poem.

4.1.4 The Metrical Structure

This analysis of the metrical patterns, following a deductive method, is based on the total structure. As indicated in the chapter on the structure of the shape of writing, it is the divergent number of the lines within the strophes that first strikes the eye. Each part is different. The length of the lines, however, gives a somewhat symmetrical impression: the lines in the first and the last parts are definitely longer than the lines of the two middle parts. Looking at the several forms of enjambements, we notice a certain similarity in their frequent occurrence in the first and the third parts, compared to the two other parts of the poem. This is probably due to the fact that the strophes are relatively shorter in the first and third parts. There is, however, a striking similarity in the occurrence of identical grammatical patterns in the lines from the second and fourth parts.

The majority of the strophes, with the exception of the connected last and first lines of the third and fourth strophes of the first part, are closed by a punctuation mark. The lack of rhymes and a definite and describable metrical pattern is also seen throughout the poem. This rhythm of the poem inevitably reminds us of prose.

The numerous formal constraints, then, which are characteristic of both quantitative and syllabic metrical systems are difficult to find in *Atlantis*, although the existing lines and strophes, the most fundamental features of the poem, clearly belong to the genre of poetry. Instead of a constant and consistent metrical pattern, however, there is a sense of rhythm emerging from the parallel grammatical structure of the sentences. As a result, Weöres' poem, because of its form, is free-verse.

There are three distinctive forms of free verse, associated with the forms implemented by Goethe, Heine and Whitman (Kecskés 1984:207-208; Wåhlin 1995:145). Naturally, placing a given poem into one of these categories is difficult, because most poems written in free verse can exhibit certain traits from all of these categories. Specific features originating from one certain type can, however, be fairly pronounced. In my opinion, in the poem *Atlantis* there are few features which are characteristic of Goethe's free verse style, as one of its main criteria, that is, the frequent recurrence of enjambements, is only slightly seen in the first and the third parts. Characteristics of Heine's free verse style are easier to recognize. In his form of free verse, the lines are separate syntagms, and the style is close to everyday speech. Characteristics, however, of Whitman's free verse style are the easiest to demonstrate. One strong characteristic of his free verse is parallelism, which functions as the main structuring principle of Weöres' poem *Atlantis*.

Surely this form of free verse was a deliberate choice by Weöres, who then consciously adapted the form to a given subject matter. The re-telling of mythical themes, that is, a reconstruction of prehistory, is supposedly the most verisimilar when using the ancient forms of poetry. But as there are no written reminiscences handed down, we must rely on logical inferences from plausible facts. The view of an originally unconstrained form is generally accepted by researchers, which means the lack of a well-ordered structure created by rhymes and a rhythmical pattern. These first forms of poetry might resemble free verse, fulfilling the only requirement of free-verse: a precise arrangement into regular lines. The early forms of poetry had a clearly syncretic character, not only aiming towards aesthetic assignation but towards an essential subject matter (Szerdahelyi 1994:36). Although originating from religious beliefs, this subject matter irreversibly turned into myth.

The poem *Atlantis* touches on the mythical spirit of the most profound truths. It does this by using the form of free verse, which, like Orphic poetry, has no knowledge about the constraint of form. Instead, "everything rests on the superhuman force of the inspiration" as Hamvas (1990:217) put it. The concept of inspiration is difficult to define and, surely, it also verges on the unconscious. The idea of Atlantis is not only an image of the sinking of this blessed island but also a descent to the unconscious. The use of free verse to represent a mythical theme is a conscious act of the poet. The descent into mythic profundity is a two-dimensional move, because the descent concludes in the very depths of individuality. It is, then, ultimately the unconscious which is represented in Weöres' free verse.

4.1.5 The Grammatical structure

Each of the four parts are composed as a whole, as seen by the consistency of the punctuation marks, and each in terms of the subject matter, is closely connected to the title. Moreover, a certain structural symmetry can be seen as a result of the three periods of the first and last strophes of the poem. These also may express deepened levels of conceptuality, that is, when the real transgresses to the unreal.

This same conclusiveness mentioned above is reflected in the strophes. Each strophe, like each of the four parts, is a semantical unit. This fact is also supported by the correctly-used punctuation marks. The sentences from time to time run freely over to the following lines, yet for the most part are contained within a single line. Placing sentences and syntagms in a linear chain indicates a type of horizontality. This is further reinforced by the predominantly compound sentences, which differ only in terms of their states of modality. The greater part of the sentences are affirmative. This is especially seen in the exclusively affirmative sentences of the second, third and fourth parts. In the first part, however, declarative sentences alternate with exclamatory and interrogative sentences. The second strophe, in spite of the exclamation mark which closes both the first and third lines, can also be seen as a question.

This linear or horizontal construction, however, implies not only a free flow of a chain of sentences, but also a similar or even identical structuring of the syntactical units. Examples of these types of parallel grammatical structures are: *a sok zene, a sok madár* 'this music [lit. this much music'], these many birds' in the first part; *a fény, a szél* 'the light, the wind' in the second part; and *nézz messze, nézz messze* 'look far, look far' in the third part. Similar parallel structured syntagms are also significant in the fourth part, but are somewhat longer than in the previous parts.

This structure, principally based on parallel grammatical structures, is also seen on the vertical plane, that is, in the placement of the sentences, syntagms or the words which do not necessarily follow each other. This vertical arrangement of certain word- or syntagm-contructions is especially common in the first and the third part: *világos – világos* 'clear' – 'clear'; *kerti füvön – sötét füvön* 'garden grass' – 'dark grass'. Similarly structured sentences, sometimes appearing as unvaried repetitions, can be demonstrated by many examples from the second, third and fourth parts: *Mikor a termeken végigmentem – Mikor a termeken végigmentem* 'When I wandered through the halls' – 'When I wandered through the halls'; *Nézz rám, te hajlós testű – Dalolj, eleven kút – Táncolj, kereplő derekú* 'Look at me, you, nimble-bodied' – 'Sing, living well' – Dance, rattle-waisted'; *a csonkaság fénye vidám – a csonkaság sötétje szomorú;* 'the light of the broken is merry' – 'the dark of the broken is sad'.

In addition to these characteristic traits of syntax, an investigation of the tenses may also be instructive. As shown by the verbs, both present, past and future tenses are included in the course of occurrences. The past tense in the first strophe of the first part is followed by the present tense in the next strophes. The past tense of the first two strophes of the second part are replaced by the alternate change of present and past tenses in the third strophe, where, as a result of this alternation, past and present merges into each other, and where future time is indicated first of all by the repetition of the lines *Többé nem tudok végigmenni a termeken* 'I cannot wander through the halls anymore'. This last strophe of the second part also signifies some kind of a transition from past to present which comes into play in the third part.

The fact that the represented time phases have a crucial effect on structure was especially emhasized by Roman Ingarden (1976:308-322). He distinguishes between three phases of time: homogeneous or objective universal time; concrete, intersubjective time, shared by the humankind today; and subjective time. According to Ingarden's view on time, only these two last phases can be captured in literary works, while the first-mentioned universal, "void" time, as defined by physical-mathematical circumstances, cannot be depicted. His concept of time perspective involves the actual time of the interpretation, i.e. whether the plot is presented in past, present or future time. That phase of time which the reader adapts is called the "zero-point of orientation" by Ingarden. While concrete, intersubjective time represents the time of present occurrences, Ingarden's last group, subjective time, may be associated with both an imagined, thinkable past, and with present or future time. To Ingarden, the time we identify in literary works is a continous medium, and within this structure there cannot be any interruptions. These three phases of time link to each other in an origin-less and an endless route.

"... a myth is an account of events which took place *in principio*, that is 'in the beginning', in a primordial and non-temporal instant, a moment of *sacred time* [– – –] ... the myth takes man out of his own time – his individual, chronological. 'historic' time – and projects him, symbolically at least, into the Great Time, into a paradoxical instant which cannot be measured because it does not consist of duration. This is as much as to say that the myth implies a breakaway from Time and the surrounding world; it opens up a way into the sacred Great Time" (Eliade 1991:57-58). This assessment of Eliade's may be compared with Ingarden's concept of homogeneous or objective universal time, which in his opinion cannot be depicted in literary works. In my opinion, however, Weöres' *Atlantis* is very closely related to just this void time. The transition line involving the three phases of time, uniting present, past and future in the last strophe of the second part, and the apparent present time, which disappears into the timeless in the last part, are traits in a distinctly arranged time-structure, and support my interpretation.

4.2 The World of the Text

4.2.1 The Theme

When dealing with literary works, we notice the difference between the concepts of theme and content, especially when interpretation creates obvious difficulties. While content, disclosed by the essential components of the plot, may be depicted in a concrete way and as a factual matter, theme, on the other hand, most often indirectly reflected by abstract motifs, may be described symbolically. This is because the content, as such, is directly represented by the words, and hence is affiliated to language; while theme, a symbolic form, has no characteristics relating it to language.

Claude Lévy-Strauss, in studying myth according to the methods of the structural anthropology, declares that myth by its nature has some characteristics of language, but at the same time myth functions without language, "above the ordinary linguistic level" (Lévi-Strauss 1968:210). He uses this as a basis for explaining the nature of mytholological time. *Langue* and *parole*, used as Saussureian terms, stand for reversible and irreversible time. Mythological time is to be found between these two poles, as the very essence of the timeless nature of a harmonized past, present and future. An approach like this, as a matter of fact, has similarities to the concepts of synchronic and diachronic time.

Lévy-Strauss created another link to language with his term *mythemes*, patterned after the linguistic concepts phoneme and morpheme. The *mythemes*, essential components of myth, are larger units than phonemes and morphemes. *Mythemes* function at the semantic level. If one marks the mythemes with numbers, the structure of the myth can be compared to that of a musical score, according to Lévi-Strauss. A horizontal line of these numbers corresponds to the succession of textual events, and the vertical line shows the events which are in some way connected to each other. The diagram formed by this pattern then demonstrates both the diachronic order of irreversible time, represented by the horizontal line; and the synchronic pattern of the formerly-undiscovered connections within reversible time, depicted by the vertical line. In the words of Lévy-Strauss: "Were we to *tell* the myth, we would disregard the columns and read the rows from left to right and from top to bottom. But if we want to *understand* the myth, then we will have to disregard one half of the diacronic dimension (top to bottom) and read from left to right, column after column, each one being considered as a unit" (Lévy-Strauss 1968:214).

The concept discussed above can be used to discuss theme and content, in my opinion. Content would answer to the focal points within the chain of the events indicated by the diachronic order of irreversible time, seen on the horizontal line; and theme is congruent to the vertical line of related motifs and their inherently synchronious, reversible discontinuity.

Kenyeres (1983:135) argues that Weöres goes further and further away from the original stories in his later applications of mythical theme, and that he uses the original stories only as starting points. Weöres "paraphrased the inner structure of the 'mythical way of thinking'", as Kenyeres put it. Kenyeres (1983:134) also points out that there is a certain similarity between the horizontally and vertically structured elements of myth in the model of the structural anthropology and in Weöres' myth-paraphrases. In my opinion, the poem *Atlantis* is one of these rewritings of a myth. The original plot can hardly be seen as a source of inspiration and the events only roughly, or, in some cases, not at all, follow the original plot of the myth. The occurrences and motifs related to the myth, however, may also be represented by numbers as closely as possible to the tables of Lévy-Strauss. This leads to a double accounting of the structure of the theme and the content.

These methods of structural anthropology may be of particular advantage in analyzing those poems in which theme seems difficult to define using traditional approaches. The theme of the poem *Atlantis* is undoubtedly, and formulated briefly, the very world of the title: *Atlantis*. A symbolic interpretation is guaranteed because evidence of certain events is debatable. As, however, the probability of an ancient continent cannot be entirely excluded, a belief in a theme that embraces more than one dimension is somewhat strengthened. How can this multidimensional structure be grasped? A feasible way is suggested: an analysis of the poem using a method from structural anthropology.

We have found that the primary structuring principle of the myth is the repetition of certain semantical units. These motifs or mythemes are usually short sentences or syntagms in which the very essence of the subject-matter is concentrated and which are arranged in groups based on the same semantical foundation. Sentences or syntagms, however, can also be replaced by words, particularly in poems like *Atlantis*, because here the words themselves are symbols of certain larger units of meaning. In looking at Atlantis, I propose fifteen groups to represent the main repetition-patterns. These are, however, not the same forms of the words, or synonyms, but words which, in my opinion, are associated with each other by their meaning. These words are presented in the same form as they occur in the poem and the numbers within the brackets stand for the strophes and the lines:

1: *zenét* 'music' (1:2,15); *szórakozik* 'he enjoys himself' (1:14); *dalolj* 'sing' (3:11); *táncolj* 'dance' (3:18); *vidám* 'merry' (4:2,3)

2: *láttam* 'I have seen' (1:1); *szememből kiesett a tekintet* 'the gaze dropped out from my eyes' (2:17); *nézz rám* 'look at me' (3:4); *nézz messze* 'look far' (3:8)

3: *világos* 'clear' (1:3,7); *fény* 'light' (2:2,18); *fényt* 'light' (2:11); *vakító* 'glare' (2:14,17); *előfehérlő* 'white emerging from the dusk' (3:12); *szikrázik* 'glitters' (3:15); *fény* 'light' (3:16,16); *fénye* 'the light' (4:2,2)

4: *tompaság* 'hollow' (1:5); *üresség* 'emptiness' (2:14); *esti* 'evening' (3:3,9), *homály* 'dusk' (3:12); *sötétje* 'the dark' (4:3,3); *sötétsége* 'darkness' (4:5)

5: *csarnok* 'hall' (1:5,13); *termeken* 'through the halls' (2:1,4,7,10,13,16)

6: *nevezhetőnek* 'for all nameable things' (1:6); *névtelen* 'nameless' (1:7); *világos* 'clear' (1:7); *lány képében* 'in the image of a girl' (1:8); *gyors macska* 'swift cat' (1:11); *áldozati csésze* 'offering cup' (1:11); *árnyéka valaminek* 'shadow of something' (1:11); *én lelkem* 'my soul' (2:8); *vakító* 'glare' (2:14); *hajlós testű* 'nimble-bodied' (3:4); *eleven kút* 'living well' (3:11); *kereplő derekú* 'rattle-waisted' (3:18); *bozót* 'brushwood' (4:1,4,5,6,7); *ember* 'human' (4:1,4,7); *angyal* 'angel' (4:1,4,5,6,7)

7: *heversz* 'rests' [lit. 'you rest'] (1:8); *fekszel* 'lies' [lit. 'you lie'] (1:9); *elnyújtózol* 'you strech yoursef out' (3:5)

8: *emlékemben* 'in my memories' [lit. 'in my memory'] (1:9); *emlékemben* 'in my memories' (2:18)

9: *sétálsz* 'walks' [lit. 'you walk'] (1:10); *végigmentem* 'I wandered through' (2:1,4); *jött* 'came' (2:5); *mentem végig* 'I wandered through' (2:7,10); *nem tudok végigmenni* 'I cannot wander through' (3:13,16); *járok* 'I walk' (2:14); *föl-le jár* 'walks up and down' (2:18); *bolyong* 'roams' (4:7)

10: *elnyugszol* 'takes a rest' [lit. 'you take a rest'] (1:10); *csituljon* 'may quieten' (4:4)

11: *szél* 'wind' (2:3,18); *libeg a hűs esti levegő* 'the fresh evening breeze floats' (3:3)

12: *kinti világ* 'outside world' (2:5); *kerti füvön* 'on the garden grass' (3:5); *a gyöngyös, sötét füvön* 'on the pearly, dark grass' (3:19), *bozót* 'brushwood' (4:1,4,5,6,7)

13: *sírtam* 'I wept' (2:9); *szomorú* 'sad' (4:2,3)

14: *fekete, sötétkék és arany* 'black, dark-blue and gold' (3:2); *ég sárgája* 'yellow evening sky' (3:9); *egy csillag buzog pirosan* 'a star bubbles reddening' (3:10); *előfehérlő* 'white emerging' (3:12)

15: *ezért tudsz szeretni engem* 'that is why you can love me' (3:17, 21)

This grouping of the motifs, though patterned differently, is aimed to correspond to that of Lévy-Strauss' vertically arranged chain of mythemes. Using these fifteen groups presented above, new aspects of the theme of the poem are likely to be exposed.

Easily discernible references to similar meaning are found in the sixth group. This is the sphere of the self between the named and the unnamed, also shown by the question: *más vagy-e? vagy én vagyok?* 'are you somebody else? or are you myself?'. When the named is replaced by the unnamed, then reality loses its contours and becomes an abstract idea. The girl is not real, only an image of a girl, and at the same time this form is connected to the probably mythological image of a cat. A closer study of the correspondence between mythical cats and their *alter ego*s, the *les grands sphynxs* in Baudelaire's sonnet, *Les Chats*, and this image of a cat in Weöres' *Atlantis* could certainly be very instructive. Jakobson's and Lévy-Strauss' well-known grammatical analysis of Baudelaire's poem emphasizes the unity of the female and the masculine parts in it. According to popular belief, as this animal hunts in darkness, it is connected to dark powers, and also possesses magical powers, for example, the power to transform itself. In the sonnet *Les Chats* the cat is able to enlarge time and space to cosmic proportions. Within this expanded time and space the cat metamorphoses to the sphinx. Weöres' poem, in my opinion, involves a similar change. The image of the cat, as a symbol of the feminine in psychology (Aeppli 1943:368), is the first step of transformation. It is followed by the religious symbol of the offering cup, closely related to the act of sacrifice, and here can also be seen as a sacrificing of individuality. The next phrase, *árnyéka valaminek* 'shadow of something', expands this, symbolizing double human nature as the result of the sacrifice, that is, the unconscious, different nature, hidden deepest in the self, being discovered. The dismay over this sudden disclosure is expressed by the question: *más vagy-e? vagy én vagyok?* 'are you somebody else? or are you myself?'.

It is in the second part where the nature of the shadow becomes explicit and also where the question from the first part gets its answer. Here the second person singular changes to first person singular: *én lelkem* 'my soul', because "the light showed its mighty face". An identification between the shadow and the first person singular is now within easy reach. As a result of the metamorphosed unity of the grammatical persons, the "nimble-bodied", the "living well" and the "rattle-waisted" of the third part refer to the main character. This grammatical oneness seems obvious in spite of the fact that both the first and second person singular are present in this part. The memory of the shadow, the real nature of the self, connecting to the first part, is mirrored in the water of the well. Narcissus lost himself in it. This same element of losing himself is suggested by the image of the living well, in which the first and second person singular become united. As a result the suppressed glowing music from the first part realizes its purpose, as the first person singular, spell-bound by the music, within the idea of the girl, which is phrased by the words *hajlós testű* 'nimble-bodied', *eleven kút* 'living well' and *kereplő derekú* 'rattle-waisted', becomes completely and inevitably lost.

To whom is the fourth part addressed, then? According to its first line, to the brushwood, to the human and to the angel, to something which cannot be called by one single name, for there is no single name for it. This nameless idea of something fastens itself to the nameless of the first part. In parallel opposition, these units of three concepts, each illustrated by a single line, are kept apart in the three last lines. Yet, in this disconnection, they perpetually turn to each other in a kind of nostalgic longing. The idea of the brushwood, figuratively used for the entangled, the disordered, the chaotic and also for the dark, mysterious feminine part of the man, is contrasted with the idea of the angel, which symbolizes the ordered, divine will, the immaterial and the androgynous nature of the man. Between these two poles stands the human, who by nature is neither solely brushwood, nor angel, and he, for this reason, is only able to temporarily fill the gap between these two extremes.

This category of the nameless, although paradoxically named by many names, asserts itself the most out of the fifteen categories. A further expansion of its meaning is provided by the third category, where the words *világos* 'clear' and *vakító* 'glare', also possible terms for the nameless, also connects to this former group. The word *világos* 'clear', occurring twice in the first part, is, however, quite ambiguous. In the given contexts it actually may function both as a noun and as an adjective. If understood as an adjective, it expresses the idea that everything in the poem is self-evidently clear and not in the least mystical. This dismisses the mystic content of the title. In the case of it being a feasible noun, *világos* 'clear' expresses that it is the girl who is clear and that she can even be named by this word. This possible meaning becomes still more intensified as a result of the word *vakító* 'glare' twice in the third strophe of the second part. A parallel arrangement occurs as well with the words *én lelkem* 'my soul', also appearing twice in the third strophe. This emphasizes a close contextual relationship between these two words.

It is in this second part the word *fény* 'light' first turns up and as the most often repeated word, it also becomes the main motif of the poem. As it is phrased by the same word continuously, it can also be interpreted as the only nameable thing in the poem, as opposed to the sixth group of the unnameable, which is expressed by a variety of words. Nevertheless, as the words *világos* 'clear' and *vakító* 'glare' are also affiliated with the sphere of the unnamed, these two representations of the named and the unnamed become unified through the focal word *fény* 'light'.

All through the poem, however, the counterpart of light, darkness, stands by, represented by the fourth group. This is an apocalyptical darkness, the undiscernible obscurity of the original chaos. When the light, however, makes its first appearance in the second part, it obviously takes the lead from that time on. There is also a star in the evening sky of the third part, which is the same as light.

This contrast between darkness and light becomes most intensified in the second and the third lines of the fourth part. How can light be both sad and merry at the same time, paralleling the simultaneous sadness and merryness of the darkness? A contextual approach, referring to the second and the third parts, may help explain these paradoxical statements. Man is sad within the wholeness, in the radiating light of the second part: *belül sírtam* 'I wept inside', because he is alone in the light: *üresség ben járok* 'I walk in emptiness', or as expressed in the fourth part: *a teltség fénye szomorú* 'the light of the whole is sad'. Although reflected by a star in the third part, the light becomes broken in the fourth part. Its light is now merry, because in the sensual act of the dance the desire for the other part ultimately becomes calm: *a csonkaság fénye vidám* 'the light of the broken is merry'. Or as Fry (1957:159) put it: "For the human rhythm is the opposite of the solar one: a titanic libido wakes when the sun sleeps, and the light of day is often the darkness of desire". An interpretation along these lines must by necessity be followed by a similar interpretation concerning the third line. As the total absence of the light denotes a disordered chaos, then *a csonkaság sötétje szomorú* 'the dark of the broken is sad', and against the light the dark, that is, the shadow, the other part of the human becomes visible, which means that man is not alone any more: *a teltség sötétje vidám* 'the dark of the whole is merry'.

This train of thought continues, clearly, within the second group of the main repetition patterns. The verb *láttam* 'I have seen' in the first part relates to the darkness, including the hollowness of the deep of the hall and also the shadow. The mighty light of the second part still shows the emptiness, that is, that sight which, caused by the sunlight, is now gone: *szememből kiesett a tekintet* 'the gaze dropped out from my eyes'. It is the shining star of the third part which brings back the light, when the metaphor for the girl, the living well comes to light, whose eyes meet the star and also those of the main characters mirrored in the well.

The only word of the eighth group *emlékemben* 'in my memories' relates to the scene of the events. In spite of the fact that the word in this form only occurs twice in the poem, once in the first and once in the second part, the whole poem is affected by it. The use of the first person singular, related to the title, makes it even more ambiguous.

The words of the eleventh group are also associated in some way with memory, but the word *szél* 'wind' in the second part, because of its syntactical connection to the words *emlékemben* 'in my memories' and *fény* 'light', extends the idea to apocalyptical dimensons.

Both the image of the girl and that of the wind can be implied by the verbs of the tenth group: *elnyugszol* 'takes a rest' and *csituljon* 'may quieten'. This latter, as indicated by the only line written in the second person plural in the poem, refers to everyone, without, however, signifying the real incidental of this plural.

There is a close connection between the verbs of this tenth group and the set of the verbs of movement in the ninth group. While the first verb *sétálsz* 'walks' [lit. 'you walk'] concerns the image of the girl, the last one in the group *bolyong* 'roams', similar to the verb *csituljon* 'may quieten' in the former group, includes every individual. And while the verbs *végigmentem* 'I wandered through', *mentem végig* 'I wandered through', *nem tudok végigmenni* 'I cannot wander through' and *járok* 'I walk' give voice to the first person singular and hence refer to human activity, the verb *föl-le jár* 'walks up and down' in the last line of this second part exhibits the movement of natural forces as reflected within the memories of the man. All the above verbs of motion connote some kind of an aimless movement. There is no point in the girl's walk through the events, nor in the wandering through the halls, nor to the up and down walk of memories. Likewise, the wandering of the human is aimless. Only the "inrush of the outside world" into the halls, as phrased in the second part, has purpose. In the same group, including the almost Edenic picture of the garden grass in the third part and the image of the brushwood in the fourth part, this army-like inrush of the outside world, in my opinion, becomes a deliberate mediator of some very important thought. Looking at the halls and the outside world as possible metaphors for the human soul and the memories inrushing in it, a probable interpretation could refer to the awakening of self-consciousness in the human, represented by the adventure of discovering himself between the brushwood and the angel in his real guise, as a human.

The scenes of the fifth part, *csarnok mélye* 'the deep of the hall' and *termek* 'halls' used figuratively are metaphors of the innermost world and the memories of the human. It is the first image of the girl that turns the images of the outside world and the garden grass, belonging to the twelfth group, to memories. The lines *belőled isznak / a legdúsabb pillanatok* 'the wealthiest moments / drink from you' can also be interpreted as a metaphor of remembrance. The colors depicted in the fourteenth group are also visions of memories. Nowhere else in the poem is there such frequent recurrence of color as in this third part. The contrast of light and darkness in the other three parts is followed by the multicolored image of the meeting between the opposite parts of the self. We know that colors not only exercise an influence on one's frame of mind, but can also express certain frames of mind. Psychology attaches great importance to the meaning of color. Colors reveal a subject matter by how they figuratively visualize a certain feeling. Red, for example, usually means joy, love or happiness. The star in the poem *Atlantis* is red, too, under which the first and second person unite.

The line of the last group *ezért tudsz szeretni engem* 'that is why you can love me' occurs twice in the poem, within the third part, the first time as the words of the star, the second time as the words of the teller. The star is liked for its light, and the teller is liked for his song, which decides the rhythm of the dance. Along with Bata (1979:117) we could say that "the principle of the creation is masculine". It is the opposition between the feminine and the masculine, the antagonism of passivity and activity that comes up here, which at the same time also binds the two sexes together: in love and in desire. This sentence connects the two main motifs of the poem: the sphere of the light, which is also represented by the most frequent word of the poem *fény* 'light', and the sphere of the self, which is also represented by the largest group of words expressing the same figurative meaning. As a result of this vertical structural pattern the real theme becomes much less ambiguous: the theme is not the sinking of the ancient mystical island, Atlantis, but a descent into the secret dimensions of individual consciousness.

4.2.2 The Poem as Part of Weöres' Lifework

It was not very often that Weöres wrote the date of composition on his poems.

There was, naturally, a particular reason for this: he worked for a long time on his poems and because of this only the publishing date can be determined without any doubt. The first part of the poem *Atlantis,* titled *Áhitat* 'Longing' was first published in the volume *Elysium* in 1946. Later this title changed to *Tüzes csőrű madarakat* 'Birds with flame-colored beaks' (Kenyeres 1983:100). In contrast to the majority of the poems, the entire poem *Atlantis* in the three-volume *Egybegyűjtött írások* 'Collected Writings', is undated. This is probably due to the fact that the four separate parts were written at different times. Nevertheless, most of the poems of the *Elysium* were written during the beginning of the forties, mostly in 1944.

The poems published in this volume, with few exceptions, borrow their origins from surrealism. One of these is the poem *Eidolon*, later titled *Az áramlás szobra* 'The Statue of the Stream', which because of its exceedingly unusual idea associations, soundly provoked the general literary public of that time in Hungary. In the debate that followed the publishing of the poem, the poet József Fodor hit the nail on the head when he concluded that "the poet is free to stand on his head, but the public is free to be taken aback. The poem will give voice to the collective soul" (Eidolon 1993:23). Kenyeres (1983:115) wrote as follows about the poem: "[...] with its chain of memories and associations, with its dreamlike veil, the poem Atlantis was connected to surrealism".

The most illuminating definition of surrealism is that of André Breton (1946:45-46), formulated in 1924: "Surréalisme, n. m. Automatisme psychique pur par lequel on se propose d'exprimer, soit verbalement, soit par écrit, soit de toute autre manière, le fonctionnement réel de la pensée. Dictée de la pensée, en l'absence de tout controle exercé par la raison, en dehors de toute préoccupation esthétique ou morale. [...] Le surréalisme repose sur la croyance à la réalité supérieure de certaines formes d'associations négligées jusqu'à lui, à la toutepuissance du rêve, au jeu désintéressé de la pensée. Il trend à ruiner définitivement tous les autres mécanismes psychiques et à se substituer à eux dans la résolution des principaux problèmes de la vie".

The poem *Atlantis* obviously bears the marks of this literary movement. These marks, however, are not to be compared to those of the poem *Eidolon*, which Weöres also considered to be an experiment (Eidolon 1993:25), but essential characteristics of surrealism are easy to find in the *Atlantis*, too. These characteristics are, for example, the "dreamlike veil" that Kenyeres mentioned, the non-reality of the seemingly real images and the subject-matter, which includes the entire universe. Poems like the *Tavasz-ünnep előestéje* 'The Eve of the Spring-feast' or the *Anadyomené*, which, like *Atlantis*, are inspired by some mythical theme, are not only artifacts of some poetic experimentation. These poems are characterized by a deliberate immersion in the most essential questions of human existence. The distinctive marks of surrealism, such as the use of irregular sentences, the omission of punctuation marks, and collocations contrary to reason, are not seen in *Atlantis*. Instead of these traits of surrealism, I will emphasize those characteristics of the Symbolist style. The tension created by the difference between the concrete and the abstract levels in a symbol aids in expressing the most complex human emotions. Because of the fact that *Atlantis* is created from symbols, a thematic approach involving a denotative method must be replaced by a connotative one.

The twenty pieces of the poem *Dalok Naconxypan-ból* 'Songs from Naconxypan' (EI:330-335) show characteristic features of both symbolism and surrealism. Contrary to Bata (1979:60), who declares that these pieces are not representative of the surrealist style, there are, in my opinion, several indications of this. It was a surrealist painting by Lajos Gulácsy which inspired Weöres to write the poem. This picture is reflected in the particularly dream-like visions in the poem, the seemingly real images of something non-real, the free associations, and the semantic dissonances of Weöres' poem. In addition, there are symbols present which contribute to the poem's symbolic character. Meaning is not dependent on conceptual factors related to these images of reality, but on those feelings and assumptions which these images arouse. The images in the small songs of the poem are not coherently connected to one another. They are instead like the pictures of a montage or the constantly changing images of a dream.

Aside from their style, these poems are also connected by their thematic points of view. Many pieces of the poem *Dalok Naconxypan-ból* 'Songs from Nacoxypan' recall the voices of a sunken world, as in the 16th verse:

Ki sírva faggatsz, hű baráti lélek,
vigasztalásul ennyit mondhatok:
a víz alatti házban éldegélek,
fölfalnak tengermélyi csillagok.

You true friendly soul, who question me weeping,
this I can say to comfort you:
I live in the house under the water,
the stars in the depth devour me.

According to Bata (1979:61) it is the image of the original oneness and completeness that we sense in the poem. This wholeness of human existence, because it belongs to the sphere of the unconscious, is impossible to realize, as it is worded in the twentieth verse:

Ez a vers is valóság, akár az álmod.

Az élet szív és kés egy szín alatt.
Szemeddel az egész tengert halászod
s horoggal mit fogsz? egynéhány halat.

This poem is as real as your dream.
Life is heart and knife at the same time.
You fish in the whole sea with your eyes
and what do you catch? One or two fish.

The work *A teljesség felé* 'Towards the Absolute' (EI: I:635-690) is the actual completion of this theme of original wholeness. The next-to-last line of *Atlantis* points to this: *mert az angyal bozótként fordul a teljesség felé* 'for the angel like the brushwood turns towards the Absolute'. This work from 1945 is a poetic representation of Béla Hamvas' and Katalin Kemény's translation on the *Vedanta* (Szőcs 1990:475-476). It is dedicated to Hamvas: "it was he who brought about harmony in me" as Weöres said in the preface. The first part, *A forrás* 'The Source' talks about the primary knowledge of ancient times, that is, the existential wholeness, from which, in the next part *A kard* 'The Sword', the individual fate had broken away and which feels an eternal nostalgia for its loss. In the third part, *The fészek* 'The Nest' "the most essential form of the disintegration of primeval wholeness is that it became female and male. [– – –] In the same way as the female-body and the male-body need completion, the female-soul and male-soul are broken. The woman does not know about the light, the man does not know about the fervour. The woman wants creating-power, the man wants life-giving power. [– – –] Which of them is worth more: the woman or the man? No matter. Either one of them can reach the last step: the wholeness. But each reaches it in a separate way: the man by developing his own, limited existence into a more open, whole one; the woman, by becoming like a soft fervour settling on the last, soft, warm nest". The fourth part, *A szárny* 'The Wing' puts the unconscious territories of the human mind into words: the essential of the human mind does not show itself through words, but as settled or unsettled figures in a space which belongs to the other world... Everything is covered by the oneness of an undefineable clearness and hollowness, a brightness and obscurity which could mostly be called a 'tuneless music'; this is the music emanating from the angels, the music of the spheres". This connects, in my opinion, to the *Atlantis*' sphere of thought. The part, *Tíz erkély* 'Ten Balconies' of the last chapter presents the idea of perfect completeness as a harmonized dialectical structure of opposite concepts:

A teljes lét: élet-nélküli.
A teljes öröklét: idő-nélküli.
A teljes működés: változás-nélküli.

A teljes hatalom: erő-nélküli.
A teljes tudás: adat-nélküli.
A teljes bölcsesség: gondolat-nélküli.
A teljes szeretet: érzés-nélküli.
A teljes jóság: irány-nélküli.
A teljes boldogság: öröm-nélküli.
A teljes zengés: hang-nélküli.

The absolute existence is: existence without life.
The absolute eternity is: eternity without time.
The absolute action is: action without change.
The absolute power is: power without strength.
The absolute knowledge is: knowledge without information.
The absolute love is: love without feelings.
The absolute kindness is: kindness without direction.
The absolute happiness is: happiness without joy.
The absolute sound is: sound without tunes.

The loss of original oneness is also the theme of the work, *Mahruh veszése* 'The Loss of Mahruh'. According to the introductory part of the poem, Mahruh was once an enormous star, which, because of an explosion, broke into pieces. The Earth arose from one of these pieces. The poet Rou Eroun, or 'Purple Flame', as he called himself, lived in the time immediately before the catastrophe, and wrote down the history of this time. A fictitious poet living in a fictitious time – it is once again the domain of myth, when time and space disappear in the obscurity of an unconscious collective memory, or as worded in the introduction: "In this poem, man and memory are older than Earth". And the poet, in keeping with his profession, preserves this ancient memory for posterity by his work, because poetry can never die. Certainly, that is the reason why this poem of Rou Eroun can be read today.

In the ten pieces of the *Grádicsok éneke* 'The Song of the Stairs' (EI II:395-407) the lost oneness is found within the macrocosmic wholeness of love. Losing oneself in the rapture of the body is the same as the freeing of the soul being immersed in universal harmony:

Szomjúság lenti kútjai fölött
a bizalom csóvája szétterül
és angyalok csengve tükrözik egymást:
Örömöm kétszerezze örömöd.

Above the wells of thirst beneath
the brand of confidence lies prostrate

and the angels tinkling mirror each other:
my joy will redouble your joy.

The poem *Néma zene* 'Silent Music' (EI II:456-459) was written in 1963. Characteristics of the surrealist style can easily be found in this poem. A visual arrangement of the lines is similar to concrete poetry and the most important details, accordingly the poet, are stressed in some typographical way, often with the use of italics, as illustrated below:

zsoltár kezdődik újból

a látat*atlan tisz*ta világért
mely nem az évekk*el süllyedt* habokba
a redőtlen szerel*mi kor*szakért ami folyton elsötétült
így szülte a *tört ént* a világtalan
s a törzs *nem is meri* egymásban feloldani többé
a semmiből éle *sen ki*ált a

mélybe merült

If we follow only the italics, we read as follows: *atlantisz elsűlyedt mikor történt nem ismeri senki* 'atlantis sunk when it happened nobody knows'. This masterly arrangement creates a twofold thematic structure. Not only are the diachronic events of irreversible time represented by the horizontal level, but the steadiness of a reversible time is also represented by the italics on the vertical line.

4.2.3 Weöres' Philosophy of Poetics

"I think that those poems which are usable as the ploughshare is are going to be worth something once (if there are some that are this way at all). Their use is the same as their models, that is, to release the human mind from individualistic peregrinations and ups and downs, opening up his eyes to new, more profound and superior vistas, and calling his attention to universal and everlasting values. Only if he understands this teaching, can the man of the Machine Age remain human: he does not have only a stomach, a groin and a practical ability for gathering, similar to the animals; he must possess the sphere of his subconscious instincts, his true consciousness (which, as suggested by the neglected instincts, decreased to an organ of satisfaction); and his higher consciousness, the intuitive spiritual sphere (which he does not think exists any more). Only in this way can he achieve harmony with others and the powers he has; otherwise he is going to destroy himself and the powers he possesses are going to wipe him out. The intention of modern art is to open up, to aim for a more explicit, more complete humanity. – If my poems can do something along these lines, then it is good that they exist; as far as their greatness and modernity concerned, they can go to the dunghill" (WW:194). This passage, quoted from a letter written in 1957, could also be called a summing up of Weöres' entire philosophy of poetics. It could demonstrate that those critical issues which used to accuse him of being apolitical were not based on real facts. He could at best be accused of being superior to politics in all its forms, in my opinion, because he practiced politics at the highest level: the level of purest humanity.

The journal *Sziget* 'Island', published for the first time in 1935, takes its origin from this level of humanity. Its founders were Károly Kerényi, professor of classical philolology in Pécs and Béla Hamvas, the philosopher. Though Weöres did not subscribe to the journal and he did not even know Hamvas then, the basic ideology of the journal had a very strong influence on him. The *Sziget* 'Island' sprang up during the steadily increasing threat of Fascism in Europe. The title implied that the only means of rescue for the main treasures of human culture was to re-locate them on an island, away from the ravages of a genocidal, racial, Hitlerian politics (Kenyeres 1983:87). Many artists in the journal found the ideals of a primeval oneness and harmony through mythology. In spite of myth's illusory and irrational form and the fact that it could not solve the problems of society, it promised the survival of mankind's culture to those without any other hope. The ideology of the *Sziget* 'Island', was also a place of refuge, and gave a home to numerous writers who had lost all they had. Hamvas, who was banished from Hungarian literary life by the official culture policies for most of his life, and Weöres, who endured this historical period as the deepest nadir, belonged to this group of writers.

The only escape from the chaos of war, and from an inner crisis, as shown by the letter above, is a freeing of the subconscious territories of the instincts and the intuitive territories of the spirit. This is the only way of transforming a disordered chaos into the harmonious order of the cosmos. In Weöres' poetry the idea of the island reveals itself through his myth-paraphrases, which, true to the nature of the myth, bring us closer to the oldest period of humankind, the Golden Age.

The work *A teljesség felé* 'Towards the Absolute' describes four main periods in the history of mankind. The oldest is called the Golden Age, "when the life of the human is quiet and happy, simple, without any secrets, in total harmony with the ethereal powers and nature" (EI I:676). In the following Silver Age this substratum breaks and in the third period, the Bronze Age, the distance between human existence and individual life increases. In the Iron age, which is the fourth period, there is no contact between these two any more, or it "appears as not more than a flash or a dream". Other characteristics of the Iron Age are as follows: "truth is replaced a by hundred different sorts of opinions, science by rummaging among information and popularized mass education. [– – –] The law is replaced by all kinds of orders which have nothing to do with morality, but are based on the management's interests; [– – –] The brutality of Iron Age man is only matched by his incompetence; he projects, arranges, and manages everything, but all these things turn into confusion" (EI I:676-677). Though these periods, according to Weöres, do not belong to historical time, but to an ideal sphere of time, the last period of the Iron Age can obviously be interpreted as the time of the Second World War, when this work was written. The only way out of the disorder of the Iron Age is to call up the memory of the lost Golden Age, which unlike harmony can only be conceived intuitively.

In his work *Scientia Sacra* Béla Hamvas (1995a:20) phrases these same thoughts as follows: "The knowledge concerning bygone days is about to be lost forever. Only the blurred memory of the Golden Age remains; which is homesickness, hoping to balance a more and more increasing brutality of life. [– – –] The most important thing dropped out of the mind, which usually remains; the senses, able to make distinctions between existence and life; and instinct disappeared, which is able to bring existence of life into being". Are there any means of restituting the original unity of existence and life? And if it can possibly happen, by whom can it be made? In the essay, *Poeta metaphisica*, Hamvas (1987:177-178), makes a comparison between religion and poetry. Religion is dualistic, as all its categories are epitomized antinomies, such as: human and God, God and devil, good and bad, body and soul. Poetry does not have this restriction. To the poet everything is one and the same thing: "The world is the same, the thing is the same, the human is the same and everything together is the same thing. When the artist lifts the world from life to existence and his transcendental instinct moves it over into eternity, then this 'over' does not mean 'from one thing into an other'. Here there are never 'two' and never 'over'. [– – –] The transcendental instinct is a giftedness with which the poet is able to show the phenomenon as a phenomenon, as a complete thing, in the world-wide horizon of it, in its total reality...".

Similar to the Sziget-circle ideals from ancient Greek culture, these thoughts of Hamvas are rooted in Greek philosophy. The inspired poet in the *Ion* of Plato is only able to create in an unconscious condition. Moreover, in the dialogues of *Phaedo* and *The Republic*, when speaking of the immortal soul, Plato refers to an eternal knowledge, a reminiscence of something or anamnesy, that is, a kind of knowledge which existed before birth. It is the ideas, which exist apart from time and space, which are the media of this eternal knowledge. True reality does not appear as a changeable world of conceivable physical objects, but instead as constant ideas which cannot be conceived by our senses.

In Plato's ideal state there was no place for poets. The future generation must be protected from the mendacious poets, who can only reflect and imitate ideas, not express them in a direct way. This means that they are always three steps away from truth and can hence never reach it. Plotinos' views on poetic reflection are directly opposite to those of Plato's. According to Plotinos' theses, the oldest principle is the principle of the One. This One is the basis of all existence, from which, most likely from a divinal center, ideas and the most primordial images of reality emanate. The poets can share in this emanation and become capable of directly expressing a reality beyond the senses.

The aesthetics of Romanticism includes related ideas. Contrary to the ideas of Classicism, Romanticism aimed at exploring the subconscious. Johann Gottfried Herder, for example, thought that only the poet can give voice to the fundamental and innermost essence of the soul with metaphors as the only means. Herder was among those very first poets who began to collect pieces of folk-poetry, which he regarded as manifestations of the collective consciousness of man, that is, the common soul of a people (Jonsson 1971:86-90). August Wilhelm Schlegel had a recovery of the symbolical forms of primeval language in mind. He emphasized the primary roles of metaphor, symbols and myth (Jonsson 1971:109-110). It is in Friedrich Schelling's philosophy that the concept of the subconscious presents itself for the first time. According to his view, the creative artist gives absolute ideas a symbolic shape (Jonsson 1971:111-112). These ideas later became crystallized in Freud's psychoanalysis.

The poetry of the Symbolists aimed for a description of the absolute reality which lies beyond all visible things. The sonnet *Correspondances* by Baudelaire is related to the tenets of Emanuel Swedenborg's *Clavis hieroglyphica*, as aspects of objective and subjective reality are tied to general symbols (Jonsson 1971:143). In Henry Bergson's philosophy a non-objective reality cannot be perceived according to the laws of logic, but only by intuition (Jonsson 1971:154). Benedetto Croce, basing his ideas on the concept of intuition, emphasizes the synthesis of form and subject matter, which reveal themselves as metaphors, in his aesthetics (Jonsson 1971:155-156). Looking at the movements of the *avant garde*, Surrealism attached great importance to associations and dreams within poetry. Surrealism, the aim of which was to express a reality above our visible and conceivable reality, made the unconscious its central concept under the influences of Bergson's theory on intuition and Freudian psychoanalysis.

It is obviously this latter that we associate with the concept of the subconscious. In dealing with this poem by Weöres, however, I think, that Jung's theories on the collective unconsciousness and archetypes are more significant. The collective unconscious is reflected in folktales and myth in the same way as it is reflected in dreams. That is why these domains of psychology must not be neglected (Thompson 1972:192-193). "Man darf heutzutage wohl den Satz aussprechen, daß die Archetypen in den Mythen und Märchen, wie in Traum und in psychotischen Phantasieprodukten erscheinen", as Jung put it in the work which he wrote together with Károly Kerényi (Jung 1941:107). We may say that research on myths in modern literature history are in general based on Jung's studies.

The concept of the archetype originated in Plato's doctrine of ideas (Jung 1995:103). This same doctrine discusses the category of anamnesis, or the collective unconscious according to Jung's terminology. In Jung's view the archetype is an original intuition of the human which manifests itself as symbols (Thomson 1972:192). Parallels with the metaphor and intuition theories mentioned above are easy to draw. Jung (1965:81) makes a distinction between the subconscious of the individual and the collective subconscious. The former is unique in each and every individual and appears in the forms of dreams and fantasies. The latter represents primordial, common images of mankind which appear as reminiscences. While the individual unconscious goes back to birth, the collective unconscious connects to prenatal time. That is why the individual unconscious is measurable in time, but the collective unconscious, a timeless factor, exists without any ties to historical time (Jung 1965:95). This essential timeless characteristic appears in myth. "Die mytischen Bilder gehören zur Struktur des Unbewußten und sind unpersönlicher Besitz, von dem die allermeisten Menschen viel eher besessen sind, als daß sie Ihn besäßen" (Jung 1941:223).

Weöres stressed on several occasions the fundamental influence of an unconscious, intuitive way of seeing his work. We must allow for this fact when interpreting his poems. His myth-imitations belong to this category, in particular those where the theme indicated by the title develops along the vertical line of context. This verticality, this "star-like gravitation of thought", as Weöres put it (Bozóky 1993:236), a nearly gnostic view of depth and height, connects very closely to Jung's theories on the collective unconscious and archetypes. As a result, an examination of certain common characteristics is essential.

The archetype of water is the most common symbol of the unconscious, according to Jung (1995:122). In *Atlantis* the image of water connects partly to an ancient island which probably sunk into the sea, as suggested by the title, and partly to the symbol of the well in the third part. As a symbol of the island, it has a place in the profundity of the collective unconscious, in the nostalgia of a lost Golden Age. "The myth of the lost paradise still survives in the images of a Paradisian island or a land of innocence; a privileged land where laws are abolished and Time stands still" (Eliade 1960:33). While Plato, in the *Timaeus*, explains that the myth of Atlantis is nothing more than the utopic

160

desire for a better world (Forsyth 1980:51-52), Jung (1964:49) accentuates the compensatory role of the dreams. Both a fulfillment of utopic desire and a compensation of any kind could function as a means of regaining lost harmony. As opposed to the symbol of the island Atlantis, which reflects the collective unconscious, the symbol of the well refers to the individual. Bata (1979:117) lays stress upon the individual unconscious when he points out the metaphysical aspect in Weöres' poetry. The image of the well, symbolizing the girl, may also suggest the original feminine nature of poetic inspiration, worded as follows in the third part of the *Atlantis*: *belőled isznak / a legdúsabb pillanatok* 'the wealthiest moments / drink from you'.

From a Jungian perspective the word *emlék* 'memory' evidently corresponds to the unconscious, here both the collective and the individual forms of it. The memory relating to the image of the *kemény ágy* 'hard bed' in the first part inevitably relates to dreams, which further reinforces the Jungian interpretation.

Subliminal is Jung's term for the existing, but deliberately neglected, suppressed thoughts in our mind. If unexpectedly overtaken by a sensual effect, these almost-forgotten thoughts may surface (Jung 1964:36). In the first lines of *Atlantis* the sight of the birds and listening to music arouse the memories. The image of the bird, which often symbolizes the immortal soul, can also be seen as the transcendental and is hence a help in removing the cover from the unconscious. Assisted by the bird, a mediatory person is able to give expression to the unconscious. The Sibirian shaman in his bird-like shape is such a person (Henderson 1964:151). This image of the bird in the first part of *Atlantis* foreshadows that of the angel in the last part, where by winged desire the human is then placed in the highest spheres. The term *medium* of Henderson's, describing the intermediary chain of the unconscious, is not so far from what both Lévy-Strauss and Kenyeres call the *mediator* (Lévy-Strauss 1968:221-27; Kenyeres 1983:136). Jung writes in the following manner about the archetype of the child: "Es ist daher ein die Gegensätze vereinigendes Symbol, ein Mediator, ein Heilbringer, d. h. Ganzmacher" (Jung 1941:122-123). This Medium-Mediator in *Atlantis* is the human, standing between the brushwood and the angel; or the child, the fruit of the ecstasy of love depicted in the third part, and the only appropriate character, who, replacing two former characters, is able to mediate between them.

Personality, according to Jung, is comprised partly by the conscious part, which he calls the *ego* or the *persona* and partly by the unconscious component, the often-cited *shadow* of the self. The *persona*, which refers to the mask used in ancient Greek drama, is in fact our visible face which is shown to the world. Behind this face, however, there is the invisible shadow, a secret, repressed part of the personality. The last word of the second strophe in the first part, the *nevezhető* 'nameable' foreshadows the *névtelen* 'nameless', the

161

first word of the next strophe. The *persona* or the *ego* here contrasts its *shadow*. It is perfectly clear who the nameless is: this nameless takes on the image of a girl, who, at the beginning, "rests beside the door". A parallel to this image is the mythological Kore, about which Jung (1941:219-220) writes as follows: "In der praktischen Beobachtung tritt bei der Frau die Korefigur als unbekanntes junges Mädchen auf [...] Eine häufige Nüance ist die Tänzerin, zu deren Ausgestaltung oft Anleihen bei Kenntnissen gemacht werden: dann erscheint nämlich das Mädchen als Korybantin, Mänade oder Nymphe". This memory of the nameless, however, does not belong to pleasant memories, which the image of the hard bed and the girl lying beside the door indicates. This scene may also refer to an animal resting beside the door (it could be a cat), as worded in the next-to-last strophe. Animals, as symbols of the instinctual life of the self, are frequently seen in myths and folktales (Jung 1965:79; Franz 1964:207). The last image of the nameless in this first part is the *árnyék* 'shadow'. The "nameable" appears in this image as well, as a question. Are the nameable and the nameless one and the same?

The nature of the shadow reflected by the self is mostly negative, according to Jung. It represents the dark side of the soul. It appears very often as a thirst for power or as erotic fantasies (Franz 1964:172). The feminine image of the shadow in the male unconscious is called *anima*, compared to *animus*, which is the male image of the shadow in the female unconscious, in Jungian terminology.

Two poems in Weöres' sonnet-cycle *Átváltozások* 'Metamorphoses' are closely connected to these Jungian terms: the first titled *Animus*, and the second titled *Anima*. These frequent motifs of Weöres' are dealt with in a separate chapter in Kenyeres' (1983:285-304) work on Weöres. Kenyeres references Otto Weininger's work, *Geschlecht und Charakter* and also Jung's psychoanalytic theory, which in all probability influenced Weöres in his construction of the motifs. There is, however, a basic difference between Weininger's and Weöres' view of the motifs, as Kenyeres points out: while Weininger contests that there is a female personality, to Weöres the *animus* and the *anima* are equally important, because as they supplement each other, they together endeavor to reach the Absolute.

The *árnyék* 'shadow' which could also take the image of a girl, could then be interpreted as the *anima*, i.e. the female part of the man. What are the main characteristics of Weöres' *anima*? Thinking of the *gyors macska* 'swift cat', the *hajlós testű* 'nimble-bodied' and the *kereplő derekú* 'rattle-waisted', it could symbolize the subconscious slumbering instincts of man, but not the dark female side of the personality, as Jung defines the *shadow*. In Weöres' view the *shadow* is *világos* 'clear' and also *vakító* 'glare'. Many other poems suggest the same view and several critics, such as Kenyeres (1983:291) made the point unmistakably clear, namely: Weöres saw greater possibilities in woman than in man. When Mátyás Domokos once made a remark that in his opinion it is the feminine principle which has the upper hand in Weöres' poetry, Weöres answered as follows: "I think it is rather the principally female: a woman, as a matter of fact, possesses more possibilities than a man: she is mother, wife, meretrix, regina". Or as he put it in piece 145 in the *Rongyszőnyeg* 'Rag-carpet' cycle:

A nő: tetőtől talpig élet.
A férfi: nagyképű kísértet.
A nőé: mind, mely élő és halott,
úgy, amint két kézzel megfoghatod;
a férfié: minderről egy csomó
kétes bölcsesség, nagy könyv, zagyva szó.

Woman is: life from top to toe,
Man is: bumptious ghost.
Woman's: all the living and the dead,
as you can take them in your hands;
man's: a bunch of doubtful wisdom,
large book, jabbering words.

The continuation of the interview given to Domokos is worth noting: "Which is the greatest metamorphosis of mythology? That of Theresias, the blind prophet and oracle – and specifically as the lead character of Oedipus Rex. For seven years he was a woman, a hetaira. The poet, as he is between the two limits of creating and maternity, although imperfectly, is of both genders, too. The myths talk about this secret knowledge...". This androgynous nature of man is found in the poem *Xenia* (EI: II:445) foreshadowing another character of Weöres', *Psyché*:

Nő voltam s uramat kényes testemre fogadtam
mint érzékeny húros hangszer a mesteri játszót
hogy pici éles csillagokat szikrázzon a vérem
csiklandó puha talpamtól a hajam gyökeréig,
hangyasereg bizsergett kagylóim kék-erü mélyén,
comb-köze, nyak, fülcimpa, tenyér, mind mézet adott-vett,
büszke hasamban sok rejtőző angyali bölcső
kéjtől tátogatott, izgulva feszült ki a mellem,
táncot járt a farom, hő nedv a szemen meg az ajkon
lázas lankadozástól, gyöngyöt sírt sima bőröm,
nyitvafeledt számon szökellt ki szívdobogásom:

ó hogy irígylem a gaz ringyót! most férfi vagyok csak.

I was a woman and I welcomed my lord on my slender body
as a sensitive, stringed instrument welcomes the masterly player
so that my blood should sparkle tiny, garish stars
from my ticklish, soft soles to the roots of my hair,
an army of ants prickled in the blue-veined hollows of my shells,
the thights, the neck, the ear-lobes, the palms, all bought and sold honey,
from pleasure gasped many hidden angel-cradles
in my proud belly, my breasts strained in excitement,
my backside danced a dance, there was hot moisture on the eyes and lips,
from the fevered slackening, my smooth skin wept pearls,
my heart leapt into my open-leaved lips:
o!, how much I envy the dirty strumpet! I am only a man now.

Though less free-spoken and symbolic, the third part of *Atlantis* also expresses erotic fantasies, those instincts which represent the dark, negative part of the
anima according to Jung. In Weöres' poem, however, a star is shining, and this
fact turns darkness to light, the negative to positive. Moreover, the moonlight
on the landscape can also refer to the unconscious as it denotes that the control
of the conscious loosened and is now replaced by the unconscious (Franz
1964:215).

Obviously, each contact with the *anima* creates something positive in
the *Atlantis*. The suppressed memory, also expressed by the trope of *kemény
ágy* 'hard bed' in the first part is followed by *káprázat és a szerencse* 'the
mirage and the fortune', suggesting not only the pleasures of the body, but also
the moments of inspiration.

In Jung's view, personality is like a circle, and the center is the unconscious, where dreams are born. Two other parts of the personality are the
conscious *ego* and the *shadow* of it. The positive side of the *anima* is capable
of creating a connection between the *ego* and the *self*, which is the *personality* in its entirety (Franz 1964:188). The *anima* can enlighten the unconscious
deeply concealed in the personality, by awakening the consciousness of the
whole personality. It can also bring out hidden abilities (Franz 1964:162). The
clear, and later glaring, shadow in *Atlantis* throws its light into the halls and
the dim light of the star lights up the garden. The king in the depths of the hall
must then be *personality* personified, the most central unconscious part of it.
The bird, the symbol of the unconscious, then belongs to the king (Franz
1964:196), like the music which in the song of the third part realizes its
purpose.

After the king meets the self in the second part, a wind begins to blow,
and the outside world invades the halls, followed by sorrow and the memory

of the light. The first meeting of the *ego* and the innermost center of it is not without conflict. Things turn chaotic (Franz 1964:166). This chaos, this emptiness, however, is most essential for the *ego*, in order to recognize itself in the shadow. This circumstance, in its turn, causes the *persona* or the mask to undergo a change and to take the form of personality in its entirety: *minden belém temette arcát* 'everything buried its face in me'. That process, during which the consciousness of the self suddenly realizes the unconscious part of itself, when the individual recognizes personality, is called individuation by Jung. This is the emptiness of chaos, and the anguish caused by the lack of harmony: *szemem száraz volt, belül sírtam* 'my eyes were dry, I wept inside', which is followed by the happiness at the union of the conscious and the unconscious, creating cosmic perfection. "Das Ziel des Individuationsprozesses ist die Synthese des Selbst. Von einem andern Standpunkt aus betrahtet, empfiehlt sich statt des Terminus 'Synthese' vielleicht eher Entelechie. Es gibt einen empirischen Grund, warum letzterer Ausdruch eventuell passender wäre: Die Symbole der Ganzheit treten nämlich häufig am Anfang des Individuationprozesses ein..." (Jung 1942:123). We may follow the same process of individuation in the love scene of the third part of *Atlantis*, where words are added to music so it changes to song, perhaps denoting the birth of the poet.

The *animus-anima* archetype not only connects the conscious in the personality and the innermost unconscious of it, but also connects personality and the collective unconscious. When the human, as the result of the love scene in the third part, appears in the fourth part, he has a relationship with the *angyal* 'angel', the symbol of the soul, in addition to the *bozót* 'brushwood', that is, the instincts. In this sense then he indicates a possible, potential wholeness. The idea of the *kathabasis*, which, according to Hamvas, is a descent to a world of potentials (Bálint 1991:2:3:131), not only includes a sensual completeness emerging from a biological act, but also a higher gain: the androgynous union of the feminine and the masculine.

Bata (1995:15), in analyzing the poem *Pastorale* by Weöres, writes that in an act of love there is an archetypical feeling. The female and the male want to be back in an original state of oneness. Further, Eliade (1960:176) defines androgyny in the following way: "Androgyny is an archaic and universal formula for expression of wholeness, the co-existence of the contraries, or coincidentia oppositorum. More than a state of sexual completeness and autarchy, androgyny symbolizes the perfection of a primordial, nonconditioned state". In his work *Scientia Sacra* Hamvas (1996:243-314) deals with androgyny in a separate chapter. His most important theses are as follows: the androgynous is identical to the timeless and is nothing else but the moment which includes eternity. The ultimate aim of uniting in love is not to reproduce oneself but to re-establish the lost state of completeness.

The wholeness represented by the androgynous, as a return to the original condition, is also a descent into the collective unconscious. The newborn human does not represent completeness yet, only the possibility of it, as he can only substitute the positions of the brushwood and the angel. There are three unities: the brushwood, the human and the angel. According to metaphysical number theories, the number three represents the concept of unity, for in it the characteristics of the two preceding units are combined in order to create a new completeness. The number four, however, further increases the wholeness of the three into absolute completeness (Hamvas 1995:225). In Jung's (1953:399; 1965:133) view, personality or the *self* is symbolized by the number four. It is the sum of the numbers three and one, giving the completeness of four. When praying, the brushwood, the human and the angel turn toward the fourth, toward the Absolute. There we may experience the *imago Dei*, which according to Jung is the archetype of the personality. In the last three lines, where everything turns towards each other, the image of God, the *imago Dei in homine* (Jung 1953:431) is mirrored in all three parts of the personality. In terms of the human, however, another motif is also included: the motif of searching and wandering among the pieces of oneness. This motif of peregrination, also mentioned by Kenyeres (1983:140) parallels the motif of the breaking up of primeval harmony and the search for the way out from the resulting chaos, in order to re-create the lost harmony.

The question: "... in which way can the human, who only for a moment, as a blink of light is able to experience harmony, achieve the completeness, the Absolute?", Weöres answered as follows: "In no way, I think. For the experience, the possession of the absolute completeness, such a basic simplicity and naivité is needed, and we no longer have any aptitude or possibility of this. The only possible approach towards the absolute is by those who stand outside the total ancient divine unity. Every human is outside this" (Hornyik 1993:82). As a poet, however, Weöres certainly made his way towards absolute completeness. It is only the poet – though not all poets – who has the gift to put the inconceivable and the insoluble into words. This special capacity goes back to the poet's view of the fundamental identity of life and existence and of the view that it is the macrocosmos of the whole universe which is reflected in the microcosmos of human personality. To the poet everything belongs to the same One. The center of the personality is also the place of the ancient archetypical structures. Within the unconscious of the individual there is the collective unconscious, which can be revealed only with the help of intuition and inspiration. Moments of intuition and inspiration shed light on the secret structures of the universe. The original truth becomes unveiled.

The idea of the *aletheia* in Greek philosophy stands for the uncovering of the truth which lies hidden beneath the surface. Talking about this idea, Hamvas (1987:177-189) argues that, owing to the poet's basic openness to the world, the world manifests itself in its true, unconcealed forms to him. The ancient oneness is reflected in the works of the poet.

We have found that the most frequent word in *Atlantis* is the word *fény* 'light', and have termed it the focal point of the poem. It is present throughout the poem. It is a reflection of the universal oneness, and helps to reveal the real character of hidden things. This idea of illumination is seen in Neo-Platonic philosophy and in Heidegger's hermeneutic ontology. According to Heidegger it is the enlightenment (Lichtung), which changes the state of concealment into revelation (Unverborgenhet) or *aletheia* (Bókay 1997:302-306). At the same moment that the poet discovers the revealed within the seemingly concealed, he changes chaos into harmony. Heidegger is of the opinion that the hidden truth of all things has its greatest expression in poetry. Poetry illumines the basic structures of human existence. It involves the recognition of the self in the world.

The idea of 'Evidence' is frequently seen in Weöres' interviews. In Bata's formulation the evidence involves "moments concerning basic truth", that is, "everyone's common experiences", expressed by the structures of music and myth. In evident structures "an innermost infinity is revealed, identical to the outer infinity, for everything is one and the same thing" (Bata 1979:95-96). All the philosophical concepts mentioned above, in my opinion, are represented in Weöres' views on evident structures. He declares as follows: "... the man representing the evident works in this way: he does not propose things very often, he is happy at the fact that things are as they are, he does not strive for any advancement or change, but only lives in his simple and cosmic world" (Hornyik 1993:84).

5 The Search for the Absolute

I

(1) Madárka sír, madárka örül,
míg piros gerendái közül
néz a hatalmas –

(2) Küldd néki töretlen álmodat,
míg magad vagy a vadász, meg a vad,
nem szűnhet kerge futásod.
Győznöd se lehet, veszned se szabad:
a hályogos sürüség alatt
vermed hasztalan ásod.

(3) Kinyílik a táj,
lehunyódik a táj –
az üresség öntözi szélét!
A rét, a liget,
itt mind a tied,
de nem lelhetsz soha békét.

(4) Az élettelen avar is röpül.
Ne hidd, hogy a rögben alhass.
Madárka sír, madárka örül,
néz a hatalmas.

(5) A mult se pihen:
új percek méreg-csöppjeiben
elomolva őrzi részét.
A holt vadlúd, bár tolla se lebben,
röpül a zúgó szárnyu seregben
s röptében üli fészkét.

(6) A jövő nem vár, előre arat:
a most ömlő sugarak
a holnapi gyermek
rózsás bőréről csiripelnek.

(7) Ne kérdd a veremtől jussodat.
Te vagy a vadász és te vagy a vad
s távol, a hatalmas: az is te magad.

Ő odafönn
merev csillámu közöny,
és sorsba burkolt lénye idelenn
rengés, mely sohasem pihen,
s a két arc: az Igaz és a Van
összefordul mámorosan,
mint a Nap meg a tenger
nézi egymást ragyogó szerelemmel.

(8)   Küldd néki töretlen álmodat!
mert szived éber-álma,
mint légen a pára,
átlódul a pályán
s fönn sajog a menny hajnal-koronáján.

(9)   Madárka sír, madárka örül,
míg piros gerendái közül
néz a hatalmas –

(10)   Kereplőként űzöd körbe magad,
rab vagy, de keserved álma szabad
s igazad az álom, a röpke!
A szikla, ha rávésed jajodat,
többé nem szikla: élő te-magad
s föllibben a fellegekbe!

(11)   Kinyílik a táj,
lehunyódik a táj –
az üresség öntözi szélét!
Sugarak izzó füzére alatt
meglelheted százszor sirodat,
mégsem lelhetsz soha békét.

(12)   Az élettelen avar is röpül.
Ne hidd, hogy a rögben alhass.
Szél körme kapar a sír körül,
és vallat a fény, a hatalmas.

(13)   Te vagy a vadász és te vagy a vad
s a pálya is, minden te magad
– madárka sír, madárka örül –
piros gerendák közül kidagadva

tág szemmel nézel magadra.

II

(1) Rikolt a páva veled,
tipeg az éjbe veled,
elveszti nyúlt vonalát
a futórózsa veled,

(2) odafönn villámló kútnál
remegő gyöngy közt aludtál –
kikkel egy-éjbe jutottál,
mindannyival oda futnál.

(3) Rikolt a páva veled –
rád-kúszó rózsa remeg,
a mező nyers illata
nedves csókjára pereg.

(4) Sír a liliom,
a sáska is –
hogyha lehetne,
szánna is.
Csak a könny csorog
a szirmon, a fán –
ki merne sírni
igazán?

(5) Ki merne súgni neked
arról, hogy mi lett veled?
melyik ég rejti helyed?
őrzi-e gyöngyeidet?

(6) Ki egét elhagyta, lássa:
habos örvény a lakása,
fedelének éj az ácsa,
sötétség a kalapácsa.

(7) Tipeg a páva veled,
remeg a rózsa veled,
fáradtan rád-hajlanak,
megosztják alvó-helyed.

(8)   Itt minden örömbe
      bogárka vész,
      s a fájdalom mélye
      tiszta méz.
      Hét szín mozog itt
      és hang-özön:
      egyetlen, arany csend
      volt odafönn.

(9)   Szinek közt gyúl a szemed,
      hangok közt zsong a füled –
      kivánsz-e bucsuzni, mondd,
      vagy itt lenn jobb a helyed?

(10) Odafönn villámló kútnál
      remegő gyöngy közt aludtál –
      remegő gyöngy közt a kútnál
      tán már aludni se tudnál.

(11) Hegyekkel játszik az út,
      a tücskök dobja pereg,
      rád-kúszó rózsa remeg,
      Rikolt a páva veled –

III

(1)   Tűzhabos, bársonyos tereken át
      keresem szárnyának pille-porát.
      Ormokon,
      kő-fokon
      kutatom fátyla nyomát.

(2)   Lehelletét
      szél verte szét,
      lángja kormát vas-pohárban
      őrzi a sötét.

(3)   Jégszirmos hegyeken át,
      csatakos völgyeken át
      kérlelem, keresem:
      ápolná kegyesen

sápadt kis mécsesem fénysugarát.

(4)   Ide se lát!
Ide se lát!
Alszik és álmában épít
ablaktalan tükör-palotát!

(5)   Hasztalan üldözöm zajban, csendben,
nem érem el soha: itt van bennem,
vad futásommal ő űzi magát,
mécsesem fénye az ő kicsi foglya,
vézna, ijedt fény, mégis beragyogja
a végtelen tükör-palotát.

(6)   Rögökön, fellegen, kék vidéken
siető léptemmel el nem érem:
szivemben szövöget
napokat, éjeket,
a kinti sokszinü szőnyeget
benn szövi mind,
bennem szőtt szőnyegen
odakinn keresem,
míg ezer mintája szüntelen
körbe kering.

(7)   De néha meglátom
– igaz-e vagy álom –
mikor a kerek táj télbe hajolt
s a jeges réteken
minden csak sirverem
s lenn fekszem, földdé vált fekete holt.
Homályos tereken,
idegen egeken
sebzetten bukdos a légen által
és rekedt, színtelen víjjogással
lezuhan a jég alá!
lezuhan a jég alá!
A mélység föllazul,
villogó gyöngy-habot ont
és megint elsimul,
és minden fekete, holt.

(8)   Lehelletét
szél verte szét,
lángja kormát vas pohárban
őrzi a sötét.

(9)   Jég alatt, nem múló percemen át
őrizem simuló pille-porát.
S a fényben szűntelen
szaladó éveken
tű-fokon
csókolom
ujja nyomát.

I

(1)   Little bird cries, little bird rejoices,
while from his red planks
the mighty one looks down –

(2)   Send him your unbroken dreams,
when you yourself are the hunter and the wild,
your giddy run cannot stop.
You cannot win, nor can you get lost:
under the blurred thickness
you dig your pitfall in vain.

(3)   The land opens up,
the land closes –
vastness waters its verges!
The meadow, the grove,
everything is yours,
but you never can find your peace.

(4)   The lifeless leaves do also fly.
Do not hope, you can sleep in the soil.
Little bird cries, little bird rejoices,
the mighty one looks down.

(5)   Not even the past rests:
in new minutes poisoned drops
crumbling it keeps its share.
The dead wild-goose, yet with no flap of feathers,

flies in the flock of buzzing wings
and builds its nest while flying.

(6)   The future does not wait: it harvests in advance:
the beams that stream today
chirp about the rosy cheek
of tomorrow's child.

(7)   Do not ask for your rights from the pitfall.
You are the hunter and you are the wild,
and you are the mighty in the distance, too.
He above there
is coldness stiffly glancing,
and his being wrapped up in destiny down here
is a quake that never rests,
and the two sides: Truth and Being
turn to each other in rapture
like the Sun and the Sea
looking with glorious love at each other.

(8)   Send him your unbroken dreams!
for the light sleep of your heart,
like haze in the air,
swings over the line
and aches above the crown of the rising sun.

(9)   Little bird cries, little bird rejoices,
while from his red planks
the mighty one looks down.

(10)   Like a rattle, you hunt yourself around,
you are a slave, but the dream of your grief is free
and your truth is the dream, the fugitive!
If you cut your pain on the rock,
it is not a rock any more: it turns into yourself
and flies off to the skies!

(11)   The land opens up,
the land closes –
vastness waters its verges!
Under the glowing chaplet of the beams
you may find your grave a hundred times

yet cannot find your peace.

(12)   The lifeless leaves do also fly.
Do not hope, you can sleep in the soil.
The claws of the wind scratch around the grave,
and you are questioned by the light, the mighty.

(13)   You are the hunter and you are the wild
and the line, too, you are everything
– little bird cries, little bird rejoices –
bulging from red planks
wide-eyed you watch yourself.

II

(1)   The peacock screams with you,
it trips to the night with you,
the rambling rose loses
its lengthened line with you,

(2)   above there at the shining well
amongst trembling pearls you slept –
with whom you spent the same night
there you would now run back to.

(3)   The peacock screams with you –
the rose trembles climbing on you,
the rough smell of the meadow
drops on its watery kiss.

(4)   The lily is in tears,
and the locust, too –
if it were possible
it would feel pity for you.
Only the tears run
on the petals, on the trees –
who would dare to cry indeed?

(5)   Who would whisper to you
about what happened to you?
which heaven hides your place?
does it care for your pearls?

(6)   He, who his heaven abandoned, may see:
his home is a lathering whirlpool,
the night is the carpenter of his roof,
the darkness is his hammer.

(7)   The peacock trips with you,
the rose trembles with you,
tired they bend on you
and share your sleeping-place.

(8)   Here, little beetle
falls into every joy,
and the deep of sorrow is
pure honey.
Seven colors move here
and a stream of sounds:
a single, golden silence
it was above there.

(9)   Among many colors shine your eyes,
among many sounds hum your ears –
do you want to leave now, say,
or do you have a better place down here?

(10)   Above there at the shining well
amongst trembling pearls you slept –
amongst trembling pearls at the well
maybe you could not sleep any more.

(11)   The road plays with the hills,
the drum of the cricket rolls,
the rose trembles climbing on you,
the peacock screams with you.

III

(1)   Through fire-foamy, velvety places
I look for the butterfly-dust of his wings.
On the peaks,
on the capes
for the shadow of his veil I search.

(2)   His breath in the air
       is dispersed by the wind,
       the black of his light is kept
       in an iron-cup by the darkness.

(3)   Across ice-corollaed mountains,
       across muddy valleys
       I beg him, I seek him:
       kindly take care of
       the gleam of my little misty night-light.

(4)   Not even here he sees!
       Not even here he sees!
       He sleeps and in his dream builds
       a mirror-palace without any windows!

(5)   Vainly I chase him in noise, in silence,
       I can never catch him: he is within me,
       it is himself he chases in my wild scamper,
       his little prisoner is the gleam of my night-light,
       a puny, frightened light, which still shines into
       the endless mirror-palace.

(6)   Through the soil, through the clouds, through the blue country
       I don't catch him with my hasty steps:
       in my heart he weaves
       the days and the nights,
       the outward many-coloured carpet
       he weaves inside,
       on the carpet weaved within me
       I look for him outside,
       while his thousand figures
       ceaselessly wheel around.

(7)   But sometimes I glimpse him
       – is it true or is it a dream –
       when the whole country came round to winter
       and the icy meadows are merely graves
       and underneath I lie like a black corpse turned to earth.
       Through shadowy places,
       on foreign spaces
       wounded he tumbles in the air

and with a throaty, toneless screaming
he falls under the ice!
he falls under the ice!
The depth slackens,
gleaming pearl-foam it sheds
and again it gets smooth
and everything is black and dead.

(8)   His breath in the air
is dispersed by the wind,
the black of his light is kept
in an iron-cup by the darkness.

(9)   Through never-ending minutes beneath the ice
closely I keep his butterfly-dust.
And through ceaselessly running years in the light
on the needle-point
I kiss
his finger-mark.

(*Harmadik szimfónia.* 'Third Symphony'. In: EI I:348-354)

5.1 The Text

5.1.1 The Structure and Shape of the Writing

The poem *Harmadik szimfónia* 'Third Symphony' in the *Medusa*-volume can be found under the title *Háromrészes ének* 'Song in Three Parts'. Apparently, this earlier title is much more explicit in conveying the most specific characteristics of the composition, i.e. that the poem consists of three parts. The thirteen verses of the first part, the eleven verses of the second part and the nine verses of the third part show specific structural parallels: each consecutive part is made up of two strophes less than the previous part.

There is very little regularity in the number of lines in the various strophes. Strophes consisting of three lines, appearing only twice in the first part, are the shortest. The longest is the strophe consisting of sixteen lines in the third part. The other strophes are composed of four, five, six, seven, eight, ten and eleven lines, respectively, but there is no strophe which consists of nine lines. The majority of the strophes, i.e. fifteen strophes from the entire poem, are, however, made up of four lines. There is only one strophe containing seven lines, and one strophe each consisting of ten, eleven and sixteen lines, respectively.

In contrast to the irregular pattern of the number of the lines in the strophes of the first and third part, the arrangement of the lines in the central second part is perfectly symmetrical. The three first and last strophes are both built up of four lines each, similar to the composition of the middle three strophes. The two eight-line strophes are also symmetrically arranged on both sides of this central unit of three four-line strophes. The symmetrical pattern of this second part then can be illustrated in the following way: 4, 4, 4, 8, 4, 4, 4, 8, 4, 4, 4.

Regarding interpunctuation, we cannot find any irregularities. Punctuation-marks are present when needed, both at the end of the lines and in the middle of the lines. Enjambements are frequent throughout the poem, but are somewhat more common in the longer strophes. Moreover, each strophe is definitively closed by a punctuation-mark.

The structure of the shape of writing in the poem *Harmadik szimfónia* 'Third Symphony' is characterized by proportionality and symmetry. In accordance with this principle, the formal axis of the second part, i.e. the three middle strophes consisting of four lines each, also represents the center of that symmetry and proportionality formed by the two irregularly-patterned first and third parts and the regular middle part.

5.1.2 The Represented Elements of Reality

As they are often repeated, certain parts of the poem need to be considered for the dominant motifs. Such is the unvaried repetition of the first and the ninth strophe in the first part: *Madárka sír, madárka örül, / míg piros gerendái közül / néz a hatalmas* – 'Little bird cries, little bird rejoices, / while from his red planks / the mighty one looks down'. The first and the third lines from this passage are repeated in the fourth strophe, but only the first line in the last strophe of this first part. The line *Madárka sír, madárka örül* 'Little bird cries, little bird rejoices' is then repeated four times. The three lines *Kinyílik a táj, / lehunyódik a táj – / az üresség öntözi szélét!* 'The land opens up, / the land closes – / vastness waters its verges!' are repeated exactly in the third and in the eleventh strophes. This same type of occurence appears in the two lines of the fourth and the twelve strophes: *Az élettelen avar is röpül. / Ne hidd, hogy a rögben alhass.* 'The lifeless leaves do also fly. / Do not hope, you can sleep in the soil'. The line *Te vagy a vadász és te vagy a vad* 'You are the hunter and you are the wild' occurs in this form in the seventh and the thirteenth strophes and in a somewhat varied form in the second strophe. Returning to the eleventh strophe, the last line of the third strophe is somewhat varied: *de nem lelhetsz soha békét* 'but you never can find your peace' – *mégsem lelhetsz soha békét* 'yet you cannot find your peace'. The first line *Madárka sír, madárka örül* 'Little bird cries, little bird rejoices', however, partly because it gives the lead and partly because it is the line most often repeated, can be regarded as the leading motif in this first part of the poem.

The line *Rikolt a páva veled* 'The peacock screams with you' is repeated three times in the second part of the poem. This same form occurs in the first line of the first and third strophes and in the last line of the last strophe. This motif of the peacock, connected to another verb – the verb *tipeg* 'trips' in the second line of the first strophe, connected in its turn to the first line – is revived in the first line of the seventh strophe, too. Other repetitions are contained in the first two lines of the second and the tenth strophes: *odafönn villámló kútnál / remegő gyöngy közt aludtál* – 'above there at the shining well / amongst trembling pearls you slept'. The form in which the motif of the rose appears in the third and the eleventh strophes is consistent: *rád-kúszó rózsa remeg* 'the rose trembles climbing on you'. The leading motif of this second part is obviously the line *Rikolt a páva veled* 'The peacock screams with you'. This is demonstrated by the fact that this is the most often repeated line and that the symmetrical arrangement of the lines, as the first and the last line of this second part, reflect the same sense of regularity as we have seen in the chapter on the structure of the shape of writing. The symmetrical arrangement of the lines *odafönn villámló kútnál / remegő gyöngy közt aludtál* 'above there at the shining well / amongst trembling pearls you slept', as the first lines of the second and tenth strophes, further reinforces this principle of proportionality.

A tendency of simultaneous decrease and increase of the repetitive structures can be observed in the third part. A tendency of decreasing structure is indicated by the only repetition in this last part; a tendency of increasing structure is indicated by the number of lines which are repeated. The second and the eighth strophes are composed of four identical lines: *Lehelletét / szél verte szét, / lángja kormát vas-pohárban / őrzi a sötét* 'His breath in the air / is dispersed by the wind, / the black of his light is kept / in an iron-cup by the darkness'. Similar to the two symmetrically arranged lines in the second and tenth strophes of the former part, these two identical strophes of the last part can also be found in the second and the next-to-last strophes. All these circumstances plainly demonstrate that these four lines function as the leading motif of the last part.

The represented elements of reality in the three parts are then grouped around three leading motifs. The leading motifs of the first and second parts, both composed of a single line, are followed by the four-line leading motif of the third part. Although there are four main motifs repeated in the first part, the number of these motifs decreases to three in the second part and to one in the third part. This single main motif of the third part is, however, seen in four lines. This amount corresponds to the number of the main motifs in the first part and also to the number of recurrences of the leading motif. The focal point of the symmetry, based upon the varied occurrence of four units, is formed by the second part, where the main motifs correspond to the three parts of the poem and also to the title.

This regular repetition of motifs, like the musical term of the title, suggests a composition principally based on music. In 1933, in a letter to Mihály Babits, Weöres wrote: "I attempt to bring musical forms into poetry [– – –] I have mastered the theory of the symphony, too: in the first part I raise a set of themes, images and rhythms, then I vary them through two or three parts, by plunging the stuff of the first part into several dispositions each time. It will be very difficult" (Weöres 1990:64-65). This difficult task, however, is also a challenge which greatly raises Weöres' experimental spirit, resulting in the volume *Tizenegy szimfónia* 'Eleven Symphonies' in 1973. The form of the symphony is based on the form of the sonata. There are three themes: exposition, performance and repetition. The leading melodies and the minor motifs are brought out in the exposition; the performance is the most vivacious but also the most harmonious theme; and the repetition is composed in a manner very similar to the exposition.

Apparently, this arrangement of symphonic themes is similar to the structure of the poem *Harmadik szimfónia* 'Third Symphony'. The four main motifs of the first theme, followed by the harmoniously structured second theme, and the four-line epilogue echoing the four motifs of the first part are characteristics of this poem which arise from musical structuring.

This musical inspiration defines the arrangement of the elements of represented reality. But what occurrences are unravelled by these recurrent motifs? Obviously, the leading motifs are of prime necessity in presenting a thematic analysis, but the minor motifs are also most essential in shedding light upon the hidden contexts. The motifs mostly come from the reality sphere of the outside world. The scene of the land in the first part is followed by the well in the second part and the endless places of the third part. But all these scenes occur on two different levels. They are both above and below at the same time. The land, which "verges the vastness waters", dissolves in an endlessness, while the "rock flies to the clouds", the "well is above" and the whereabouts of the "shadowy places" remains indeterminate. The unity of the two dimensions of above and below is revealed by the movement in which the "lifeless leaves and the dead wild-goose fly", the "dreams swing over the line", the "rock flies to the clouds", the "peacock trips" and "seven colors move". In the third part, where the former second person singular is transformed to first person singular, this motif of movement is also changed into a different motif, that of the search. It is the search of something undefinable, in which a "thousand figures ceaselessly wheel around" and which at the end "falls under the ice". Something dies, but there are not any clues as to what.

Or does the first part clearly state the true reason for the search: *de nem lelhetsz soha békét* 'but you never can find your peace'? Or do the lines of the second part *melyik ég rejti helyed? / őrzi-e gyöngyeidet?* 'which heaven hides your place? does it care for your pearls?', possibly contain the main thought? Or perhaps the butterfly-dust of a vanished bird is the object of the search. A further possibility is that of the vanished girl's in the following lines: *kutatom fátyla nyomát* 'for the shadow of his veil I search' – *csókolom / ujja nyomát* 'I kiss / his finger mark'. – In this last case, naturally, we must not take gender into account, for, as there are no different forms in Hungarian for the feminine and the masculine in third person singular personal pronouns. One thing, however, is certain: something is lost, and it is up to the reader to solve the puzzle.

Notwithstanding, this is not an easy task for the reader, which means that the ambiguity will remain. The only aspect which is comprehensible is the incomprehensible. This is seen not only in the constant movement between the dimensions of below and above but, as worded in the first and the third part, within time's motion as well: *A múlt se pihen* 'Not even the past rests' – *S a fényben szüntelen / szaladó éveken / tű-fokon / csókolom / ujja nyomát.* 'And through ceasessly running years in the light / on the needle-point / I kiss / his finger-mark'. Movement, in its real sense, is difficult to grasp, especially combined with the moment of the search, and even more so, when the object of the search is unknown. Weöres made a statement concerning this state of inexplicability: "The poem, 'Song in Three Parts', on the other hand, does not have any content which can be narrated, as everything is in flight and in constant change, which makes direct understanding impossible" (Liptay 1993:419).

If the elements of represented reality offer so few clues as to under-standing, can the elements depicting the inner world of the individual perhaps more clearly elucidate what is most essential? Which elements give us insight into the inner world of the individual? Without doubt, the motif of the dream spans the three parts of the poem: *Küldd néki töretlen álmodat!* 'Send him your unbroken dreams!' – *rab vagy, de keserved álma szabad* 'you are a slave, but the dream of your grief is free', as we can read in the first part; *remegő gyöngy közt aludtál* 'amongst trembling pearls you slept' – *megosztják alvó helyed* 'and share your sleeping place' – *tán már aludni se tudnál* 'maybe you could not sleep any more', as stated in the second part; and *Alszik és álmában épít / ablaktalan tükör-palotát!* 'He sleeps and in his dream builds / a mirror-palace without any windows!'; – *igaz-e vagy álom* – '– is it true or is it a dream –', within the third part. In the motif of the dream the inconceivable might be explained. We might assume that the inconceivable originates from the dream, in which events in a seemingly illogical order follow each other.

The question of whose dream is depicted is still unanswered. As discussed above, the second person singular in the first and second part is followed by the third person singular in the third part. Judging from the deep emotional content which reveals itself in the third part, we might assume that all three parts in fact deal with the first person singular. Consequently, the *Harmadik szimfónia* 'Third Symphony' belongs to the category of poems where the poet apostrophizes himself. Béla Németh G. (1970:630) wrote that the focus in this type of poem is the second person imperative. The following sentences demonstrate this: *Küldd néki töretlen álmodat* 'Send him your unbroken dreams' – *Ne hidd, hogy a rögben alhass* 'Do not hope, you can sleep in the soil' – *Ne kérdd a veremtől jussodat* 'Do not ask for your rights from the pitfall', in the first part; *Ki egét elhagyta, lássa: / habos örvény a lakása, / fedelének éj az ácsa, / sötétség a kalapácsa.* 'He, who, his heaven abandoned, may see: / his home is a lathering whirlpool, / the night is the carpenter of his roof, / the darkness is his hammer'. When, however, the second person singular changes to the first person singular in the third part, we cannot see any further self-apostrophizing sentences. There is no need for them either, because by this time the real identity of the second person singular is ultimately revealed.

Most essentially, however, the main motif of the dream, which in the first two parts was related to the addressed second person singular, suddenly, in the third part of the poem, becomes transferred to the third part singular: *Alszik és álmában épít / ablaktalan tükör-palotát!* 'He sleeps and in his dream builds / a mirror-palace without any windows!'. The mighty in the first part still looked down from his red planks, i.e., he who was awake then sleeps in this last part of the poem. The lines *Küldd néki töretlen álmodat!* 'Send him your unbroken dreams!', in the first part are echoed by the lines *Alszik és álmában épít / ablaktalan tükör-palotát!* 'He sleeps and in his dream builds / a mirror-palace without any windows!' in the third part. These lines, in my opinion, depict the intertwining of the grammatical persons in the dream. It is their only common domain. This meeting within dreams is also expressed by the lines in the third part: *De néha meglátom / – igaz-e vagy álom –* 'But sometimes I glimpse him / – is it true or is it a dream –'.

First we saw how the second person singular changed to first person singular in the third part. In addition to this change of the grammatical personas, there is another change, when the third person singular merges into the first person singular, as shown by the lines in the third part, most particularly in this metamorphosis: *Hasztalan üldözöm zajban, csendben, / nem érem el soha: itt van bennem* 'Vainly I chase him in noise, in silence, / I can never catch him: he is within me'. Furthermore, in the first part we could already see how the first person singular becomes identical to the third person singular: *Te vagy a vadász és te vagy a vad / s távol, a hatalmas: az is te magad* 'You are the hunter and you are the wild / and you are the mighty in the distance, too'.

In addition to the motif of the dream, we must also take into consideration the motif of death, which appears in the third part: *s a jeges réteken minden csak sírverem / s lenn fekszem, földdé vált fekete holt* 'and the icy meadows are merely graves / and underneath I lie like a black corpse turned to earth'. The death expressed by these words is, when carried over to dream, not a real one, as worded in the same strophe: *– igaz-e vagy álom –* ' – is it true or is it a dream –'. Seen in the leading motif of this third part, this image of death then becomes much more definitive: *Lehelletét / szél verte szét, / lágja kormát vas pohárban / őrzi a sötét* 'His breath in the air / is dispersed by the wind, / the black of his light is kept / in an iron-cup by the darkness'. The words 'iron-cup' indicate the sepulchral urn, as Bata (1979:75) also pointed out. Other allusions to death are seen in these recurring words: *lezuhan a jég alá!* 'he falls under the ice!'. When everything grows black and dead in the depths afterwards, the image of the black corpse turning to earth, depicted in this same strophe, emerges, creating the wane of the first person singular. The person, searched for between the lines, falls under the ice, and the main character keeps the memories left after him under the ice, as worded in the last strophe: *Jég alatt, nem múló percemen át / őrizem símuló pille-porát* 'Through never-ending minutes beneath the ice / closely I keep his butterfly-dust'.

After revealing these images of the inner world, are we closer to the most essential content of the poem? Possibly. But the basic dilemma remains: to what extent can a rendering of a dream, the common factor that unites the different grammatical personas, correspond to factual events? I think it is valid to the same extent that an interpretation of the outside world is trustworthy. That is, in dreams the images of the outside world are reflected, which means that these images of the inside and the outside world are to the same degree real or unreal. As pointed out earlier, the land, the well and the places, the three main scenes of the three parts, are all situated on two levels of the upper and lower spheres at the same time. This sense of a two-tiered reality also includes another pair of opposite values: the land, the well and the places do not exclusively refer to the elements of the outside world, as they are also scenes representing the inside world of the individual.

The contrasts between above and below, outside and inside reality, and between the oneness of the first and second person singular opposed to the otherness of the third person singular are all related to the global structure. Apart from these dissimilarities between different poles, however, there are tropes or pairs of tropes expressing opposite concepts simultaneously. The little bird cries and rejoices too, you are both the hunter and the wild, you are free, but also a slave, as worded in the first part. Joy and sorrow, sounds and silence, farewell and sojourn are opposed in the second part. There are also many contrasts in the third part, such as the following: mountains – valleys, soil – clouds, days – nights. Taking these tropes into account, I think that in the *Harmadik szimfónia* 'Third Symphony' it is the contrasts that organize the structure of the text. This is, however, as Tamás (1978:82) also pointed out, a kind of contrast where the contrasting parts are, as a matter of fact, not opposed to each other. Instead, like opposite poles they attract each other in order to create an ultimate unity. The bipolarity of the contrast based on opposition is thus replaced by a dynamic based on the attractive force between the different parts. As a result of this dynamic character of contrast the opposite concepts become homogeneous.

This idea of the dynamic character of contrast creates a starting point for a discussion of the focus of the poem. Still, the initial question will be raised as to whether it is really possible to reveal specific focus in a poem where everything is in continous movement and change. That is, is it really possible to find a focal point for the most significant idea of the poem? We may suppose that the three leading motifs represent the focus. Because of the three leading motifs of the three parts, however, there is little likelihood of this possibility. It is more likely to attempt to place the focal point in the middle of the poem, in line with Weöres, who declared that the *Harmadik szimfónia* 'Third Symphony' "circles around itself like a solar system". Using this solar suggestion of arrangement, the most central part of the second part and also of the whole poem, has focal quality: *Ki egét elhagyta, lássa: / habos örvény a lakása, / fedelének éj az ácsa, / sötétség a kalapácsa* 'He, who his heaven abandoned, may see: / his home is a lathering whirlpool, / the night is the carpenter of his roof, / the darkness is his hammer'. I do not want to omit this possibility. This, in my opinion, involves the most essential idea, definitively placed in the synthesis of the third strophe as well: because something has been lost, the soul's peace has also disappeared. Notwithstanding, this idea of the focus is not wholly satisfying. Placing the focus strictly in the middle, in my opinion, excludes the most fundamental constant, the activity of movement. Indeed, this entire central strophe indicates a sense of movement. Both the verb "abandoned" and the image of the "lathering whirlpool" in the first and the second lines are associated with movement, similar to the last two lines, whose tropes also depict a state of restlessness.

As we have seen before, the motif of the dream is common to all three parts. As a result, focus could ultimately be placed on this motif of the dream. I think, however, that even this variant of the focus disregards the dynamics of movement that gives the parts of the symphony the inexplicable sense of floating and flying. The images of real life are reflected in dreams, in which we could not find any focal point. Consequently, it would be difficult to establish the focus on the dream. Also the question of whose dream the poem is about remains unanswered.

These hypotheses presented above superficially touch upon the theme. They cannot, however, arrive at any answer concealed in the very nature of this theme. At this point we arrive at the most significant outcome: the main theme can be touched but it can never be grasped. This is so for the simple reason that the main theme is from the very beginning inconceivable. Both the leading motif, the dream with its ceaselessly vibrating images, and the most central strophe emphasize this inconceivability. This strophe, as mentioned above, is dynamic and static at the same time, and thus suggests the solution: the focus is concealed in the dynamics of movement and is as unnameable as what is lost. The motif of the search manifests itself in many ways, as everything relates to movement. Similar to the search inside – "he is within me", according to the third part –, the focus exists in some indefinable place, depending on the reader. As a result, the focus moves to the reader. Focus is on that place where the reader thinks it fits best. This is the dynamic of focus as it combines the concepts of contrasting qualities with the moment of reception, and then grasps it in the most comprehensive way.

5.1.3. The Rhetorical-Stylistic Structure

According to Elemér Hankiss (1970:159) "...the literary work is a complicated structure of tensions which grow and weave into each other, and it is also a structure of a set of tensions in which rich emotional-conceptual energies are concentrated and are transmitted to the reader". With the phrase 'set of tensions' Hankiss means a connection of two different poles, and he names four groups representing this connection:

1. relations based on a logical-conceptual level, for example that of cause and effect
2. relations based on an associative level, as in case of the metaphor or the symbol
3. relations based on a formal level, like the chiasmus, the antithesis or the anastrophe
4. relations based on phonetics, like the rhyme and the rhythm

Such tensions and sets of tensions are characteristic of the poem *Harmadik szimfónia* 'Third Symphony'. The contrast between opposite values, which causes a tension, is also a main structuring principle for the poem at hand. Each of these four types of Hankiss' sets of tensions, in my opinion, are represented in the *Harmadik szimfónia* 'Third Symphony'. In the first line, where the little bird both cries and rejoices and where the clauses contradict each

186

other and the event itself is problematical – can a bird cry, at all? – , the tension comes from logically-conceptually based relations. This same first line also gives us an example of relations based on an associative level. Obviously, the trope "little bird" can be interpreted as a symbol of some abstract idea. If it denotes a person, however, such as the main character, then it becomes a metaphor. But at the same time it is also a personification, as it imbues an animal with human attributes. Hankiss' third group, which concerns the relations based on a formal level, can be seen in the antithesis of the parallel-structured clauses in the first line. Relations based on phonetics will be illustrated in later chapters dealing with metrical and grammatical structures.

If there is so much tension discernible within a single line, then how much tension is accumulated within the entire poem, where the tension points not only occur within the same line but also exercise a mutual influence on the global structure? The term *síkváltás* 'shift of levels', defines the tension created by the interaction of contrasting grammatical and stylistic structures, according to Hankiss (1985:488-521). That is, different levels of interpretation which exist in the literary work, and which are realized simultaneously, create an oscillation between our levels of perception (Hankiss 1985:522-558). The trope metaphor in poetry, where levels of images and levels of possible meanings interact, is the most common example of this oscillation. I think that this metaphorical character of the tropes must be emphasised in an examination of the *Harmadik szimfónia* 'Third Symphony' in the first place.

"The terms of science are abstract symbols which do not change under the pressure of the context. They are pure (or aspire to be pure) denotations; they are defined in advance. [– – –] But where is the dictionary which contains the terms of a poem?" (Brooks 1947:210). This question of Brooks', in my opinion, can clearly be applied to Weöres' poem *Harmadik szimfónia* 'Third Symphony'. How can we approach his metaphors? Ted Cohen looks at the metaphor as a medium which expresses the identity between the poet and the reader: "When I offer you a metaphor I invite you to attempt to join a community with me, an intimate community, whose bond is our common feeling about something" (Cohen 1997:233). Consequently, the message implied in the metaphor cannot be separated from the reader. Each individual reader creates his own individual meaning. As a result, there are no homogeneous interpretations, and ambiguity refers not only to the text but also to that contact the text creates with the reader.

I believe that when dealing with the rhetorical-stylistic structure of the *Harmadik szimfónia* 'Third Symphony', this twofold ambiguity must be especially emphasized. The dynamic structure of the set of tensions makes a static and clean-cut explanation of the tropes completely impossible.

There is, however, one other reason which makes the interpretation of the tropes in the poem difficult. Because most of the metaphors are simple – in absentia – metaphors, it often becomes complicated to decide the actual impli-cations of the metaphor. In opposition to these simple metaphors, in the complete – in praesentia – metaphor both the tenor and the vehicle, the elements of identification, are present thus facilitating interpretation. The trope *madárka* 'little bird', however, is in want of a subject which it can be identi-fied with. Obviously, this semantical concentration on one word makes the mind work more intensively in order to construe a meaning. Beáta Thomka argues that metaphors which only contain one component are connotatively much more exciting and forceful than metaphors consisting of two compo-nents. However, as she also says, these simple metaphors are exceedingly rare in Hungarian poetry. According to Thomka, this phenomenon is due to the fact, that "unlike the European trends of the period (the twenties and the thir-ties [note from the writer], a logical, figurative, conceptual, grammatical and semantical coherence is constantly forceful in Hungarian poetical language. Such a distance between the components, usual in other poesies of this time, becomes not in the least wedged in, in terms of Hungarian poetry" (Thomka 1992:119). This poem of Weöres, however, could be an exception to this prob-able tendency.

On account of the trope *madárka* 'little bird', an oscillation is set up between several levels. As we cannot find any subject with which the little bird can be identified – there are no obvious structural clues – we are obliged to look for it in the entire poem. Nevertheless, this search does not reach any ulti-mate answer of the question. Hence, based on the poem, the concept of the identified subject cannot be proved. Because it goes beyond the physical limits of the poem, the answer must be searched for within the mind of the reader.

Thomka (1992:120), drawing attention to the Hungarian archaic idiom *lélekmadár* [lit.] 'soul-bird', also sheds light upon the close connection of the concepts *lélek* 'soul' and *madár* 'bird'. This image of the bird connected to the soul might be associated with another image of flying, which the Hungarian turn of phrase *elszállt belőle a lélek* – [lit.] 'the soul has flew out of him, i.e. *meghalt* 'he died' – gives expression to. The fact that the image of the bird also stands for the soul in the symbol-system of other nations, further supports this hypothesis concerning flight (Biedermann 1991:134). This idea of the bird is, however, not only symbolic, but also an archetype, a plausibility which Thomka (1992:120) also indicates. As the original shapes of mind are preserved in the archetype, it is also a primaeval form.

If, after these introductory remarks, we examine the metaphorical struc-ture of the trope *madárka* 'little bird', the relation indicated earlier, that of an identification based on the little bird, becomes somewhat problematical. If the bird represents the archetype of the soul, then the soul must be regarded as the first form, or the basis of identification, and the bird then represents the iden-tified subject. This simple metaphor then joins the identified and the subject, creating identification, and also becomes a means of expressing an irreversible content.

The dynamics of movement concealed in the simple metaphor *madárka* 'little bird', make this trope very effective. But are the other simple metaphors of the poem just as forceful as this one? The word *hatalmas* 'mighty', for example, can also be described as a simple metaphor. We are not informed about the identity of this mighty in the beginning, nor at the end. Bata (1979:72) points out that the trope *piros gerendák* 'read planks' denotes the rays of sunlight, i.e. the sunbeam. This seems very likely in the first strophe, but this suggestion turns out to be a little uncertain in the last strophe of this first part, where the image of the red planks is no longer connected to the mighty one.

One thing, however, is certain. The tropes, through interplay, mutually modify each other's meaning. By relating the metaphors in the first strophe to one other, for example, a complex trope is created. As a complex trope freely combines all the signification-levels, these complex tropes strongly reinforce the connotative message.

Hankiss (1985:535-540) identifies two different kinds of oscillation, i.e. the horizontal, taking place along the line of the signs of language, and the vertical, occurring between the levels of reality and that of the mind. In terms of the two verbs of the first line, *sír* 'cries' and *örül* 'rejoices', oscillation takes place horizontally, along the line of the signs, but also vertically, because reality and the image of it reflected in the mind occur on different levels. The oscillation patterns of the next strophe are also horizontal and vertical: *míg magad vagy a vadász meg a vad* 'when you yourself are the hunter and the wild'; *Győznöd se lehet, veszned se szabad* 'You cannot win, nor can you get lost'. According to Hankiss (1985:538-539) "the real source of the esthetical-literary force is not the horizontal but the vertical oscillation. [– – –] that is, while a repetition on the horizontal level is only a formal-grammatical mechanism, the vertical oscillation, brought in motion by this former, is already a medium for the contentual, conceptual and experimental substance of the work of art".

This statement of Hankiss, in my opinion, has a twofold implication for the poem *Harmadik szimfónia* 'Third Symphony'. The vertical oscillation between the tropes makes its impact not only in an immediate context, but also relates to the entire poem. The same trope in a new context becomes saturated with new meaning. As a result we experience an oscillation taking place between the different contexts. Thus, the *hatalmas* 'mighty' of the first strophe relates to different subjects in the seventh and the twelfth strophes: *s távol, a hatalmas: az is te magad* 'and you are the mighty in the distance, too', *és vallat a fény, a hatalmas* 'and you are questioned by the light, the mighty'. The last words of the leading motif in the second part *Rikolt a páva veled* 'The peacock screams with you' are repeated in the seventh strophe: *Tipeg a páva veled* 'The peacock trips with you'. The acoustic image in the first motif is followed by the visual image in the second. In these two contexts, the common component, the peacock, as a single metaphor, is attached to different meanings.

The verb *remeg* 'trembles' is frequently seen in this second part. It is first connected to the *gyöngy* 'pearls' [lit.] 'pearl', and later to the *rózsa* 'rose'. These possible metaphors are also elements of the personifications in which the pearls and the rose, like a human, tremble. Tropes embraced in other tropes, as complex tropes, hence place complex contents into words. The noun *jég* 'ice', represented in various contents carries different meanings. In the third strophe it belongs to an upper reality: *Jégszirmos hegyeken át* 'Across ice-corollaed mountains', in the seventh strophe we can find it on the earth: *s a jeges réteken* 'and the icy meadows', [lit.] 'and on the icy meadows', and the in repeated lines of this same strophe and also in the first line of the last strophe, it relates to the lower spheres: *lezuhan a jég alá!* / *lezuhan a jég alá!* 'he falls under the ice! / he falls under the ice!; *Jég alatt* 'beneath the ice'. These examples give a clear picture of vertical oscillation, because they reflect not only an alternating attention between different significance units but also reflect the natural form of vertical movement.

Our investigation of the oscillation patterns may be further widened to include the unity of the three parts. However independent each of the parts are, we can still recognize a certain structure of coherences between the tropes of the three parts. Obviously, this tendency towards cohesion is connected to a sense of movement. The idea is indicated from the very first by the pivotal image of the bird. Both the little bird and the dead wild-goose fly, similar to the lifeless leaves and the rock in the first part. The toddling of the peacock portrays movement, too, and colors and sounds are in motion, along with the trembling rose and the pearls in the second part. When the rose "trembles climbing on you", this awareness of movement is also transmitted to the reader. The motif of the wing, indicating the trope synecdoche, relates to the image of the bird in the third part. Here, the idea of movement is expressed by the motif of the search after a possible bird which is now gone. The numerous complex tropes arise from this convergence of tropes referring to flight. The metaphors, the personifications, the synecdoches and the other tropes, through mutual interaction, infinitely increase the tension which arises from the various associations. Because the expressed idea of movement is not a static concept, this oscillation between the different imaginative levels appears in a form which reflects its immanent and manifold complexity.

5.1.4 The Metrical Structure

According to László Bárdos, the musical character of the *Harmadik szimfónia*

'Third Symphony' is not so much due to its metrical and rhythmic aspects, but rather to the repetition of certain themes (Liptay 1993:421). Repetitive structures are involved in the entire motif-structure of the poem. As pointed out earlier, the structure of the poem originates from the musical structure of the sonata. We have also traced the three main motifs of the three parts, which form the backbone of the composition.

In contrast with Bárdos, perhaps, I still believe that the musical character is not confined to the repetition of the motifs and the themes. Weöres also comments on the fact that it was the sound of the metrical foot paeon in the line *lezuhan a jég alá!* 'he falls under the ice!', that first caught his attention, that is, the alternate change of the arsis and the thesis, characteristic features of this metrical form (Liptay 1993:421). It is to be noted that while Bárdos draws attention to a deep despair disclosed by these two lines, Weöres, on his part, does not experience any tragic tone. Instead, he is interested in the movement concealed in the rhythmic pattern. A hypothesis of the whole poem originating from this Greek metrical foot is then not merely an unfounded supposition. This indicates the origin of this form, which only later became imbued with inconceivable meaning as a result of these poetic forms of movement.

Without doubt, rhythm mainly comes from the repetition of certain motifs. The musical term of the title also indicates that rhythm will play a part in the poem. I do not believe, however, that the poem can be traced back to these repetitions of motifs. We know that at that time when this poem was written, Weöres was very much preoccupied with expressing the possibilities deriving from the rhythmic pattern of the poem. In 1939, in a letter to Babits, for example, he writes about his attempts: "I experiment with about twenty different kinds of metrical feet, in order to test the several tones they can lend to the Hungarian poem.[– – –] As all the devils of rhythm were locked up in the Hungarian language. – In cases of works of some length I imagine this 'fashionable' versification as follows: a rhythmic theme emerges, then a subject-matter; and as soon as this subject-matter asserts itself, the rhythmic theme begins to change; [...] the rhythmic theme then might take another form; or a counter-theme might abruptly interrupt it, according to the subject-matter (Weöres 1990:155). In his thesis *A vers születése* 'The Birth of the Poem' (EI I:217-260), written in the same year, Weöres declares that a metrical form might be the basis of the poem, which only later is followed by an appropriate subject-matter.

We ought to compare these statements to a letter written to Várkonyi (1976:388-389) in 1943. In this letter it is precisely the *Harmadik szimfónia* 'Third Symphony' Weöres uses to demonstrate his new ideas concerning writing: "I have at last found the content to fit the form, but it does so in an entirely new manner. This content has no logical sequence, the flow of ideas is like that of the main and secondary themes of a piece of music: they never become concrete and they remain at the intuitive level. These indefinite thoughts are pursued within a poem by several rhythms, brought into focus now from this direction, now from that" (Transl. by Kenyeres 1984:93:40).

The poem *Harmadik szimfónia* 'Third Symphony' can be seen to demonstrate these thoughts, where the source of inspiration is still the rhythm, but contrary to Weöres' former manner of writing, where "the content appeared merely as a vine-support for the form" (Várkonyi 1976:388), this rhythm can now adapt itself to individual content and become equal to it. As pointed out before, in line with Weöres, everything floats in this content, which makes it nearly inconceivable. And because the form adapts itself to the content, this floating movement must be studied within the framework of the rhythmic pattern. Weöres, commenting on the metrical foot paeon, points to this same motion of rising and falling.

In the following I make an attempt to illustrate the rhythmic pattern of this movement. The Auftakts are denoted by X, in accordance with Szerdahelyi's (1994:14) scheme.

The paeon-line that first caught Weöres' attention consists of a paeon primus and a simple paeon or cretic:

– ∪ ∪ ∪ | – ∪ –
lezuhan a jég alá!

The other exclamatory sentence of the poem also has this pattern of the paeon, although in accordance with the formula of the fourth paeon:

∪ ∪ ∪ –
Ide se lát!

The four different forms of the paeon can be seen in many places in the poem. In the two first lines of the last strophe it alternates with a mollossus and an anapest:

– ∪ – | – – – | – ∪ – | –
Jég alatt, nem-múló percemen át

– ∪ – | ∪ ∪ – | – ∪ – | –
őrizem simuló pille-porát.

In some cases the paeon stands independently as the last metric foot of the line. In her work Erika Szepes (1996:2:96-104) devotes a separate chapter to this occurrence of the paeon. She points to the fact that three-syllable Hungarian metres, with a stressed first syllable, coalesce with the metrical foot cretic at the end of the lines, and thus create a simultaneuous rhythm. Examples from the *Harmadik szimfónia* 'Third Symphony' are the two first lines of the seventh strophe of the first part, and two lines from the seventh strophe of the third part:

X | – ∪ ∪ – – || – ∪ –
Ne kérdd a veremtől jussodat.

∪ ∪ ∪ ∪ – || – ∪ | – ∪ –
Te vagy a vadász és te vagy a vad

∪ ∪ – | – ∪ –
s a jeges réteken

– – – | – ∪ –
minden csak sirverem

Apparently, a strong sense of rhythm is reinforced as a result of these identical metrical feet occurring at the end of the lines. However, these regular patterns are often replaced by other metrical units, with the only exception being the four-line strophes of the regularly arranged second part. The metrical agreements of the final metrical feet of these lines in most cases include the entire last foot, as in the first strophe where all the final metrical feet are choriambs:

∪ – ∪ | – ∪ ∪ – ,
Rikolt a páva veled,

∪ – ∪ | – ∪ ∪ –
tipeg az éjbe veled,

– – ∪ | – ∪ ∪ –
elveszti nyúlt vonalát

∪ ∪ – | – ∪ ∪ –
a futórózsa veled

We can recognize the correspondences between each of the four-line strophes in this second part. Parallel metrical feet at the end of the lines are also frequent in the longer strophes, but in those occurring in each second line, and in the first lines of the fourth strophe:

‒ ∪ ∪ ∪ ‒
Sír a liliom,

X | ‒ ∪ ‒
a sáska is –

‒ ∪ ∪ ∪ ‒
hogyha lehetne,

‒ ∪ ‒
szánna is.

The above examples inevitably draw attention to a very important matter. Correspondences between the last metrical feet of the lines in most cases coincide with correspondences between the rhymes. This fact is not to be confused with the traits of the arsis and the thesis, because in Hungarian verse, as a rule, masculine rhyme is always connected to masculine rhyme and feminine rhyme to feminine rhyme. In the poem *Harmadik szimfónia* 'Third Symphony', however, we not only experience the harmony of the rhymes, but also that of the metrical feet at the end of the lines. As a result, rhythm becomes more rhythmic, and rhymes become more perfect. The general characteristics of the poem can be illustated by an example taken from the fifth strophe of the first part:

X | ‒ ∪ ∪ ‒
A múlt se pihen:

X | ‒ ‒ | ‒ ‒ | ‒ ∪ ∪ ‒
új percek méreg-csöppjeiben

∪ ∪ ‒ ∪ | ‒ ∪ | ‒ ‒
elomolva őrzi részét.

X | ‒ ‒ | ‒ ‒ | ‒ ∪ ∪ | ‒ ‒
A holt vadlúd, bár tolla se lebben,

∪ ‒ ∪ | ‒ ‒ | ‒ ∪ ∪ | ‒ ‒
röpül a zúgó szárnyu seregben
‒ ‒ | ‒ ∪ ∪ | ‒ ‒
s röptében üli fészkét.

194

The rhyme-pattern of the strophe is as follows: *a a b a a b*. As seen, the end rhymes of the two first lines are repeated at the end of the fourth and the fifth lines. When, however, the metrical feet at the end of the first two lines are two choriambs, the fourth and fifth lines end with two spondees or adonic colon if the caesura has been omitted. Consequently, identical rhymes, if not contiguous to each other, may be part of different metrical feet.

In those cases when it appears as the final metrical foot in the line, the choriamb needs special mention. The essential motion of flying is clearly represented in the closely joined long and short syllables of this metrical foot. There are many examples of this foot in the introductory first part:

X | – ⏑ – ‖ X | – ⏑ ⏑ –
Madárka sír, madárka örül,

X | ⏑ – ⏑ – | – ⏑ ⏑ –
míg piros gerendái közül

– ⏑ ⏑ – | –
néz a hatalmas–

X | – ⏑ ⏑ –
Kinyílik a táj,

⏑ ⏑ | – ⏑ ⏑ –
lehunyódik a táj

⏑ – | – – – – ‖ – ⏑ ⏑ –
Kereplőként űzöd körbe magad,

– – ‖ ⏑ ⏑ – – | – ⏑ ⏑ –
rab vagy, de keserved álma szabad

⏑ ⏑ – – | – ⏑ ‖ ⏑ – ⏑
s igazad az álom, a röpke!

X | – ⏑ ⏑ | – – | – ⏑ ⏑ –
A szikla, ha rávésed jajodat,
X | – – – ⏑ ‖ X | – ⏑ ⏑ –
többé nem szikla: élő te-magad

$--- \cup \parallel - | \cup - \cup$

s föllibben a fellegekbe!

The variety of metrical feet illustrated above demonstrates Weöres' intimate knowledge of the most difficult poetic measures, as the dispondee $(----)$, the ionic a minore $(\cup \cup --)$, the fourth epitrite $(--- \cup)$ and the ditrochee $(- \cup - \cup)$.

The end-rhymes and the repetitive metrical patterns lend a very special rhythm to the poem. Both of these features change all the time but return later as similar rhymes or similar metrical feet. They can be seen to be reminders of something we have experienced earlier, which in its turn reinforces the over-all sense of rhythm. The rhymes at the end of the first lines of many strophes in the first part demonstrate this: *Madárka sír, madárka örül* 'Little bird cries, little bird rejoices' – *Az élettelen avar is röpül* 'The lifeless leaves do also fly', *Küldd néki töretlen álmodat* 'Send him your unbroken dreams' – *A jövő nem vár, előre arat* 'The future does not wait: it harvests in advance' – *Ne kérdd a veremtől jussodat.* 'Do not ask for your rights from the pitfall'. There are examples of this relationship in the second part as well: *Rikolt a páva veled* 'The peacock screams with you' – *Ki merne súgni neked* 'Who would whisper to you' – *Színek közt gyúl a szemed* 'Among many colors shine your eyes'; and in the third part: *Tűzhabos, bársonyos tereken át* 'Through fire-foamy, velvety places' – *Jégszirmos hegyeken át* 'Across ice-corollaed mountains' – *Ide se lát!* 'Not even here he sees!' – *Jég alatt, nem múló percemen át* 'Through never-ending minutes beneath the ice'. To this we must add that these initial lines in the strophes of the second and the third parts, without exception, also rhyme with the last line of the same strophe, which in its turn also reinforces the characteristic sense of rhythm.

We can see that not only similar metrical patterns at the end of lines, but also within successive lines build independent units which often recur after certain lines or strophes in the same or similar form. These are coherences which also relate to the inner parts of the verses, as shown by the following lines in the third part:

$- \cup -$

Ormokon

$- \cup -$

Kő-fokon

$- \cup -$

tű-fokon

– ∪ –
csókolom

However, in the poem *Harmadik szimfónia* 'Third Symphony', as in many other poems of Weöres', the quantitative metrical pattern of the lines is placed with another metrical system created by a regular repetition of the same number of syllables, where the first syllable of the metrical unit is always stressed, i.e. the accentual-syllabic metre. István Szerdahelyi (1994:153), referring to Erika Szepes' numerous metrical analyses of Weöres' poems, points to the fact that individual rhythmic patterns which result from a simul-taneous occurrence of the quantitative and the accentual-syllabic metre often seen in the Hungarian poetry of today, were first used by Weöres. The second part of the *Harmadik szimfónia* 'Third Symphony' offers many examples for further study of this particular merging of two different metrical systems:

∪ – ∪ | – ∪ ∪ –   3 | 4
ki merne súgni neked

– – – | ∪ – ∪ –   3 | 4
arról, hogy mi lett veled?

∪ ∪ – | – ∪ ∪ –   3 | 4
melyik ég rejti helyed?

– ∪ ∪ | – ∪ ∪ –   3 | 4
őrzi-e gyöngyeidet?

As we can see, the metrical feet amphribach, choriambs, mollossus, anapests and dactyls show themselves to be the regular metrical occurrences of accen-tual-syllabic meter. Determining the primary metrical system involves some difficulties. Presumably, both are present and we can also agree with Erika Szepes' and István Szerdahelyi's (1988:122) view: "Sándor Weöres combines the two metrical systems in such a masterly manner that we never can locate the basic rhythm, against which, 'in addition', the other is heard". Experimentation was an ongoing personal pursuit throughout Weöres' entire career. On one occasion, for example, indisputably in a much-too-modest and self-critical manner, he declared as follows: "Well, I look upon Ady, Babits, and Kosztolányi as poets, in the full sense of the word, but I take myself to be an experimentalist. I am some sort of an intermediary between the poet and the researcher. I don't really feel poetry is what I am doing. It is much more research and experimentation." (Domokos 1993:349-350). This is a character-istic of the *homo faber*, as Kenyeres (1983:236) also indicated.

Without doubt, the repeated themes or motifs are very important to the sense of a poem's rhythm. The compositional form of the symphony is exhibited through this parallelism. However, as described above, it is not only the arrangement of the parts that coheres to music, but also the poem's metrical structure. Weöres was of the same opinion. His answer to György Czigány's (1993b:307) question, why he (Weöres) named the twelve symphonies as symphonies, is as follows: "For two reasons. The first reason is because the word symphony simply means sound. These symphonies are acoustical poems. From another perspective, I call them symphonies because they fit into compositions consisting of four, or sometimes three or five, themes".

5.1.5 Grammatical Structure

The identical lines, metrical feet and rhymes like lines of waves follow each other in the poem *Harmadik szimfónia* 'Third Symphony'. This same undulation is reflected in the grammatical structures. We might, as a starting point, note the many copulative compound sentences. An essential characteristic of the independent clauses of these compound sentences is their open intonation pattern. This is an essential characteristic in both the logical and grammatical sense, as the pattern clearly indicates the openness of the former clause, in line with the intent of the speaker (MMNyR II:408). The grammatical rhythm, in my opinion, comes mostly from this continous backwards reference. There is, however, an opposite direction of the reference-patterns, i.e. within the pattern where each clause has a reference to the following one. The clauses exercise mutual influence over each other and this also reinforces the intensive rhythmic sense.

Many subsequent clauses have the same type of grammatical structure. Some examples from the first part: *Madárka sír, madárka örül* 'Little bird cries, little bird rejoices', *Kinyílik a táj, / lehunyódik a táj* 'the land opens up, / the land closes, *Te vagy a vadász és te vagy a vad* 'You are the hunter and you are the wild'; some examples from the second part: *Tipeg a páva veled, / remeg a rózsa veled* 'The peacock trips with you, / the rose trembles with you', *Színek közt gyúl a szemed, / hangok közt zsong a füled* 'Among many colors shine your eyes, / among many sounds hum your ears'; and some examples from the third part: *Jégszirmos hegyeken át, / csatakos völgyeken át* 'Across ice-corollaed mountains, / across muddy valleys'.

Many sentences also contain a parallel grammatical structure. The two unvaried exclamatory sentences in the third part are obvious examples of this: *Ide se lát! / Ide se lát!* 'Not even here he sees! / Not even here he sees!, *lezuhan a jég alá! / lezuhan a jég alá!* 'he falls under the ice! / he falls under the ice!'. A similar parallel structure can be demonstrated in other subsequent sentences, although sometimes these sentences include an accumulation of words belonging to the same part of speech, such as the two subsequent adjectives and the two subsequent nouns of the first lines of the third part: *Tűzhabos, bársonyos tereken át / keresem szárnyának pille-porát. / Ormokon, / kő-fokon / kutatom fátyla nyomát* 'Through fire-foamy, velvety places / I look for the butterfly-dust of his wings. / On the peaks, / on the capes / for the shadow of his veil I search'. In spite of these discrepancies, the parallel grammatical structure is clearly recognizable.

This last example, however, leads us to other syntactical fields, i.e. those of the parts of speech. As seen in this example, the same parts of speech, following each other, create copulative compound syntagms. Further accumulation of the same parts of speech can be based on the opposite values of the components, such as the antitheses depicted by syntagms *vadász meg a vad* 'the hunter and the wild', *Igaz és a Van* 'Truth and the Being', *Nap meg a tenger* 'The Sun and the sea' in the first part. The third part also includes many examples of the repetition of the same parts of speech. These occur, actually, in nearly each verse: *kérlelem, keresem* 'I beg him, I seek him', *zajban, csendben* 'in noise, in silence', *vézna, ijedt fény* 'a puny, frightened light', *Rögökön, fellegen, kék vidéken* 'Through the soil, through the clouds, through the blue country, *napokat, éjeket* 'the days and the nights', *igaz-e vagy álom* 'is it true or is it a dream', *fekete, holt* 'black and dead'.

As we can see from the examples, these compound structures are characterstic of the relationship between words, clauses and sentences. Sometimes, however, we may wonder if these numerous, seemingly coordinated relationships are instead perhaps subordination-relations. Very often, in fact, we cannot locate any conjunctions. This fact, obviously, creates room for ambiguity. An example of this is taken from the second verse of the first part: *Győznöd se lehet, veszned se szabad: / a hályogos sűrűség alatt / vermed hasztalan ásod.* 'You cannot win, nor can you get lost: / under the blurred thickness / you dig your pitfall in vain'. It is easy to decide the coordinating relation between the two first clauses. It is more difficult, however, to define that between the second and the third clauses. The colon between these clauses does not make the decision easier. It indicates a new unit, no longer part of the former enumeration. Naturally, we could use the conjunction *és* 'and', and thus refer to a similar coordinating connection other than between the former clauses. But the conjunction *tehát* 'then, hence, consequently' could also be used, which would create a resultative compound connection between the clauses. Our next example will demonstrate a case where two clauses can function in a subordinating relation, in the sixth verse of the third part: *Rögökön, fellegen, kék vidéken / siető léptemmel el nem érem: / szívemben szövöget / napokat éjeket* 'Through the soil, through the clouds, through the blue country / I don't catch him with my hasty steps: / in my heart he weaves

/ the days and the nights'. Here we could also point to a coordinating compound relation, between the clauses connected by the colon. But, in substituting the conjunction *mert* 'because, as, since', we could then refer to a clausal clause.

Other examples of subordinating structures are as follows: *míg piros gerendái közül néz a hatalmas* 'while from his red planks / the mighty one looks down, *míg magad vagy a vadász, meg a vad* 'when you yourself are the hunter and the wild', in the first part, and the examples *míg ezer mintája szüntelen / körbe kering* 'while his thousand figures / ceaselessly move around', *mikor a kerek táj télbe hajolt* 'when the whole country comes round to winter'. Because both clauses of the complex sentences denote events taking place at the same time, these clauses, similar to the clauses within the compound sentences, refer back to each other. This time-based, simultaneous relation between the clauses of the complex sentence further reinforces the rhythm. We may, however, also note that subordinating relations are less frequent than coordinating ones.

The clauses within these compound sentences, running as equal parts next to each other, also strengthen the rhythmic impression. But do the semantical units function in the same way? Owing to the fact that any rhythm goes back to some dynamic motion, a semantic study of the verbs will be most illuminating. All the verbs in the poem belong to the category of active verbs, mostly denoting continuous, incomplete action, such as, for example, the following verbs: *néz* 'looks down' [lit. 'looks'] in the first part, *rikolt* 'screams' in the second part, and *keresem* 'I look for' in the third part. These verbs, as they express a permanent state and because they also contrast the often occurring states of change, are very important verbs in terms of expressing subject-matter. But this permanent state, expressed by verbs reflecting a progressive aspect, often becomes interrupted by other forms. In my opinion, there are four chief cases of these occurrences:

1. antonyms within the sentence
2. negative particles connecting the verbs
3. progressive aspect verbs denoting movement
4. momentaneous verbs

In the parallel syntagms *Madárka sír, madárka örül* 'Little bird cries, little bird rejoices' in the first part, the two verbs are antonyms, similar to the syntagms *Győznöd se lehet, veszned se szabad* 'You cannot win, nor can you get lost' and *Kinyílik a táj, / lehunyódik a táj* 'The land opens up, / the land closes'.

The verb *lel* 'find', often occurring in different forms in the second part, belongs to the second group above. It is opposed to the different forms of the verb *keres* 'looks for' in the third part. The verb *lel* 'find', together with a negative particle, however, signifies a meaning similar to the verb *keres* 'looks for' has: *de nem lelhetsz soha békét* 'but you never can find your peace', *A múlt se pihen* 'Not even the past rests', *meglelheted százszor sírodat, mégsem lelhetsz soha békét* 'you may find you grave a hundred times, yet you cannot find your peace', in the first part, *tán már aludni se tudnál* 'maybe you could not sleep any more', and in the second part, *nem érem el soha* 'I never can catch him', *siető léptemmel el nem érem* 'I don't catch him with my hasty steps'.

The verbs belonging to the third group above have a clear relation to nouns, such as the antonyms *vadász* 'hunter' and the *vad* 'wild'. There is movement involved in these nouns, in the same way as it is in many verbs. In the first part we meet the verb *röpül* 'flies' very often: *Az élettelen avar is röpül* 'The lifeless leaves do also fly', [...] *röpül a zúgó szárnyú seregben* '[...] flies in the flock of buzzing wings'. This movement is reinforced by the noun originating from the same root: *röptében* 'while flying', in the fifth strophe and the adjective *röpke* 'fugitive', in the tenth verse. The movement is incomplete in the first line of the tenth verse, too. *Kereplőként űzöd körbe magad* 'Like a rattle, you hunt yourself around'. This movement becomes somewhat slower when the second part comes down to the earth: *tiped a páva veled* 'The peacock trips with you', *mindannyival oda futnál* 'there you would now run back to'. The image of searching is expressed by the verb in the line of the fifth strophe in the third part: *Hasztalan üldözöm zajban, csendben* 'Vainly I chase him in noise, in silence'. The nouns of both this and the next verse also increase the sense of movement; *vad futásommal* 'in my wild scamper', *siető léptemmel* 'with my hasty steps'. The verb *kering* 'wheels around' in the sixth verse denotes movement, too: *míg ezer mintája / szűntelen körbe kering* 'while his thousand figures / ceaselessly wheels around'. As shown by examples above, those verbs denoting movement reflect the dichotomy of above and below. First the flying turns to toddling in the second part, changing into a chase which occurs both above and below.

The two verbs *remeg* 'trembles' and *pereg* 'drops', relating to several contexts in the second part, are also connected to movement. Unlike the verbs discussed above, these verbs do not express an external movement, taking place outside, but instead express movement as an internal activity within the very concept of the verb. Due to the conditional form of the verb *fut* 'runs' in the last line of the second strophe, restricted movement is described: *futnál* 'you would run'. This verb relates to the involuntary trembling of the rose or the running of tears, as worded in the fourth verse. The verb *csorog* 'runs', however, may also be associated with the verb *pereg* 'drops' in the third verse, as tears may also 'drop' in Hungarian.

Possibly, these are the momentaneous verbs of the fourth group, as they intensively increase the dynamism of the poem. The verbs do this by transforming permanent movement to a movement indicating a beginning, an end or the momentary character of this. Very often, however, we have difficulty in deciding if it is the beginning or the end of the movement that is denoted, for example *elomolva őrzi részét* 'crumbling it keeps its share', in the fifth verse of the first part or *Ki egét elhagyta, lássa* 'Who, his heaven abandoned, may see', in the sixth verse of the second part. These verbs, namely, stand at the same time for a discontinuation and a creation of a new state. Similarly, with the verb *lezuhan* 'falls' in the second exclamatory sentence of the third part, an occurrence of a completed and an uncompleted movement is expressed.

Momentaneousness lasting only a moment is phrased by the verb *lebben* 'with no flap' [lit. 'makes a flapping movement'] in the fifth verse of the first part and by the verb *föllibben* 'it flies off' in the tenth verse. The adjective *villámló* 'shining' [lit. 'lightning'] in the second verse of the second part is also associated with the verb. Its momentary character, similar to the compound noun in the first verse of the third part, *pille-por* 'butterfly-dust', relates to movement.

This investigation has an emphasis of the different forms of movement, expressed by the verbs, as its objective. These verbs include the contrasting poles of above and below. These terms express the opposition between the aimless but unrestricted, and the constrained movement involuntarily bound to the same place, in other words, the contrast of static and dynamic movement.

In examining phonetic aspects of a poem, alliterations must first be mentioned. When repetitions of certain sounds are very frequent, the emotional effect created by this is striking. This is also due to the principle of sound-symbolism. Consonants, as an example of the trope *figura etymologica*, are repeated in the second verse of the first part: *míg magad vagy a vadász, meg a vad* 'when you yourself are the hunter and the wild'. The consonant *k* in the first two lines of the tenth verse reflects not only a circular movement, but also the harassment caused by it: *Kereplőként űzöd körbe magad, / rab vagy, de keserved álma szabad* 'Like a rattle, you hunt yourself around, / you are a slave, but the dream of your grief is free'. The contrast to the consonant *l* within the words of the last line of this same verse, associated with the idea of the unconstrained movement of flying, is striking: *s föllibben a fellegekbe* 'and flies off to the skies!'. A similar opposition can be revealed through the sounds *k* and *sz* in the twelfth verse: *Szél körme kapar a sír körül* 'The claws of the wind scratch around the grave'. The consonant *m* at the beginning of the words in the last verse, – *madárka sír, madárka örül* '– little bird cries, little bird rejoices' in combination with the consonant *m* in the former line, *minden te magad* 'you are everything', can also imply that you self are the little bird, too.

The consonant *r* beginning the words of the third verse in the second part must also be noted: *Rikolt a páva veled – / rád-kúszó rózsa remeg* 'The peacock screams with you – / the rose trembles climbing on you'. These consonants have, however, a special correlation to the consonant *r* within the words of the next lines: *nyers* 'rough', *pereg* 'drops'. The high frequency of the consonant *r*, although not in the initial position, is characteristic of the next verses, too: *csorog* 'run' [lit. 'runs'], *szirmon* 'petals', *merne* 'would dare', *sírni* 'to cry', *arról* ' about what', *rejti* 'hides', *őrzi-e* 'does it care' [lit. 'takes care of'].

Alliterations, as seen in the third verse of the third part, can further reinforce this intense feeling of the rhythm: *kérlelem, keresem: / ápolná kegyesen* 'I beg him, I seek him: / kindly take care of'. The rhythm becomes even stronger when it is connected to this same consonant in words in this verse: *hegyeken* 'across [...] mountains', *csatakos völgyeken* 'across muddy valleys', and *kis* 'little'. The many other alliterations and sound-congruencies within the words of this third part function in the same way. For example, there are many alliterative words beginning with the consonant *sz* in the sixth verse. Many of these words appear as the last words in the lines: s*zövöget* 'weaves', *szőnyeget* 'carpet', *szőnyegen* 'on the carpet', *szűntelen* 'ceaselessly'. The many instances of the consonant *k*, both as alliteration and arranged within the words common to both the first and the last lines of this same verse, function like a frame for the verse: *Rögökön, fellegen, kék vidéken* 'Through the soil, through the clouds, through the blue country' – *körbe kering* 'ceaselessly wheels around'. In the fifth line of the seventh verse this same acoustic rhythm is seen: *s lenn fekszem, földdé vált fekete holt* 'and underneath I lie as a black corpse turned to earth'.

Several rhythmic patterns are clear in the two identical verses of this third part. The couplet rhymes of the two first lines also rhyme with the last line. The consonant *l*, which initiates the two first words of the first and the third lines, alliterates them as well, similar to the alliterating words caused by the consonant *sz* in the second line. The focal quality of this strophe is, as a result, indicated by the acoustical patterns.

All alliterations, however, cannot be presented here. But, as shown above, these alliterations, together with the rhymes, are as essential to the rhythm as parallelism and the metrical structure.

5.2 The World of the Text

5.2.1 The Theme

According to E. D. Hirsch (1976:26-54), before interpreting a given work, we must establish the intention of the writer. Establishing the most probable meaning involves the reader deliberately and intuitively reconstructing the individual message of the writer. This psychological manner of interpretation implies a subjectivity in the interpretation process. The reader, in order to understand what the writer wanted to say, identifies himself with the writer. There is, on the whole, only one meaning, and it is the writer's. Paradoxically then, "objectivity in textual interpretation requires explicit reference to the speaker's subjectivity" (Hirsch 1976:48).

Wolfgang Iser (1993:319-341), casts doubt on Hirsch's view, and he asserts that the reader, using his imagination, must create his own individual experience of the work. The main point is to understand the intention of the writer, but not by deliberately identifying with him. The reader, according to Iser, forms his own opinion, based on his own experiences.

Wellek & Warren (1966:142-157) list several hypotheses as to what a poem is, and in some cases their ideas are related to those of Hirsch and Iser. Wellek & Warren, however, express another opinion, than these critics. According to Wellek & Warren, the work is not an experience of the reader, because "every individual experience of a poem contains something idiosyncratic and purely individual". The work is not the experience of the writer, either, because "we have no evidence to reconstruct the intentions of the author except the finished work itself". Wellek & Warren look at the poem as the realization of a collective experience based on the norms and the values of a given society.

These three different views concerning the act of interpretation have three different focal points: the writer, the reader and the collective experience of a given society. Weöres' view concerning interpretation is easy to trace in his statements. These statements also reflect his *ars poetica*. In terms of the relationship between the reader and the text, for example, he writes as follows: "The final form of the poem is always realized in the reader's mind. If he cannot relate to or against it, the poem remains a dead thing on the paper. The reader must be a co-worker. And a little bit of a poet, too. Using these means, he understands the ambiguous poem in its ambiguity" (WW:255). In the preface of the volume *Tűzkút* 'Well of Fire' he made the following statement: "I do not aim for entrance, nor for annoyance of those who shudder at the unusual; and I do not care if they understand me, either" (EI I:7). In piece 116 of the *Rongyszőnyeg* 'Rag-carpet' cycle, although its intent is to answer a hostile review, he ignores the readers, too:

Csak játék, mondja dalomra a kortárs,
s a jövő mit se szól rá, elfeled.
Verseimet ajánlom a falaknak,
úgy írtam, ahogy nekem jólesett.

It's only a joke, say my contemporaries,

and the future doesn't say anything, but forgets about me.
I dedicate my poems to the walls,
I wrote in the way it pleased me.

Consequently understanding, to Weöres, is an emotional category, not an intellectual category as it is for Hirsch, Iser and Wellek & Warren. "I want something else: I want to beam a living power, which shakes the instincts, the feelings, the intellect, the imagination, the spirit, and the whole individual; with not only the person reading the poem, but the poem reading the person, too. I want to x-ray you and rouse you in order to rearrange your closed, limited existence to an open, social, cosmic and infinite self" (EI I:7). Or as he writes in the poem *Harmadik nemzedék* 'Third Generation':

> Mit bánom én, hogy versed mért s kinek szól,
> csak hátgerincem borzongjon belé.
> [– – –]
> s még azt se bánom, ha semmit se mond.
> Csak szép legyen, csak olyan szép legyen,
> hogy a könny összefusson a szememben ...

What do I care why and to whom your poem speaks,
only that my backbone will shiver from it.
[– – –]
and I do not even care if it does not say anything.
Only that it will be beautiful, so beautiful,
that tears will gather in my eyes.

It is not so much the readers he criticizes when he dedicates his poems to the walls, but rather the reader's lack of understanding. This understanding is not the same as success, as we can read in the preface of the *Tűzkút* 'Well of Fire': "I do not yearn for success and glory in the present, and still less in the future. The poets think posterity is an infallible divine court of justice, though it is a snivelling suckling who would be glad for me to change its wet diaper; it would not hand out a laurel wreath to me. It would wrestle with me, like a little child with his father, and it would become stronger through this wrestling" (EI I:8). In other instances Weöres also stresses the act of wrestling with the poem: "The benefit of the poem is that it makes the soul more diversified, more flexible, more interesting. It does this to both the soul of he who writes it and he who reads it. The poem aims roughly at the same thing as the training of athletes. The poem is the training of the soul, which makes the muscles of the soul flexible and usable" (Ungváry 1993:141).

According to these citations above, understanding is based on emotions but it cannot take place without effort. Only with effort can it involve a common experience for both the writer and the reader, and the "social, cosmic and infinite self" might then be born. Similar to Wellek & Warren, who underlined the role of intersubjectivity in the relation between the author and the writer, Weöres talks about a union between the poet and his readers, based on shared feelings: "It is good to feel this community of fate with people, with the readers" (WW:235).

In one of his letters to Várkonyi (1976:360), Weöres mentions the concept of a non-reflective philosophy, "where it is not the chain of thoughts, but the object that philosophizes". In his monograph on Weöres, Kenyeres (1983:125) discusses in detail the concepts of reflective and non-reflective lyrics and the forms of these seen in Weöres' poetry. Kenyeres argues that in reflective lyrics thoughts about emotions are expressed, and the poet, who voices the feelings, is present throughout. In non-reflective lyrics, however, it is the emotions themselves which are directly expressed. While in reflective lyrics our mind unceasingly oscillates between the object and the subject, non-reflective lyrics, lacking a subject, only express the object: "These emotions, expressed in a non-reflective manner, appear at the suggestive level of the poems while entirely different subjects are treated on the semantic level... [– – –] Poems such as these do not need to speak of emotions: the emotion is grasped through the course of reading" (Kenyeres 1984:50). That is, in the presence of a cognitive consciousness the poem is reflective, but without this consciousness, emotions can be manifested in their most pure form.

Reflective lyrics, according to Kenyeres, make a person conscious of his own feelings, but, as he also points it out, "it only broadens the consciousness of perception, but not that of perceptivity: and this difference is of importance in connection with human acts, because the consciousness of perception does not go beyond the inner circle of the individual spiritual life; however perceptivity is directed outwards, it refers to the object and to the world, and represents a part of the act" (Kenyeres 1983:126). I think that the non-reflective philosophy of Weöres, in which the object philosophizes, intersects with Kenyeres' non-reflective lyrics. A relation with the object and the world also means a relation with the reader, where the main point is not to make a person conscious of his own feelings but to make a person ready to change these feelings. Consequently, non-reflective lyrics more profoundly exercise an influence on the reader than reflective lyrics.

Weöres avoided reflective lyrics according to Kenyeres (1983:132). He did this partly through his myth-paraphrases, where a general subject is expressed, and partly through his lyrical experimentations with language, the *játékversek* 'play-poems' as Kenyeres' (1974:291) terms them, such as the *Rongyszőnyeg* 'Rag-carpet' and the *Magyar etüdök* 'Hungarian Etudes' cycles. In this last group subject matter is embraced by the formal elements.

As the sense of form in general represents a primaeval human spirit of creation, formal elements directly reflect the emotional matter.

Does the poem *Harmadik szimfónia* 'Third Symphony' then belong to this category of non-reflective poems, in spite of the fact that it is neither a myth-paraphrase nor a play-poem? The subjects, i.e. the second person singular in the first and the second part and the first person singular in the third part, in fact indicate reflective lyrics. However, these grammatical restrictions lose their importance because they contradict themselves: *Te vagy a vadász és te vagy a vad / s távol, a hatalmas: az is te magad* 'You are the hunter and you are the wild, / and you are the mighty in the distance, too'. The subject thus turns into a general subject, similar to the general subjects in the myth-paraphrases and in the play-poems. This theory of a general subject is further reinforced by the central strophe of the second part, the topographical focus. Using third person singular, this verse includes the only sentence of the poem which has a message to every individual:

Ki egét elhagyta, lássa:
habos örvény a lakása,
fedelének éj az ácsa,
sötétség a kalapácsa.

He, who his heaven abandoned, may see:
his home is a lathering whirlpool,
the night is the carpenter of his roof,
the darkness is his hammer.

Similar motifs repeated in parallel structure is a characteristic of ancient poetry which in its turn gives evidence of mythical inspiration. The combination of two metrical systems expressed by a distinct form, similar to the play-poems, expresses the primaeval human spirit of creation.

Taking these characteristics into consideration, I believe that the poem *Harmadik szimfónia* 'Third Symphony' can rightly be classified as a non-reflective poem in which emotions directly appear. Consequently, an interpretation of a non-reflective poem must be approached in the same way, through the interpreter's own emotions. However, the writer's and the reader's subjectivity taken together includes their intersubjectivity as well. This is the point where the writer and the interpreter meet. The non-reflective text is reflected by the emotional scale of the reader, or, in Weöres' words, the poem reads the reader, too. Not only the poet, but the reader, too, so to speak, becomes unmasked with every new reading. An interpretation based on emotions can never be conventional, originating from former interpretations. We can find many examples of such non-conventional interpretations in the case of

Weöres' poem. These interpretations do not have much in common. We must also be aware of the assumption that the more true-hearted an interpretation is, the more genuine it is. This assumption gave birth to many different interpretations.

Zsuzsa Beney's (1990:201-208) interpretation of the poem reinforces what has been said above concerning the non-reflective poem. Beney was seventeen years old when she first read the poem, but the feeling that she calls *bűvölet* 'enchantment', which she felt with that first reading, has never left her, and it re-appears with each new reading. Her frequent use of the word *bővölet* 'enchantment' – three times, for example, within the first two pages – , shows that she regards it as the most essential aspect of the poem: "The aesthetic experience it gave me is a sense of its homogeneity in the first place, an enchantment in which the feelings stop short before they penetrate down to the depth of the thoughts, in order to revive, for the writer, its most essential meaning, by omitting thoughts, not in conceptual but in the other spheres of the soul" (Beney 1990:202). Thus, directly expressed feelings bring on the spell, or as Beney (1990:208) puts it, further on: "This feeling is a poem, born in the poem and it does not leave the poem, in the same way that the philosophy of the poem does not leave the medium of the poem: impossible to translate into the language of philosophy, it is instead the philosophy of poetry". When she was seventeen years old, the poem, in Beney's words, stood for an "unconscious pleasure", and this feeling remained for her. In this poem, namely, there is the possibility of tracing a first reading, which means that no matter how much experience the mature individual has, a reading of the poem always remains a first reading.

The theme of the poem has remained the same for Beney over time. The theme for her is always connected to her younger days, and she associates the last lines with youth and the passing of it: *S a fényben szűntelen / szaladó éveken / tű-fokon / csókolom / ujja nyomát* 'And throughout ceaselessly running years / in the light / on the needle-point / I kiss / his finger mark'. According to Beney, the most important line in the poem is the phrasing of the individual's feelings about the world and of his relationships to other people. Dealing with the third part, perhaps in relation to her view on a theme about the days of youth, she refers to love.

This association to love connects Beney's interpretation to one of Bata's (1983:1075-1078) interpretations. According to Bata – and this is also in line with the primary structuring principle we pointed out earlier –, the structure of the poem is based on oppositions, where "the Soul and the Sea, the sky and the earth, the man and the woman and every other contrasted thing long to unite with each other, looking with glorious love to one another". These "binary oppositions", in Bata's terminology, indicate the theme: the union of the two cannot create the desired oneness of the two, because the result of every union is, of necessity, a new entity. As Bata puts it: "Thesis and antithesis can never be one, because the third that follows is always the synthesis". Nevertheless, if there is any energy at all uniting the thesis and the antithesis, binarity then becomes oneness. The only form of such energy is love, according to Bata and he goes so far as to discuss Jesus Christ: "Reviving this lyrical hero in the poem is the metaphysical intention of Weöres' lyrics". Jesus Christ is the only person in whom this threefold essence is united. The main point of Beney's interpretation, in Bata's approach, is then focused on Jesus Christ, in whom love becomes personified.

Certainly, Bata's interpretation opens up new perspectives. First, there is the question of Weöres' religion. Of the many occasions Weöres declared his religious belief, the most well-known is the interview he gave to László Cs. Szabó (1993:40) for the English radio: "There is only one man, I think, and he is Jesus Christ. Other people exist or do not exist in so far as they are identical or not identical with Jesus". Pál Szerdahelyi (1994:565), Weöres' one-time pastor in Csönge regards him as a free-thinking religious man who was always rather weak at dogma. Thus, the fact that Weöres was Presbyterian is of no importance any more, because along with other religions, he was also influenced by Catholicism. In his article Szerdahelyi (1994:565) also thinks back to Weöres' reflections on the Holy Trinity: "In connection with one of our discussions, for example, he open-heartedly talked about his doubts, too, that is, he cannot believe with all his heart and accept without reservation the dogma of the Holy Trinity. [– – –] He cannot, namely, understand how God can exist as three persons, Father, Son and the Holy Spirit and that these three persons are still one single God at the same time".

The lines cited above, in my opinion, shed new light upon Bata's interpretation. According to his interpretation, it was the threefold essence involved in Jesus Christ's person that Weöres tried to find, i.e. the real union of the Father, the Son and the Holy Spirit. This was, nevertheless, an union which he did not really believe. We may thus catch a glimpse of another aspect, the question of faith and doubt expressed by the frequent motif of the dream. This is a type of interpretation clearly suggested by the following lines of the first part: *s a két arc: az Igaz és a Van / összefordul mámorosan, / mint a Nap meg a Tenger / nézi egymást ragyogó szerelemmel* 'and the two sides: Truth and Being / turn to each other in rapture / like the Sun and the Sea, / looking with glorious love at each another'. Weöres' statements do not contradict this: "My poetry is religious poetry, after all" (Győr 1993:106), because true faith could not endure any constraints from him, not even the constraint of the concept of faith: "This is a faith without tenets, which does not even include that there is a God. We know God, as the creator, as the source of existence, the *being*. I feel that the statement 'God exists' is contradictory if the being takes its origin from him [...] If we say that 'God exists', then we, actually, have two Gods:

God and the *Being* above him, a category of existence above him. That is why I dare not say that God exists ... " (Hornyik 1993:99).

In discussing the poem *Harmadik szimfónia* 'Third Symphony', Attila Tamás does not mention God or Jesus. Instead he talks about the sorrow of being separated from something and about the ceaseless search for this lost thing. It is the nostalgia for the completeness and the absolute that is, according to Tamás (1978:79-88), seen in the poem. Imre Bori (1984:46) uses the dialectics of opposite images to reach the "third thing", desired harmony. In contrast with Bori's view on harmony, Bata (1979:73) talks about an impression of crisis in his monograph. Kyra Rochlitz (1996:45) is on the whole of the same opinion when she writes that it is the very "way the poem is" which makes harmony impossible to reach.

There is a common feature in these interpretive-strategies: they all want to approach the theme of the poem. I think that the numerous and different discussions which build on this intention are a natural and welcome result of an interpretation of a non-reflective poem. Bata, in each of his two interpretations mentioned above – written in 1979 and 1983 – emphasizes different aspects. In another article about Weöres' symphonies, written in 1998, Bata, in addition to earlier discussed aspects, points to the structural aspects of the thesis, the antithesis and the synthesis. According to this view, the sphere embracing the whole universe in the first part is transformed into another sphere, which depicts human existence on the Earth in the second part. The synthesis of the third part describes the separation of the body and the soul at the moment of death (Bata 1988).

Thus, there are not only different interpretations from different interpreters but also different interpretations from the same interpreter. This might remind us of the dynamics within the poem, which we referred to above. We have also shown that because of the elements of represented reality that cannot be grasped, the focus of the dynamics moves to the reader. We must approach the poem in a similar manner in order to determine its theme. Because emotions are as incomprehensible as images of reality, theme must also be interpreted through its intersubjective reationship to the reader. The possibility of several themes being observed by the same reader cannot be omitted. The reader may not feel it necessary to point out the most important one, because he believes that all the themes do not exclude each other and that they function in a mutual relationship and in an indissoluble unity with each other.

Before presenting my theory on the theme of the poem *Harmadik szimfónia* 'Third Symphony', I will cite Weöres' own words: "The Song in three parts is very much related to the Psalms" (Liptay 1993:419). Further, he also said that the book of Psalms always occupied his attention in two respects: as penitence and as the grace of God. Károly Alexa (1994:[774]) in the concluding remarks of the collection of psalms entitled *Magyar Zsoltár* 'Hungarian

Psalm', writes as follows: "The psalm is lyric, entirely and originally [...] Everything is symbolic, and everything is spiritual in it [...], it can express things that cannot be put into words: joy, a guilty conscience, a cursing temper, and it can express what the human is and who God is. It can express what and how weak the former is and what and how mighty the latter is". Thus the psalm, as a genre, and as the means for expressing the inexpressible, caught Weöres' attention. The poem *Zsoltár* 'Psalm' (EI II:41), written in 1947, is one of his psalm-paraphrases:

Mindig bízom Istenben. Mintha ezer ház ablaka égne, úgy lakik Ő, míg üresnek látszik az utca.

Körülálltak a vadállatok csorgó szájjal: s úgy voltam, mint ki a tárt torkok felett repül a szélben!

Bolondként rámkiabáltak, s megtöltött éber csönddel az én Uram.

Mézes bort itatott velem és adott igaz asszonyt; s akik önmaguk istenei, magukat falják és elfogynak.

Ugyan mit ártanak énnekem, kit a Hatalom szétold a tiszta szavakban?

És mi módon veszítenek el, mikor mint kagylót és szivacsot vet fel az örvény?

A magukba rogyók lángjára kosár borul, falára penész. De él, aki az eleven tűz fészke fölött jár.

At all times I have faith in God. As if there were a thousand lights in the windows, as he lives, while the street seems empty.

The beasts surrounded me with watering mouths: and I felt like somebody who flies above wide open throats in the wind!

Like madmen they shouted at me, and my Lord filled me with wakeful silence.

He gave me wine with honey and he gave me a true wife; and those who are their own gods, they devour themselves and they waste away.

What harm can they do me, who by Might are dissolved in pure words?

And how do they put me to death, when the whirlpool casts up me like a mussel or a sponge?

Baskets fall onto the flame of those who drop down into themselves and mould falls on their walls. But he who walks above the nest of living fire is alive.

The poem *Harmadik szimfónia* 'Third Symphony' is related to the psalm form. Nevertheless, it is not a psalm-paraphrase like the poem *Zsoltár* 'Psalm' cited above. It differs from Weöres' psalm-paraphrases in two respects: first, it has an individual form which does not adhere to that of the psalms, and second, it does not name God directly. I touched upon Weöres' thoughts concerning the Holy Trinity earlier in the chapter. Maybe by not mentioning God's name, Weöres' own doubts are reflected. Possibly the *Hatalom* 'Might' in the *Zsoltár* 'Psalm' could be identified with the *hatalmas* 'mighty one' in the *Harmadik szimfónia* 'Third Symphony', but in contrast to a named *az én Uram* 'my Lord' in the former poem, God is unnamed throughout in the *Harmadik szimfónia* 'Third Symphony'. Thus, doubting God's existence, or rather transporting this existence into a dream, is, in my opinion, one of the most essential themes of the poem.

Another interpretation, still focusing on God, must also be mentioned. There is no doubt of God's existence, according to this explanation, but there is doubt concerning his readiness to help. These thoughts are expressed in the following lines of the first part: *Ő odafönn / merev csillámú közöny* 'He above there / is coldness stiffly glancing'. The desperate exclamation in the third part *Ide se lát! / Ide se lát! / Alszik és álmában épít / ablaktalan tükör-palotát!* 'Not even here he sees! / Not even here he sees! / He sleeps and in his dream builds / a mirror-palace without any windows!' can also be understand as an echo of his indifference towards human destiny. These lines involve extremely bitter accusations. This God is not involved in the fate of the human. That is why he does not need any windows and the reason, why his palace is built by mirrors, is to mirror himself. That is, he does not care about anyone but himself. These lines portray a selfish, conceited, unfeeling and narcissistic God. In other respects, the words *tükör-palota* 'mirror-palace' could contain another meaning: the human, standing outside, mirrors himself in it. The mirror-palace can reflect the true face of the human. This other essential theme represents the idea of an indifferent God.

There is a further interpretation supported by the most central verse of the poem: *Ki egét elhagyta, lássa: / habos örvény a lakása, / fedelének éj az ácsa, / sötétség a kalapácsa* 'He, who his heaven abandoned, may see: / his home is a lathering whirlpool, / the night is the carpenter of his roof / the darkness is his hammer'. According to this depiction, it is the human himself, who lost something, possibly his faith in God. In this case, it is not God, but the human who is indifferent. God is dead – he died in the sorrow caused by disbelief: *sebzetten bukdos a légen által / és rekedt, színtelen víjjogással / lezuhan a jég alá! / lezuhan a jég alá!* 'wounded he tumbles in the air / and with a throaty, toneless screaming / he falls under the ice! / he falls under the ice!' When the human realizes what he has lost, it is then too late. That is why he is always condemned to search for that he had once lost. Finally, he must resign himself to his fate: there is only the memory of an eternal moment left.

This third thematic possibility is closely related to what Weöres says about penitence and the grace of God. I think that both these concepts are seen in the *Harmadik szimfónia* 'Third Symphony', i.e. penitence for the lost spiritual home and a plea for the grace of God: *Kérlelem, keresem: / ápolná kegye-sen / sápadt kis mécsesem fénysugarát* 'I beg him, I seek him / kindly take care of / the gleam of my little misty night-light'. A god who left for the eternal darkness is, however, helpless, because he cannot redeem the world, and because of this the last hope is lost.

All these different hypotheses of the theme of the poem originate from the images of represented reality. There is, however, a common feature throughout, which is the feeling of hopelessness and a sort of nostalgia. From this we can conlude that a reading based on semantical coherencies reveals the negative aspects of the theme.

When, however, we begin with the primary structuring principle, that is, the principle of contrast, we feel that the meaning of the words becomes perfectly indifferent. The continuously-repeated thesis-antithesis relations, so to say, wear down the meaning. It is only the form of the words that remains untouched. By form I mean all the types of rhythm, that is, the parallelism, the poetic measure and the rhythm created by the acoustic elements. Because we cannot conclude any non-ambiguous meaning using the words themselves, the words become of secondary importance. Rhythm, then, is not only related to the text but also to that process in which the words lose their meaning turning the different rhythmical appearances of the poem into a symphony. As a result of this rhythmical regularity, the oppositions create a basis for the harmony we feel emanating from the poem. As long as we have rhythm, we have life. A total hopelessness exists only when the rhythm is gone. The musical rhythm, then, shapes hopelessness into hope and gives the theme a positive perspective. A negative semantic context becomes positive through the form itself, and, similar to music, the poem becomes a source of pleasure.

Bata wrote that oppositions can only be dissolved by Jesus Christ and that thesis and antithesis together do not create an additional antithesis, but instead, through the energy belonging to Jesus, create a unity from these two. The uniting energy is love, the most essential aspect of Jesus Christ's character, according to Bata (1983:1076). Weöres' religiosity needs to be understood in this way. He himself said as follows: "I write in order to display and to better approach this element of Jesus from somebody, from anybody, from myself or some other people"(Cs. Szabó 1993:40). As love, this appointed element of Jesus, is not a category for the intellect, but for the emotions, the only way to comprehend it is with our feelings. The hypotheses concerning the theme above, both those concerning the semantical elements and those concerning the musical form, support this manner of interpretation. Weöres' own words also shed light upon the most essential aspect in which the theme, in its deepest complexity, is reflected: "It is a particular experience of God which we bear within us and which I express with my art. I try to fetch from that almost unnameable well of the subconscious, where we practically cannot see any difference between things any more. [...] This is a sphere of soul, from which my poetry arises, from my intention, and where there is no earthly reason for any separation. The artist is able to give this experience to the people, and from this, much hard-heartedness can be dissolved that people now feel against each other. I am working hard to bring this sphere of man within reach by the means of visualization, and not by a type of thinking" (Győr 1993:108).

5.2.2 The Poem as Part of Weöres' lifework

The poem *Harmadik szimfónia* 'Third Symphony' was first published in the volume *Medusa*, in 1943, in the same volume that contained the *Rongyszőnyeg* 'Rag-carpet' cycle, which included 120 pieces at that time, a number that increased to 160 in the two-volume *Egybegyűjtött írások* 'Collected Writings', published in 1970.

The years 1943 and 1944 brought about several decisive changes in Weöres' life. In 1944 he left Pécs for Budapest and in these years also found his own individual voice (Kenyeres 1974:276). Though Hamvas in his memorable critiques of the *Medusa*-volume rejected many of its poems, he still recognizes the true poet in Weöres: "... Weöres is a poet for whom the maturity of the human must be on a level with that of the poetry. In poetry of full value the states of human fate and the stages of poetry must coincide with each other. They do this in Weöres. That is why Weöres is a poet of full value. He is the only one like this amongst the other poets of today" (Hamvas 1990:215).

Most of the poems in the *Medusa*-volume were written between 1939 and 1943. The shadow of the Second World War did not such an effect on this volume as on the volume *Elysium*, published in 1944. In poems with titles such as *Háborús jegyzetek* 'War Notes', *Elesett katonák* 'Fallen Soldiers', *Szirénák légitámadáskor* 'Sirens with Air-raid' and the poem *A reménytelenség könyve* 'The Book of Hopelessness' the shock caused by the war is expressed. This is unlike the poems of the *Medusa*, which are related to other spheres of thought. These poems give evidence of a process where perfectly shaped formal elements join a content which can be expressed by words and hence become of equal significance. This unique poetical experience is discussed in the previously cited letter to Várkonyi (1976:388-389).

The fact that the poem *Harmadik szimfónia* 'Third Symphony' is very much inspired by the Psalms, has been indicated earlier. Other poems in the *Medusa* also have similies to the Psalms. Actually, compared to other volumes of Weöres, most of his poems dealing with God and religion in general are to be found in this volume. According to Hamvas, the two first poems *Ha majd testemre rög borul* 'When my body is in the soil' (EI I:299) and *Nem nyúlsz le értem* 'You do not reach down for me' (EI I:300) are reminiscences, and it would have been better to burn them (Hamvas 1990:214). I do not want to refute his opinion. However, as several motifs of these poems written in 1942 foreshadow the *Harmadik szimfónia* 'Third Symphony', written a year later, we must deal with these poems, too. The first lines of the poem *Nem nyúlsz le értem* 'You do not reach down for me' read as follows:

Nem nyúlsz le értem, Istenem,
kezem hiába tartom.
De én mindig szólítalak,
mint gerle, hívó hangon.

You do not reach down for me, my God,
in vain I hold my hands.
All the time I call you, though
like a turtle-dove, with a calling voice.

The poem *Vonj sugaradba* 'Draw me in your rays' also alludes to certain motifs of the *Harmadik szimfónia* 'Third Symphony':

Vonj sugaradba, Istenem!
mint madár a fészkére szállnék hozzád,
de látod, a rét örömei közt
elpattant a szárnyam csontja.

Draw me in your rays, my God!
like a bird on his nest I should fly to you,
but, see, amongst the joys of the meadow,
I broke my wings.

In the words a *rét örömei* 'the joys of the meadow' an association can be freely made to another phrase, much more common in everyday use: *a lét örömei* 'the joys of life'. In this case, the image of the bird that broke his wings might refer to the man who, in the whirling or the whirlpool of his existence, lost his faith. This feasible parallel then connects one of the themathic lines ascribed to the *Harmadik szimfónia* 'Third Symphony'.

Many studies have dealt with the poem *De profundis* (EI I:302-303), also written in 1942. It is striking, however, that in his critique Hamvas neither refers to this poem, nor to the *Harmadik szimfónia* 'Third Symphony'. János Reisinger (1983:67) calls this poem "the poem of the pains". And in Weöres words, "the total hopelessness of life is included in it" (Liptay 1993:419). A different first line, included when the poem was published for the first time, clearly shows its religious character: *Földön élek, a mennyből kiűzve* 'I live on the Earth, driven out from heaven' (Bata 1979:41). The pain caused by the cruelty of man – also possibly the cruelty of the war – cannot be dissolved in the hope of redemption because God is helpless, too. This was one of the themes described in the *Harmadik szimfónia* 'Third Symphony'. We can also find the trope *szikla* 'rock' with a reference to a related context in both of the poems. The lines *A szikla, ha rávésed jajodat, / többé nem szikla: élő te magad* 'If you cut your pain on the rock, / it is not a rock any more, it turns to yourself', as seen in the first part of the *Harmadik szimfónia* 'Third Symphony' is closely connected contextually to the following lines of the *De profoundis*:

Sziklát zúznak, föld húsába törnek:
nem fáj az a kőnek, sem a földnek,
de fáj énnekem.

They smash the rock into pieces, they break into the flesh of the earth,
it does not give pain to the rock, nor the earth,
but it gives pain to me.

Due to the fact that God is named by name in the poem *De Profoundis*, an interpretation of it becomes much easier than an interpretation of the *Harmadik szimfónia* 'Third Symphony'. The form of the two poems are also different. Unlike the *Harmadik szimfónia* 'Third Symphony', the arrangement of the verses in the poem *De profoundis*, with six lines in every strophe, displays a regular form. The poem *Vezeklés* 'Penitence' (EI I:356), written in 1936, brings these characteristics of the two poems into harmony: this poem has a regular form but it does not name God by name. Owing to these latter characteristics, an interpretation of it is as difficult as that of the *Harmadik szimfónia* 'Third Symphony'. The tropes *madárka* 'little bird' and *hatalmas* 'mighty one' in the *Vezeklés* 'Penitence' also relate to the *Harmadik szimfónia* 'Third Symphony':
Ó tiszta ég derűs, komoly magánya!
ó távolságtól kékült levegő!
oly messze vagy, hogy a lent lebegő
madárka kettős-ívű gyönge szárnya

reád-tapadtnak látszik, te hatalmas.

O, serene and solemn loneliness of a cloudless sky!
o, air, bluish in the distance!
you are so far away, that the double-arched weak wings
of the little bird floating below

seems as they would be adhered to you, you mighty one.

A further characteristic of the poem *Vezeklés* 'Penitence', the nostalgia for a former peace of mind, thematically relates it to the *Harmadik szimfónia* 'Third Symphony'.

This same theme is seen in the poem *A Venus bolygóhoz* 'To Venus, the Planet' (EI I:347), written in 1942. The suffering that is caused by the fact that we are cast on earth becomes unendurable without faith:

Istenhez futnék s a magam gyúrta istenek
    elbotlatják lábamat –
ó jaj, tudni nem merek és hinni nem bírok!

I would run to God and the gods I clayed myself
    make my feet stumble –
oh, I dare not know, and I cannot believe!

Many poems of the *Rongyszőnyeg* 'Rag-carpet' cycle display related motifs to those found in the *Harmadik szimfónia* 'Third Symphony'. Such example is piece 21, which begins with the words *Te égi gyerek* 'You heavenly child' (EI I:385). The following line in this poem *Most sorsom a föld, hol a vágy üvölt* 'Now my fate is the Earth, with its screaming desires' is easy to associate with the line *Vendégként sétáltam én az élet kínja közt* 'I walked like a quest amongst the pains of life' in the *A Venus bolygóhoz* 'To Venus, the Planet' and with the central strophe of the *Harmadik szimfónia* 'Third Symphony'. The trope *kút* 'well' in piece 21 of the *Rongyszőnyeg* 'Rag-carpet' cycle alludes to that in the *Harmadik szimfónia* 'Third Symphony':

Idők elején álmodtalak én
világ-ölű mennyei kútnál,
fény sávjai közt, tűz ágai közt
féltő szívemben aludtál.

I dreamed of you in the beginning of the times
at the well with the world on his lap,

amongst the streaks of the light, amongst the branches of the fire,
you slept in my caring heart.

The motif of the meeting with the heavenly child in this poem of the
Rongyszőnyeg 'Rag-carpet'-cycle also includes a possible redemption:

Te égi gyerek, te angyali-jó,
mért jöttél szökve utánam?
Óvd lépteimet, mert sűlyedek, ó,
sűlyedek az éjszakában.

You heavenly child, you angel-like good,
why did you, in flight, come after me?
Guard my steps, for I am sinking now,
I am sinking in the night.

The search for faith in God relates piece 76 of the *Rongyszőnyeg* 'Rag-carpet'
cycle to one of the motifs of the *Harmadik szimfónia* 'Third Symphony':

Már csak hitet szeretnél,
szolgálnád Ég-Urát,
minden hiút levetnél,
viselnél szőrcsuhát.

Nothing else but faith you'd want
to serve the Lord above
vanity you'd get rid of
to wear a monk's habit.

In piece 144 of the *Rongyszőnyeg* 'Rag-carpet' cycle (EI I:443) we recognize
the motif of the little bird, the peacock and the wounded bird which falls under
the ice from the *Harmadik szimfónia* 'Third Symphony' and the bird with the
broken wings from the poems *Vezeklés* 'Penitence' and *Vonj sugaradba*
'Draw me in your rays':

Mikor anyából földre tettek,
hová keverték röptömet?
Embernek többé ne szülessek,
szárny nélkül élni nem lehet.

When they put me on the earth from the mother,
where did they mix up my flight?
I will not be born to a man any more,
one cannot live without wings.

Thus, many pieces of the *Rongyszőnyeg* 'Rag-carpet' cycle are thematically connected to the *Harmadik szimfónia* 'Third Symphony'. We have also found that many poems in the volume *Medusa* are directly or indirectly related to God. Weöres was engaged in psalms and he also had written many psalm-paraphrases throughout his life (Liptay 1993:419). In 1935, in a poem entitled *Zsoltár* 'Psalm' (EI I:109-110) he prays for God's grace in order to accept God's will, while still doubting his existence at the same time:

Törd meg kevélységemet,
törd meg kevélységemet,
mély megbánást adj nekem.
Nyársat nyeltem én,
derekam kemény:
mért nem szabad
súlyod alatt
meghajolnom, Istenem?

Break my haughtiness,
break my haughtiness,
give me deep regret.
I am stiff as a poker,
my waist is proud:
why can I not bend
under your power
my God?

However, it is the last verse of the poem *Zsoltár* 'Psalm' that most clearly shows a certain themathic relationship to the *Harmadik szimfónia* 'Third Symphony':

Legyen meg akaratod,
legyen meg akaratod,
ha vesznem kell, jól legyen:
tán kárhozásom
áldás lesz máson –

de ha énrám
kincset bíztál,
ments meg immár, Istenem.

Thy will be done,
thy will be done,
if I must be lost, would it be in the right way:
maybe my damnation
will be a blessing for someone –
but if you left me
a treasure,
save me then, my God.

The same motif of saving and salvation can be seen in the following lines of the *Harmadik szimfónia* 'Third Symphony': *kérlelem, keresem: / ápolná kegyesen / sápadt kis mécsesem fénysugarát* 'I beg him, I seek him: / kindly take care of / the gleam of my little misty night-light'. The tropes *sápadt kis mécsesem* 'my little misty night-light' in this poem, and the trope *kincs* 'treasure' in the *Zsoltár* 'Psalm' can be regarded as symbols for faith and for hope. A motif of belief and a hope in salvation can be seen in both of these two poems. Besides the individual who seeks for a faith in God, in the *Zsoltár* 'Psalm' however, the poet also speaks: the poet, in possession of a treasure, i.e. his talent for writing which he got from God, does not want to be lost, because if he becomes lost the gift from God would also be lost.

The poem *A reménytelenség könyve* 'The Book of Hopelessness (EI I:700-707), has a much more different approach to God. Tamás (1978:55) calls this poem the "document on Fascism", and not without reason, as the poem was written in 1944 when the last hope was lost for many people:

Ne várj csodát:
mibelőlünk meghalt az Isten,
mibelőlünk kihalt az Isten.

Hited arra jó, hogy csörgesd, játssz vele,
hogy könyörögj valakihez, ki nem több, mint egy kitömött madár,
mint egy kóró, melyen szél fütyül.

Do not await wonder:
God is dead in us,
God has died from us.

220

Your faith is good to rattle, to play with it,
to pray to someone, who is nothing more but a stuffed bird,
like a dry stalk on which the wind is whistling.

An association from a stuffed bird to a little bird is created here. In the *A reménytelenség könyve* 'The Book of Hopelessness', however, we cannot find any positive images. On that account, we might question, as to whether a faith in God is now replaced by atheism? But, as Weöres (1993b:368) once declared: "The Book of Hopelessness is one of my most optimistic poems, but nobody has noticed this yet. [...] The modern and technological man lives in waiting and in hope, in a 'later perhaps' instead of a 'now', but he, who does not wait and does not hope but instead lives in the shadow and does his work in piece, is happy, harmonious and complete in his soul". To this Weöres adds the following remarks: "Naturally, I have pessimistic poems, too, such as the *De profundis*, the *Merülő Saturnus* 'Saturn Submerging', but I do not have a single unbelieving one".

In addition to the appointed contexts of motifs, the place of the *Harmadik szimfónia* 'Third Symphony' in Weöres' life-work is also determined by the genres. The poem, according to the title, is a symphony, i.e. one of Weöres' twelve symphonies. Bata (1998:12) lets us know that these symphonies were organized between 1968-69, which means that pieces written before then were arranged together and given with specific titles. In the two-volume *Egybegyűjtött írások* 'Collected Writings', published in 1970, we can find ten such symphonies, which together with one more poem, became published in a volume entitled *Tizenegy szimfónia* 'Eleven Symphonies' in 1973. The *Tizenkettedik szimfónia* 'Twelfth Symphony', missing from this volume and written in 1970, however, is included in the three-volume *Egybegyűjtött írások* 'Collected Writings'.

This title of the volume *Tizenegy szimfónia* 'Eleven Symphonies', naturally, indicates the musical character of the included poems. These are compositions of some length, each consisting of at least three parts. Their structure originates from that of the sonata, as discussed earlier. Weöres' symphonies are, however, not only symphonies on the basis of this musical form. The musical character of these symphonies is not barely a formal category. It also becomes a component of the subject matter. This occurs through the paradoxal ambition of making music, an originally wordless form of expression, speak. Thus, Weöres undertakes the bold enterprise of shaping the unspeakable into words.

The subtitle of the *Első szimfónia* 'First Symphony' is *A négy évszak* 'The Four Seasons' (EI I:115-1120). The title of the third poem, dealing with the autumn, is *Valse Triste*, written about 1933. László Lator (1996:11) calls this poem a "symphony in miniature" and he also believes that this poem is a *tableau vivant* for the *Harmadik szimfónia* 'Third Symphony'. Lator points to the constant change of the motifs and he talks about a "serious psalm-like voice of an universal decay". Undoubtedly, the poem, similar to the *Harmadik szimfónia* 'Third Symphony' refers to the transitoriness of life and also to the motif of remembrance:

Az ember szíve kivásik.
Egyik nyár, akár a másik.
Mindegy, hogy rég volt, vagy nem-rég.
Lyukas és fagyos az emlék.

The heart of man wears out.
This summer is just like any other.
No matter if it was a long time ago or not.
Holed and frosty is the memory.

The five parts of the *Második szimfónia* 'Second Symphony' (EI I:208:215) deal with the creation of the world, and through the scenes of the Old and the New Testaments, show the path of man, who, chased out from Eden, "replaced his piece with suffering". It is also about the useless fight of man, because, as stated in the last part of the poem, *a harc az Istené!* 'the struggle belongs to God!'.

The *Negyedik szimfónia* 'Fourth Symphony' (EI II:50-54) also treats existential issues, in spite of the subtitle, *Hódolat Arany Jánosnak* 'Homage to János Arany' – János Arany (1817-1882), one of the most outstanding poets of Hungary. The first two parts, using the motifs of some of Arany's main works, imitate Arany's style of writing. In the third part, however, the poet in general, that is, Arany together with Weöres, speaks, where "he" complains of a missing reading public. In the fourth part, as Bata (1979:142) also puts it, Arany's life is recorded through Weöres' views. These lines are about man's fruitless fight with his fate. In the course of some fifty years, man, growing old, is thrown into the fire, like worthless lumber.

The five parts of the *Ötödik szimfónia* 'Fifth Symphony'(EI II:139-148) are much more optimistic. This positive content is already expressed in the titles: *Az öröm* 'The Joy', *A tánc* 'The Dance', *Az álmok* 'The Dreams', *A csillagok* 'The Stars' and *Az egyesülés* 'Being United'. The former title of the part *A csillagok* 'The Stars' was *A sorsangyalok* 'The Angels of Fortune'. Inevitably, we may have some difficulty in interpreting this poem. When Weöres (WW:128-132) explains it, he also discusses how he wrote the poem. He adapted a type of Surrealistic automatic writing, arranging the words in accordance with a series of numbers that had been fixed in advance. Meaning, as a result, becomes accidental, like the carpet of the human life, woven by the angels of fortune.

The title of the first part of the *Hatodik szimfónia* 'Sixth Symphony' (EI II:156-164) is *A teremtés* 'The Creation'. The theme in the *Ötödik szimfónia* 'Third Symphony' is continued, using the angels of fortune, the *moiras* in this part. The archaic timelessness of the second part, *Az ősidő* 'The Ancient Times' is, in the third part, *A történelmi korszak* 'Historical Time' transformed to a limited time in the human life. Ultimately, in the last part *Az állandó a változóban* 'The Constant in the Changing', time metamorphoses to space, because an incomprehensible time can only through space, i. e. the inner space of man, be formed into something comprehensible, that is the unceaselessly changing into the unchanging.

The subtitle of the *Hetedik szimfónia* 'Seventh Symphony' (EI II:229-238) is *Mária mennybemenetele, Édesanyám emlékének* 'The Assumption of Mary, To the Memory of my Mother'. The poem was originally written on the occasion of the death of Weöres' mother. In the poem she becomes identified with Maria, Jesus Christ's mother and as a result becomes to a mother to all the humans.

The *Nyolcadik szimfónia* 'Eighth Symphony' (EI II:347-353) also has a subtitle: *Krúdy Gyula emlékére* 'To the Memory of Gyula Krúdy'. Gyula Krúdy, 1878-1933, was a Hungarian writer and journalist. The third part of the symphony contains a wish of getting away from the present, and entering another time, which could also be that time when Krúdy lived.

The titles of the themes in the *Kilencedik szimfónia* 'Ninth Symphony' (EI II:433-440), subtitled *A szörnyeteg koporsója* 'The Coffin of the Monstrosity', also relate to the musical term symphony: *Andante, Variazioni, Scherzo* and *Finale*. Each of the parts have subtitles, which also indicate the theme of these parts: *Emlékezés a gázkamrákra és a keretlegényekre* 'Remembering the Gas-chambers and the Henchmen', *Néger rabszolgák éneke* 'The Song of the Negro Slaves', *Huizinga a nemzetiszocializmust a viceházmesterek forradalmának nevezte* 'Huizinga called the National-Socialism for the revolution of the vice-house-porters', *A szörnyeteg szétzúzódása* 'The Monstrosity Smashes to Pieces'. The dark ages of history and Fascism, in the first place, are depicted by these themes when "the world of man dies out but the gas-masters are alive". The *Finale,* with the subtitle *A szörnyeteg szétzúzódása* 'The Monstrosity Smashes to Pieces', points to a specific theme indicated by the subtitle: every tenth word of the part comes from a novel *Elnémult harangok* 'The Bells which Became Silent' of Viktor Rákosi (Hornyik 1993:88) and which also originated from the concept of objective automatic writing (Kenyeres 1983:108).

Though the *Tizedik szimfónia* 'Tenth Symphony' (EI II:461-464) is free verse, its three themes still dictate the rhythm: *Largo, Andante* and *Presto.*

After the two first slow parts, which are reflections on the vanity of life, the fast but also the shortest third part follows, expressing the last acquiescence of fate: *A világ négy sarka lobog, s akár a cserép, izzottam a lángban: végre kiégtem* 'The four corners of the world are ablaze, and I, like a tile, glowed too in the flame: I died away at long last'.

The four themes of the *Tizenegyedik szimfónia* 'Eleventh Symphony' (EI III:413-417) are as follows: *Csillagzene* 'The Music of the Stars', *Körséta* 'Round-tour', *Iram* 'Speed' and *Csillagzene finale* 'The Music of the Stars, Finale'. I think that these subtitles reveal a method of interpretation: this chain of words, often put together without any grammatical rules, are as a matter of fact stars, the light in which this soundless music is born. Some words, not only because of their semantic meaning, but also because they are frequently repeated, portray apocalyptical horizons both within and outside man: *végtelen* 'endless', *hatalmas* 'immense', *messzeség* 'remoteness'. The same tendency of separating the forms of the words from their meanings in order to transform the poem to music can be demonstrated using the *Tizenkettedik szimfónia* 'Twelfth Symphony (EI III:417-422), too.

In sum, throughout Weöres' twelve symphonies both the compositional arrangement of the parts according to the principles of music, and the thematic issues show common characteristics. Through these symphonies Weöres wishes to approach such subjects which are difficult to express through words. Words, because of the clear sense of logic and rationality they include, in fact cover up the most essential, non-intellectual issues one wants to voice. That is why the words must be re-composed, i.e. caught in a form which can formulate what is most fundamental. Different forms of music, like the symphony are capable of this. Weöres' symphonies create a form arising from the weight of questions concerning the ontological essence of human existence.

5.2.3 Weöres' Philosophy of Poetics

The poem *Az áramlás szobra* 'The Statue of the Stream', initially published with the title *Eidolon*, puts the content seen in the musical form of the *Harmadik szimfónia* 'Third Symphony' into words. According to Kenyeres (1983:116), Weöres, in the poem *Eidolon*,"experienced the philosophical possibilities of a concentrated poetical expression, when he asked if the essential movement can be caught by static words, and if an answering lingual duplicate, i.e. eidolon could be done on motion, as a 'fictional reality'". The concept of movement in such poems is realized by words and by a free use of the grammatical rules, through which the components building the words are connected to each other in an unusual way. Consequently, these words are very difficult both to understand and translate. The first compound word *nyug-*

mozgás [lit.] 'rest-movement', really, consists of two nouns *nyugalom* 'rest' and *mozgás* 'movement', but the first word *nyugalom* 'rest' lost its second half. A new concept had been created, where the structural union of two opposite ideas stands for the most essential issue. In my opinion, in the *Harmadik szimfónia* 'Third Symphony' where "everything is in a continuous change", according to Weöres as well (Liptay 1993:419), this same *nyugmozgás* 'rest-movement' is expressed.

As pointed out above, the representation of movement in some kind of oscillation between opposite concepts in our mind gives the result that an interpretation of a given work becomes difficult. In piece 14 in the *Rongyszőnyeg* 'Rag-carpet' cycle (EI I:382) everything is also in continuous movement, movement whose reason "only God understands":

Minden árad, fut, remeg,
rádnéz, aztán ellebeg,
rádnéz, aztán ellebeg,
csak az Isten érti meg.

Everything is rising, running and trembling,
it looks at you, and then it floats away,
it looks at you, and then it floats away,
only God understands, why.

A remote and mighty union of the "hunter and the wild", the concepts of rest and movement, and the idea that everything is identical to everything, this God included, points to the philosophy of Pantheism. But we can also clearly point to the concept of the *tat twam asi* from Hinduism, i.e. the identity of the soul and a God outside us, the complementary dualism of the *yin and yang*. The unity of the latter is represented by the *tao* in Chinese philosophy. "The tao is the law of dialectical movement in the world. Everything is in change in the world, it arises and dies, and this means that everything turns into its opposite, yet these oppositions create a oneness, and this is the inherent law of all things [...] The wise man [...] has only one duty, and this is to recognize and passively look at how the law works ..." as Tőkei (1994:156-157) explained the main thoughts of this philosophy in his concluding remarks of Weöres' translation of the *Tao Te Ching*.

Several motifs in the *Harmadik szimfónia* 'Third Symphony' are related to the philosophies of Hinduism, Buddhism and Taoism. One example is the motif of emptiness, seen in the third and eleventh verses and another example is the motif of the hope of sleep, seen in the twelfth verse. Through these motifs, we can arrive at nirvana, the ultimate union of the individual and the Brahman. Another correspondence is revealed in the lines *Itt minden örömbe / bogárka vész, / s a fájdalom mélye / tiszta méz* 'Here, little beetle / falls into every joy, / and the deep of sorrow is / pure honey'. I think that these lines symbolize the tenet of suffering, the *dukkha* of Buddhism, and the trope of honey becomes clear in Hamvas' (1992:I:417) interpretation: "It is not the mind that craves the honey, the *mahdu*, but the heart that knows that there is a Golden Age and a Paradise and a salvation, in the same way as there is mild wind and ripe fruit and song and laughter". The motif of the veil in the first verse of the third part suggests the concept of the veil of Maya in Hinduism, which covers reality with its veil and what is seen is only an image of reality, that is, illusion.

Thus, the motif of the veil can be related to a search for something that, in fact, does not exist. This is an issue which can be related to certain thoughts within Christianity. According to Bata, as cited before, the only union of the thesis and the antithesis is created by the love of Jesus Christ. We have also pointed to the fact that, unlike the psalm-paraphrases, neither God nor Jesus are named by name in the *Harmadik szimfónia* 'Third Symphony'. The dynamics between the opposing concepts, however, show a tendency of incessantly searching to define just this unnamed third subject. This third subject, however, cannot be named, because in contrast to the thesis and the antithesis, it cannot be experienced. As a result it transcends the oppositions, moving towards a permanent and transcendental reality.

In the work *Summa Theologica*, St. Thomas of Aquinas proves the existence of God in five ways. The first way is through the origin of movement. As everything that moves, as a matter of fact, also moves something else, these secondary items must be moved by some primary thing, i. e. Jesus Christ, according to St. Thomas of Aquinas. Thus, the movement of opposite poles points back to the cause of movement. Keith Ward (1987:137) writes the following concerning St. Thomas of Aquinas idea of God: "[...] the only intelligible view is to say that it is not the sort of being which could logically be caused". As a result, God is "a subsistent form, the pure act of being, fully actual cause of all derived beings" (Ward 1987:138).

Related ideas can be seen in Søren Kirkegaard's philosophy. According to him, we cannot experience God objectively, because God is a subject. That is, only he who searches God subjectively can find him. Because, however, this search takes place objectively amongst real things, there is always a feeling of uncertainty about it (BEV: 290).

Using these thoughts of Kierkegaard, another dimension of this philosophical approach opens up: to search for the non-existing amongst existing things is an absurd situation which creates anxiety and fear in us. Relating this to Weöres' poem, I think that these ideas of existentialism are most clearly reflected in the most central strophe. This strophe is an expression of how man ultimately becomes conscious about her real existential situation, that is, the fact that she is totally alone in all of her decisions. Beney (1990:206-207) argues that in this second part of the poem, the elements of nature, such as the peacock and the rose, do not leave the individual, and as a result express a sympathy for her fate. Contrary to Beney's opinion, I believe, that these lines put a feeling of loneliness into words. The word *veled* 'with you', in fact contradicts its own semantic meaning, and thus expresses the opposite state of isolation. With the use of rhyme-words at the end of the lines, the complaint of the lonely man is then echoed by the surrounding elements of nature. Nothwithstanding, Beney also points to the fact that sympathy is helpless throughout, that is, it does not give any real help. Consequently, the word *veled* 'with you' as a result of its formal arrangement, reveals another meaning than it really means. This is also a form of expressing contrast, the primary structuring principle here.

"Faith is the abandonment of man's own security and the readiness to find security only in the unseen beyond, in God. This means that faith is security where no security can be seen, it is as Luther said, the readiness to enter confidently into the darkness of the future", as Bultmann (1958:40-41) put it, while aiming at syncretize Christianity and the philosophy of existentialism. According to Bultmann, human existence is liable to God's existence. Paradoxically, however, the man, though realizing the fact that his faith in God cannot give him absolute security, keeps it as well. Only through this, namely, can he gain real freedom, which helps him to understand his own existential situation better. In addition, this understanding signifies a new openness towards the future, too: "Faith as openness to the future is freedom from the past, because it is faith in the forgiveness of sins; it is freedom from the enslaving chains of the past. It is freedom from ourselves as the old selves, and for ourselves as the new selves" (Bultmann 1958:78).

I believe that this synthesis of Christianity and the philosophy of existentialism as worded by Bultmann, is evident in the third part of the *Harmadik szimfónia* 'Third Symphony'. The motif of keeping watch over what remained also indicates the end of the search. Man at last found the *pille-por* 'butterfly-dust' in himself, the symbol of the eternal moment, the Absolute. When he understands that the Absolute is within him and it works through him, he then also understands that his duty is to bring this Absolute, the divine essence, to the surface.

6 Conclusion

6.1 Summary

As pointed out in the introductory chapters, the aim of this work is to shed light upon the focal points of the poetical form and philosophy in the poetry of Sándor Weöres. Any desire for completeness that could be indicated by the title, however, stops short of a philosophy, where there only is *A teljesség felé* 'Towards the Absolute' [lit. 'Towards completeness'] and where everything is at the same time its opposite. Thus, completeness is not unambiguously completeness, either. Or as Weöres put it in the poem *Dalok Naconxypan-ból* 'Songs from Naconxypan':

Szemeddel az egész tengert halászod
s horoggal mit fogsz? Egynéhány halat.

You fish in the whole sea with your eyes
and what do you catch? One or two fish.

The desire for completeness, then, is limited by such factors. Consequently, the analyses of the six poems are based on the thematical spheres which, in my view, most completely reflect a philosophy involved with poetical form.

Although I am aware of the fact that other spheres can also be added to these thematical spheres – the scale of this work sets limits to the desire for completeness, as well – I am dealing with four large issues: the question of impersonality, homelessness, the opposition of chaos and harmony, and the search for the Absolute. The chapter dealing with the question of impersonality approaches this theme in three ways: becoming someone else in second person singular, metamorphosing into somebody else and becoming someone else in another form. These thematical spheres are represented by the poems: *Rongyszőnyeg 76* 'Rag-carpet 76', *A benső végtelen* 'The Infinite Inside' and the *Barbár dal* 'Barbarian Song'. The topic of homelessness is illustrated by the poem *Magna Meretrix*, the poem *Atlantis* is related to the question of chaos and harmony and the *Harmadik szimfónia* 'Third Symphony' is related to the search of the Absolute.

Though based on these thematical spheres, the analyses take their starting-point from the elements of form. This reciprocal style of study can strongly be ascribed to my ambition of demonstrating a synthesis of the formal and the philosophical issues in Weöres' poetry. My investigations, however, are strongly influenced by Weöres' own views on the poem, where form and structure always played a very important part. In addition, the complex analysing methods of text-grammatics and text-stylistics, including the essential concepts of the text organization principle and focal quality also exercise a strong influence on my analyses.

The points of discussion are arranged in the same way for each of the six poems. The two main parts deal with the text and the world of the text. Starting from the text, the fields of analyses are as follows: the structure and the shape of the writing, the represented elements of reality, the rhetorical-stylistic structures, the metrical structures and the grammatical structures. The represented elements of reality, as these also define the semantic context, let us arrive at the primary structuring principle and the focal quality. These two determinants govern the following levels, too. The part dealing with the world of the text is divided into the following three sections: the theme, the poem as a part of Weöres' life work and Weöres' philosophy of poetics. This last part is also a type of summary of the previous parts.

6. 2 Discussion

As pointed out in the introductory chapters, not only the parts dealing with Weöres' philosophy aim for a sort of a synthesis, but also the conclusion of this work. While, however, the former synthesis touches primarily on one special poem, this synthesis at hand is based on several levels which are common to the six poems. In my appoach, I try to reveal common stylistic features in each of these levels, i.e. giving an approach to Weöres' individual style. Zoltán Szabó (1988:138) argues that a certain individual style is made up of structures which are to be found in every work of the specific writer studied. Due to the fact that the description of individual style, according to Szabó, is also based on stylistic analyses, we cannot claim completeness here either, as we are dealing with only six poems. The specific aspects of this thesis which relate each poems under discussion to other poems of Weöres belonging in the same context aims, however, at expanding this level of approach. In this discussion I will give a summary of the several levels, concentrating on the means by which the primary structuring principle and focal quality are represented. These two particulars will also be illustrated by some examples.

The first chapter within the main chapter of the text discusses the structure and shape of the writing. Apparently, all of the three poems dealing with the forms of impersonality are characterized by regularity, clearness, symmetry and proportionality. Each of the four strophes of the *Rongyszőnyeg 76* 'Rag-carpet 76', for example, consists of four lines, and the identical first and fourth verses create a frame for the poem:

A hársfa mind virágzik,
a csíz mind énekel,
a lomb sugárban ázik,
csak szíved alszik el.

All the limetrees are in blossom,
all the siskins are singing,
the leaves bathe in sunshine,
only your heart goes to sleep.

These same characteristics can be seen in the other poems contextually similar to the poems at hand. The next three poems, representing the thematical spheres of homelessness, chaos and harmony and the search for the Absolute, are, however, not regular, clear, symmetrical and proportional at first sight. Still, on closer inspection we cannot say that the poem *Magna Meretrix*, with eight lines in most of the strophes, the poem *Atlantis*, where several formal representations of the numbers three and seven create harmony, or the poem *Harmadik szimfónia* 'Third Symphony', with a central strophe as the focus of the symmetry, are irregular. Nor are the poems belonging to this same context irregular. The sentence in italics in the poem *Néma zene* 'Silent Music', clearly reflects this well-weighed formal arrangement: *atlantisz elsűlyedt mikor történt nem ismeri senki* 'atlantis sunk when it happened nobody knows'. We could also mention the symphonies related to the *Harmadik szimfónia* 'Third Symphony', whose formal composition originates from music. In sum, there is a regularity concerning the structure and shape of the writing in all the analysed poems. Even in poems that do not show this regularity at once, these characteristics are implicitly present.

The represented elements of reality are connected to a particular text organization principle which in its part determines the focal quality. I have pointed out contrast in the poems *Rongyszőnyeg 76* 'Rag-carpet 76', *A benső végtelen* 'The Infinite Inside', *Magna Meretrix* and the *Harmadik szimfónia* 'Third Symphony' as the main structuring principle. In two poems, *Barbár ének* 'Barbarian Song' and *Atlantis*, the text is based on parallelism. Contrast as the primary structuring principle gives rise to the focal qualities as follows: a sentence in the *Rongyszőnyeg 76* 'Rag-carpet 76' (*csak szíved alszik el* 'only your heart goes to sleep'), the title of the *A benső végtelen* 'The Infinite Inside', and an interrogative sentence in the *Magna Meretrix*. (*E világot feleségül / az ész hozománya nélkül / minek vettem?* 'Why did I marry this world / without the dowry of / common sense?'). In the *Harmadik szimfónia* 'Third Symphony', the poem where everything is in ceaseless movement and change, no focus could be established, and for this reason I decided that it belonged to the reader. Parallelism as the primary structuring principle gives the following focal qualities: in the *Barbár dal* 'Barbarian Song' it is a word – or two words owing to the two versions (*jaman!; ajaj!* 'woe is me') – , and it is a word, too, in the poem *Atlantis* (*fény* 'light'). Consequently, in poems with contrast as the main structuring principle, the focus is represented by a sentence – a hypothesis of a sentence as focus has also been raised in the case of the *Harmadik szimfónia* 'Third Symphony' – contrary to poems with parallelism as the primary structuring principle, where the focus is one word in both cases.

The rhetorical-stylistic structures also comply with the primary structuring principle. Thus, we see contrast represented in the opposition of thesis and antithesis in the *Rongyszőnyeg 76* 'Rag-carpet 76', the different quantities of the tropes of the octet and the sestet in the *A benső végtelen* 'The Infinite Inside', the opposition between the similes in the *Magna Meretrix* and the contrasting horizontal and vertical oscillation in the *Harmadik szimfónia* 'Third Symphony'. I can also find the characteristics of parallelism in the *Barbár dal* 'Barbarian Song', which are represented by parallel grammatical structures and in the repetition of the identical lines in the *Atlantis*. A profusion of tropes is a general characteristics of all the poems. Tropes combined with each other form complex tropes. In this combination, however, the single tropes lose their own meaning, in order to signify some different message. As a result the tropes become "total metaphors", as Miklós Szentkuthy (1985:143) put it. The trope *madárka* 'little bird' in the *Harmadik szimfónia* 'Third Symphony', for example, may be interpreted as a symbol for some abstract idea, but if denoting a person, it is a metaphor, and it is also a personification, if it endues an animal with human attributes:

Madárka sír, madárka örül,
míg piros gerendái közül
néz a hatalmas –

Little bird cries, little bird rejoices,
while from his red planks
the mighty one looks down –

Due to the ambiguity arising from the combination of the tropes, interpretation involves some difficulties. These difficulties in interpretation are, however, necessary in order to touch every single reader.

We must also start from the primary structuring principle when dealing with the metrical structures. There is inherently a contrast between the simultaneously present accentual-syllabic and quantitative metrical systems in the *Ronyszőnyeg 76* 'Rag-carpet 76', a characteristic feature of the *Harmadik szimfónia* 'Third Symphony', as well. "As if all the devils of rhythm were closed up in the Hungarian language", Weöres (1990:155) once stated, and this statement of his can be illustrated by many of his poems. The abovementioned contrast between the accentual-syllabic and the quantitative metrical systems in the *Harmadik szimfónia* 'Third Symphony', for example, also represent a merger of these two different metrical systems into an idiosyncratic and individual one:

∪ – ∪ | – ∪ ∪ –   3 | 4
ki merne súgni neked

– – – | ∪ – ∪ –   3 | 4
arról, hogy mi lett veled?

∪ ∪ – | – ∪ ∪ –   3 | 4
melyik ég rejti helyed?

– ∪ ∪ | – ∪ ∪ –   3 | 4
őrzi-e gyöngyeidet?

Who would whisper to you
about what happened to you?
which heaven hides your place?
does it care for your pearls?

We can find the contrasting principle in the *A benső végtelen* 'The Infinite Inside', as well. In this poem there is a contrast, for example, between the octet and the sestet concerning the iamb, the dominant metrical foot. The iambs are more regular in the octet than in the sestet. In the poem *Magna Meretrix*, it is the different rhyme-patterns between the verses which can be mentioned as an example of the contrasting principle. A rhythm originating from both the metrical structure and parallel sentence patterns and the oscillation created by it is a further manifestation of an immanent opposition in the *Harmadik szimfónia* 'Third Symphony'. But we can also find parallelism as the primary structuring principle represented by the identical intonation-patterns of the two versions of the *Barbár dal* 'Barbarian Song' and the sentences with parallel

232

grammatical structures, a characteristic of free-verse attributed to Whitman in the *Atlantis*. In the analyses I often emphasized Weöres' exceptional skill and his language experimentation on the poetical form. Weöres himself, in many instances, has declared how often he drew inspiration from the formal and the structural elements of the poem. According to Ákos Szilágyi (1984:643), in Weöres' poetry "virtuosity becomes independent and the most essential esthetical content of his life-work".

Obviously, there is a correspondence between the primary structuring principle and the grammatical structures. Contrast, for example, can be studied in relation to the vowels and the consonants in the *Rongyszőnyeg 76* 'Rag-carpet 76'. Characteristics, as the disjunctive and adversative sentences, the opposition of an indicated, grammatical subject and a logical one in the *A benső végtelen* 'The Infinite Inside' also demonstrate the contrasting principle. We can see the contrast between the complex and the compound sentences in the *Magna Meretrix* and the tension caused by the syntactical structures which can represent both complex and compound sentences in the *Harmadik szimfónia* 'Third Symphony'. Parallelism as the text organization principle is obviously present in the parallel structured sentences in the *Barbár dal* 'Barbarian Song':

Vá pudd shukomo ikede
vá jimla gulmo buglavi ele
vá leli gulmo ni dede
vá odda dzsárumo he! jaman!

Földed tüskét teremjen
tehened véres tejet adjon
asszonyod fiat ne adjon
édesapád eltemessen! ajaj!

May your land raise thorns
may your cow give bloody milk
may your wife never give you a son
may your father bury you! woe is me!

The principle of parallelism is seen in the *Atlantis*, too, expressed here by the parallel time-phases of present, past and future.

The theme of the poems discussed relates to the thematic spheres indicated in the title of the chapters, but it also relates to the primary structuring principle and the focal quality, similar to the discussion of the levels in the part on text. The focal sentence of the *Rongyszőnyeg 76*, – *csak szíved alszik el* 'only your heart goes to sleep' – indicates an impersonality transformed to second person singular. The focal sentence of the title in the *A benső végtelen* 'The Infinite Inside' expresses impersonality by the metamorphosis of the logical and grammatical subjects. The two interjections *jaman!* and *ajaj!* 'woe is me!' transform personality to impersonality by making use of an imagined language in the *Barbár dal* 'Barbarian Song'. In the focal sentence of the *Magna Meretrix, E világot feleségül / az ész hozománya nélkül / minek vettem?* 'Why did I marry this world / without the dowry of / common sense?' a feeling of homelessness is put into words, and it is through the focal word *fény* 'light', in which chaos turns into harmony in the *Atlantis*. The theme of the *Harmadik szimfónia* 'Third Symphony', however, can only be grasped through an intersubjective relation with the reader. The main structuring principle, within these specific thematic spheres, is explicitly represented by contrasting or parallel motifs in the poems at hand.

Despite the dissimilarities between them, the thematic spheres found in the six poems have some features in common. I believe that this is the motif of a search, phrased in various forms. In the *Rongyszőnyeg 76* 'Rag-carpet 76', a wish for faith and a more complete individual inner world is apparent. The poem *A benső végtelen* 'The Infinite Inside' is about the seeking of a kindred spirit, while the *Barbár dal* 'Barbarian Song' is about a search for the primaeval form of language. The object of the search in the *Magna Meretrix* is the real home, in the *Atlantis* it is the lost inner continent of the Self and in the *Harmadik szimfónia* 'Third Symphony' it is the truth under the surface of the things, i.e. the absolute essence. These specific thematic spheres represented by the common motif of the search are, however, not unambiguously seen by every individual reader. Because meaning in general is created through an individual relationship between the text and the reader, this motif of a search, in the poems at hand, could possibly be defined in another way by another reader. This essential meaning, so difficult to define, leads us to the last chapter on Weöres' philosophy of poetics.

On the basis of the six analysed poems and those which were discussed in a similar context, we clearly have a poetry which includes various philosophical influences. In addition to the strong effects of Hinduism, Buddhism and Taoism, as has been emphasized by many of Weöres' researchers, we can find clear connections to Christianity, the philosophy of existentialism, especially in its religious form, and Jung's psychoanalysis. However, the hypothesis which involves the primary structuring principle working on every level, and which concerns the last part in Weöres' philosophy of poetics, is still unproven.

The four poems in which we referred to contrast as the primary structuring principle, also demonstrate this principle when one uncovers the philosophical issues related to the poems. The positive pole *nature* and the negative pole individual *inner world* in the *Ronyszőnyeg 76* 'Rag-carpet 76' can be associated with the opposite poles of the *yin* and *yang* in Chinese philosophy. The binary opposition of the concepts *there is* and *there is not*, as phrased in the *A benső végtelen* 'The Infinite Inside' draws attention to Orphic philosophy. Within the constrained outer form of the sonnet, the profound inner form breaking through the limits of time and space and turning everything to nothing, demonstrates the pure poetry of Orpheus:

nincs puszta itt, nincs fönt s alant
hajlék se zár védett világot
de az sincs többé aki fázott.

there is no desert here, no above and no below,
no roof closes a sheltered world
but not even he exists any more who felt cold.

In the *Magna Meretrix* we found tokens of the philosophy of existentialism, presenting itself as a contrast between a wish for freedom and a sense of responsibility. The idea of a search for something that does not exist amongst things that exist, as seen in the *Harmadik szimfónia* 'Third Symphony', connects both to Christianity and to the philosophy of existentialism. In addition to these representations of the primary structuring principle of contrast, the other principle of parallelism can also be shown. In the *Barbár dal* 'Barbarian Song' the philosophy, through which the first language rerealizes an analogy between things, is an example of this principle. The conscious and the unconscious, the *animus* and the *anima*, which appear at the same time in the *Atlantis,* also demonstrate that parallelism is the main structuring principle.

Thus, the two primary structuring principles, contrast and parallelism, have a particular influence on the philosophical spheres as well. This influence, however, is not so easy to uncover as it was when dealing with the several levels of the text. Speaking of the theme, we pointed out the common element of the motif of a search. As such, this motif also embraces the possibility of a synthesis. This is a possibility that becomes realized through the interrelation of the philosophical spheres discussed above. As a result, opposite concepts are not unambiguously opposite, yet identical concepts are not unambiguously identical, either.

References

Alexa Károly 1994: Utószó. In: Magyar Zsoltár, pp. 773-[777].

Általános nyelvészeti tanulmányok XI. A szöveg megközelítései. Szerkesztő: Telegdi Zsigmond és Szépe György. Budapest, 1976.

Aeppli, Ernst 1943: Der Traum und seine Deutung. Zürich.

Approaches to Poetry. Some Aspects of Textuality, Intertextuality and Intertextuality. Ed. By János S. Petöfi and Terery Olivi. Berlin, 1994.

Austerlitz, Robert 1958: Ob-Ugric Meters. Helsinki.

Balassa, Péter 1990: A mint B. Weöres Sándor átváltozások című szonettciklusának elemzése. In: MO, pp. 369-375.

Balassi, Bálint 1994: XLII. zsoltár. In: Magyar zsoltár.

Bálint, Péter 1991: "Gőgös papjai a Lantnak" – az Orpheusz-mítosz lélektani realitásai. In: Orpheus 1991:2-3, pp. 129-141.

Barthes, Roland 1971: De l'œuvre au texte. In: Revue d'esthétique 1971:3, pp. 225-232.

Bata, Imre 1979: Weöres Sándor közelében. (Elvek és utak), Budapest.

– 1983: Weöres Sándor hetven esztendeje. In: Nagyvilág. 1983:7, pp. 1075-1079.

– 1995: Egy korai Weöres-szonett – a Pastorale elemzése. In: Élet és irodalom. 1995. március 14.

– 1998: Csak zenét... Weöres Sándor Tizenegy szimfóniájáról. In: Élet és irodalom. 1998. december 18.

Begemann, Petra 1994: Reader's strategies in comprehending poetic discourse. In: Approaches to Poetry, pp. 1-31.

Beney, Zsuzsa 1990: A Háromrészes ének-ről. IN: MO, pp. 201-208.

Bertha, Bulcsu 1993: Weöres Sándor. Bertha Bulcsu beszélgetése a költővel. In: EM, pp. 143-155.

BEV = Bevezetés a filozófiába.

Bevezetés a filozófába. Szöveggyűjtemény. Szerkesztette Steiger Kornél. Budapest, 1995.

Biedermann, Hans 1991: Symbollexikonet. Stockholm.

BM = Bonniers musiklexikon.

Bókay, Antal 1997: Irodalomtudomány a modern és posztmodern korban. (Osiris tankönyvek) Budapest.

Bonniers musiklexikon. 2., revid. uppl. Stockholm, 1983.

Bónyi, Adorján 1990: Mint csillag az égen. In: MO, pp. 34-41.

Bori, Imre 1984: Bori Imre huszonöt tanulmánya. A XX. századi magyar irodalomról. Újvidék.

Bozóky, Éva 1993: A vers: villám. Bozóky Éva beszélgetése Weöres Sándorral. In: EM, pp. 230-237.

Breton, André 1946: Les Manifestes du Surréalisme suivis de Prolégomènes à un troisème Manifeste du Surréalisme ou non. Paris.

Brooks, Cleanth 1947: The Well Wrought Urn. New York.

Bultmann, Rudolf 1958: Jesus Christ and Mythology. London.

Cohen, Ted 1997: Metaphor, feeling and narrative. In: Philosophy and litera-ture. 1997:21:2, pp. 223-244.

Czigány, György 1993a: Költészet és zene. Czigány György rádióbeszélgetése Weöres Sándorral. In: EM, pp. 73-78.

– 1993b: A szimfóniákról, az elfelejtett versekről. Czigány György rádióbeszélgetése Weöres Sándorral. In: EM, pp. 306-308.

Cs. Szabó, László 1993: Negyvenhat perc a költővel. Cs. Szabó László rádióbeszélgetése Weöres Sándorral. In: EM, pp. 27-40.

Csatlós, János 1989: Sándor Weöres – mystiker och skämtare. In: Svenska Dagbladet. 1989.02.02.

"de nem felelnek, úgy felelnek". A magyar líra a húszas-harmincas évek fordulóján. Szerkesztette Kabdebó Lóránt, Kulcsár Szabó Ernő. Pécs, 1992.

Derrida, Jacques 1967: L'Ecriture et la différence. Paris.

Dijk, Teun A. van 1972: Some Aspects of Text Grammars. The Hague – Paris.

Diószegi, Vilmos 1983: A pogány magyarok hitvilága. (Kőrösi Csoma Kiskönyvtár, 4) Budapest.

Domokos, Mátyás 1977: Ugyanarról másképpen. Budapest.

–1982: A pályatárs szemével. Budapest.

–1993: Válaszolni nehezebb. Domokos Mátyás TV-beszélgetése Weöres Sándorral. In: EM, pp. 347-364.

Dugántsy, Mária 1991: Erzä-mordwinische rituelle Klagegesänge. Uppsala.

Egyedül mindenkivel. Weöres Sándor beszélgetései, nyilatkozatai, vallomá-sai. Összeállította, szerkesztette, sajtó alá rendezte Domokos Mátyás. Budapest, 1993. EI = Weöres, Sándor 1975.

Eidolon. Ismeretlen nyelvű vers a Magyarok című folyóiratban. In: EM, pp. 20-26.

Élet és irodalom. Irodalmi és politikai hetilap. Budapest, 1957-.

Életünk. Irodalmi, művészeti és kritikai folyóirat. Szombathely, 1963-.

Eliade, Mircea 1960: Myths, Dreams and Mysteries. The Encounter between Contemporary Faiths and Archaic Reality. London.

– 1991: Images and Symbols. Studies in Religious Symbolism. Princeton, New Jersey.

EM = Egyedül mindenkivel.

Espmark, Kjell 1977: Själen i bild. En huvudlinje i modern svensk poesi. Stockholm.

Fábián, László 1977: Lantos – Weöres: Négy korál 2. In: Művészet, 1977:3. XIII. évf.

Filosofilexikonet. Redaktör Poul Lübcke. Stockholm, 1988.

Form och struktur. Litteraturvetenskapliga texter i urval av Kurt Aspelin och Bengt A. Lundberg. Stockholm, 1971.

Forrás. Kecskemét, 1969-.

Forsyth, Phillis Young 1980: Atlantis. The Making of Myth. Montreal, London.

Franz, M.-L. von 1964: Individuationsprocessen. In: Jung, Carl Gustav 1964, pp. 158-229.

Fry, Northrop 1957: Anatomy of Criticism. Four Essays. Princeton, New Jersey.

Glasenapp, Helmuth von 1943: Die Religionen Indiens. (Kröners Taschenausgabe, 190) Stuttgart.

– 1973: De fem världsreligionerna. Stockholm. 3. uppl.

Győr, Sándor 1993: Beszélgetés Weöres Sándorral. Kérdező: Győr Sándor. In: EM, pp. 107-109.

Hajdú, András 1990: A Bóbita ritmikájáról. In: MO, pp. 307-322.

Hallberg, Peter 1975: Litterär teori och stilistik. Göteborg.

Hamvas, Béla 1941: Szellem és existencia. Karl Jaspers filozófiája. (Philosophia. A m. kir. Horthy Miklós-Tudományegyetem filozófiai intézetének közleményei. 1) Szeged.

– 1987: Hamvas Béla harminchárom esszéje. Tartóshullám. Budapest.

– 1990: A Medúza. In: MO, pp. 213-217.

– 1992: Patmosz. Esszék. (Hamvas Béla művei. 3) Szombathely.

– 1993: A babérligetkönyv. Hexakümion. (Hamvas Béla művei. 5) Budapest.

– 1995a: Scientia sacra. 1. rész. 1. kötet. Az őskori emberiség szellemi hagyománya. (Hamvas Béla művei. 8) Szentendre.

– 1995b: Scientia sacra. 1. rész. 2. kötet. Az őskori emberiség szellemi hagyománya. (Hamvas Béla művei. 9) Szentendre.

– 1996: Scientia sacra. 2. rész. A kereszténység. (Hamvas Béla művei. 10) Szentendre.

Hankiss, Elemér 1970: Az irodalmi kifejezésformák lélektana. Budapest.

– 1985: Az irodalmi mű mint komplex modell. Budapest.

Havas, Ervin 1993: Hogyan lehet százféleképpen írni? Havas Ervin beszél getése Weöres Sándorral. In: EM, pp. 344-346.

Henderson, Joseph L. 1964: Gamla myter och moderna människor. In: Jung, Carl Gustav 1964, pp. 104-157.

Henrikson, Alf 1982: Verskonstens ABC. En poetisk uppslagsbok. [Stockholm].

Hirsch, E. D. 1976: Objective Interpretation. In: On Literary Intention, pp. 26-54.

Hornyik, Miklós 1993: Műhelybeszélgetés a költészetről a Hold és Sárkány szerzőjével. Hornyik Miklós beszélgetése Weöres Sándorral. In: EM, pp. 79-99.

Hozsanna! Teljes kottás népénekeskönyv. Budapest, 1984.

Humphreys, Christmas 1962: A Popular Dictionary of Buddhism. London.

Ingarden, Roman 1976: Det litterära konstverket. Lund.

Irodalomtörténet. A Magyar Irodalomtörténeti Társaság folyóirata. Budapest, 1912-.

Iser, W: 1993: Läsprocessen – en fenomenologisk betraktelse. In: Modern Litteraturteori, pp. 319-341.

Jakobson, Roman 1971: Les chats av Charles Baudlaire. In: Form och struktur, pp. 158-178.

– 1974: Poetik och lingvistik. Stockholm.

Jaspers, Karl 1950: Einführung in die Philosophie. Zürich.

Jelenkor. Pécs, 1957-.

Jonsson, Inge 1971: Idéer och teorier om ordens konst. Stockholm.

Jung, Karl Gustav – Karl Kerényi 1941: Einführung in das Wesen der Mythologie. Leipzig.

Jung, Karl Gustav 1953: Symbolik des Geistes. Zürich.

– 1964: Människan och hennes symboler. [Stockholm].

– 1965: Det omedvetna. Stockholm.

– 1995: Arketyper och drömmar. Valda skrifter av C. G. Jung. Stockholm.

Kabdebó, Lóránt 1980: Versek között. Tanulmányok, kritikák. Budapest.

Kamocsay, Ildikó 1993: Költő házaspár. Kamocsay Ildikó látogatóban Károlyi Amynál és Weöres Sándornál. In: EM, pp. 365-370.

Karinthy, Ferenc 1990: Róma, 1948. (Részlet) In: MO, pp. 274-276.

Kecskés, András 1984: A magyar vers hangzásszerkezete (Opus irodalomelméleti tanulmányok. 8) Budapest.

Kcnycrcs, Zoltán: Gondolkodó irodalom. Budapest, 1974.

– 1974: Mítosz és játék. Bevezetés Weöres Sándor költészetébe. In: Kenyeres, Zoltán: Gondolkodó irodalom, pp. 243-305.

– 1978: Weöres Sándor irodalomszemlélete. Egy antológia tanulságai. In: Jelenkor, 1978:1, pp. 69-74.

– 1983: Tündérsíp. Weöres Sándorról. Budapest.

– 1984: Sándor Weöres – poet of Cosmic Harmony. In: The New Hungarian Quarterly, 93. spring 1984, pp. 38-62.

– 1986: Weöres Sándor. In: MIT 1945-1975., pp. 333-362.

– 1990: Medúzalebegés. Weöres Sándor a Nyugattól önmagáig. In: MO, pp. 165- 174.

Kiefer, Ferenc 1976: A szövegelmélet grammatikai indokoltságáról. In: Általános nyelvészeti tanulmányok XI., pp. 197-222.

Kodolányi, János 1958: Új ég, új föld. Budapest.

Kosztolányi, Dezső 1957: Ábécé. Budapest.

Kulcsár Szabó Ernő 1992: A kettévált modernség nyomában. A magyar líra a húszas-harmincas évek fordulóján. In: "de nem felelnek, úgy felelnek", pp. 21-52.

Landgren, Bengt 1983a: mannen utan väg XXIX. En strukturanalytisk studie. In: Tidskrift för litteraturvetenskap. 1983:2, pp. 68-77.

— 1983b: Erik Lindegrens dikt "Döende vår" i Sviter. En strukturanalytisk studie. In: Tidskrift för litteraturvetenskap. 1983:2, pp. 78-92.

— 1985: Johannes Edfeldts dikt Återskenet i Bråddjupt eko (1947) Tre tolk-ningsstrategier. In: Tidskrift för litteraturvetenskap. 1985:1-2, pp. 29-39.

Lao-ce: Tao Te King. Az Út és az Erény könyve. Weöres Sándor fordítása Tőkey Ferenc prózafordítása alapján. Budapest, 1974.

Látóhatár. Zürich, 1950-.

Lator, László 19990: Vázlat Weöres Sándorról. In: MO, pp. 529-542.

— 1996: Vers, zene, verszene. In: Mozgó világ. 1996:11, pp. 109-112.

Lévy-Strauss, Claude 1968: Structural Anthropology. London.

— 1971: see. Jakobson, Roman 1971.

Liptay, Katalin 1993: Ének a határtalanról. Liptay Katalin, Bárdos László, Reisinger János beszélgetése Weöres Sándorral. In: EM, pp. 415-424.

The Loeb Classical Library. Cambridge, Mass., 1912-.

Lotman, Jurij 1974: Den poetiska texten. Stockholm.

A magyar irodalom története. Főszerkesztő: Sőtér István. 1-5. 1964-1965. Budapest.

A magyar irodalom története 1945-1975. II/1. A költészet. 1986. Szerkesztette Béládi Miklós. Budapest.

Magyar Nyelvőr. Budapest, 1872-.

Magyar Zsoltár. Válogatta és szerkesztette Alexa Károly. Budapest, 1994.

A mai magyar nyelv rendszere. Leíró nyelvtan I-II. kötet. Szerkesztette Tompa József. Budapest, 1961-1962.

Mezey, Katalin 1993: A Vigília beszélgetése Weöres Sándorral. In: EM, pp. 429-435.

MIT = A magyar irodalom története.

MIT 1945-1975 = A magyar irodalom története 1945-1975.

MNNyR = A mai magyar nyelv rendszere.

MO = Magyar Orpheus.

Magyar Orpheus. Weöres Sándor emlékezetére. Összeállította, szerkesztette, sajtó alá rendezte Domokos Mátyás. Budapest, 1990.

Modern litteraturteori. Från rysk formalism till dekonstruktion. Claes Entzenberg, Cecilia Hansson (red.) 2. uppl. Lund, 1993.

Moldován, Domokos 1993: Kodály Zoltánról. Moldován Domokos magneto-fonbeszélgetése Weöres Sándor és Károlyi Amy költőkkel. In:

EM, pp. 188-195.

Molnár, Ildikó A. 1977: Weöres Sándor költői nyelvének hangtanából. Budapest.

Mórocz, Zsolt 1996: Hamvason innen, Hamvason túl. In: Életünk 1996:2, pp. 101-114.

Mozgó világ. Budapest, 1971-.

Művészet. Budapest, 1960-.

Nagyvilág. Világirodalmi folyóirat. Budapest, 1956-.

Németh G., Béla: 1992: Többirányzatú, többfázisú korszakváltás. In: "de nem felelnek, úgy felelnek".

The New Hungarian Quarterly. Budapest, 1960-1992.

Norris, Christopher 1982: Deconstruction: Theory and Practice. London and New York.

On Literary Intention, Edinburgh, 1976.

Orpheus. Irodalmi folyóirat. Miskolc, 1990-.

Parancs, János 1990: Orpheus. Weöres Sándor köszöntése. In: MO, p. 392.

– 1994: Weöres Sándor: Tűzkút. Domokos Mátyás sorozata. Beszélgetűtárs: Parancs János. In: Forrás. 1994:5., pp. 78-79.

Paul, David 1966: Poison and Vision. Poems and Prose of Baudlaire, Mallarmé and Rimbaud. Salzburg.

Philosophy and Literature. Baltimore, 1976-.

Plotinus 1984: Plotinus. With an English translation by A. H. Amstrong. Enneads V. 1-9. In: The Loeb Classical Library, Plotinus V. Cambridge, Mass.

Revue d'esthétique. Paris, 1948-.

Réz, Pál 1993: Látogatóban. Réz Pál beszélgetése Weöres Sándorral. In: EM, pp. 51-59.

Richard, Jean-Pierre 1961: L'Univers imaginaire de Mallarmé. Paris.

Rochlitz, Kyra: Orpheus nyomában. A Teljesség felé: Salve Regina. In: Műhely, 1966:6, pp. 40-50.

Simon, István 1993: Írószobám. Simon István beszélgetése Weöres Sándorral. In: EM, pp. 263-276.

Sklovskij, Viktor 1971: Konsten som grepp. In: Form och struktur.

Steinitz, Wolfgang 1934: Der Parallelismus in der finnish-karelischen Volksdichtung. Helsinki.

Svenska Dagbladet. Stockholm, 1884-,

Szabó, Zoltán 1985: Szövegkohézió és globális stilisztikai elemzés. In: Magyar Nyelvőr, 109, 1985, pp. 479-490.

– 1988: Szövegnyelvészet és stilisztika. Budapest.

Szabolcsi, Miklós, 1957: Weöres Sándor költészetéről. A Hallgatás tornya, "harminc év verseiből", megjelenése alkalmából. In: Irodalomtörténet 1957:2.

Szathmári, István 1977: A nyelv (és benne a mondat) "felbomlása" az újabb költői stílusban. In: Tanulmányok a mai magyar nyelv mondattana köréből, pp. 189-203.

– 1983: Beszélhetünk-e szövegstilisztikáról? In: Tanulmányok a a mai magyar nyelv szövegtana köréből, pp. 320-355.

– 1990: Fejezetek a magyar költői stílus történetéből. (Castrenianumin toimitteita 38; Folia Hungarica 5) Helsinki.

Szekér, Endre 1993: Beszélgetés Weöres Sándorral. Beszélgetőtárs: Szekér Endre. In: EM, pp. 319-328.

Széles, Klára 1996: Van-e értelme a műértelmezésnek? (Ha van, mi az?) Budapest.

Szentkuthy, Miklós 1985: Múzsák testamentuma. Budapest.

Szepes, Erika 1996: A mai magyar vers. Költészetünk formakincsének leíró és funkcionális elemzése az elmúlt fél évszázad verseinek tükrében. 1. kötet [Budapest].

Szepes, Erika – Szerdahelyi, István 1988: A múzsák tánca. Verstani kisenciklopédia. Budapest.

Szerdahelyi, István 1994: Verstan mindenkinek. Budapest.

– 1996: Irodalomelmélet mindenkinek. Budapest.

Szerdahelyi, Pál 1994: "Vonj sugaradba Istenem!" Weöres Sándor vallásossága és vallásos költészete. In: Életünk. 1994: 5-6, pp. 564-575.

Szilágyi, Ákos 1984: Nem vagyok kritikus! Budapest.

Szőcs, Géza 1990: A parton Proteus alakoskodik. In: MO, pp. 472-483.

Tamás, Attila 1978: Weöres Sándor. Budapest.

Tanulmányok a mai magyar nyelv mondattana köréből. Szerk.: Rácz Endre és Szathmári István. Budapest, 1977.

Tanulmányok a mai magyar nyelv szövegtana köréből. Szerk.: Rácz Endre és Szathmári István. Budapest, 1983.

Thomka, Beáta 1992: A húszas-harmincas évek költészetének domináns poetikai, retorikai alakzatai. In: "de nem felelnek, úgy felelnek", pp. 111-121.

Thomson, Robert 1972: Psykologins historia. Lund.

Tidskrift för litteraturvetenskap. Lund, 1971-.

Tüskés, Tibor : Weöres és a Sorsunk. In: MO, pp. 177-191.

Tőkei, Ferenc 1994: Utószó. In: Lao-ce: Tao Te King, pp. 151-158.

Ungváry, Ildikó 1993: A vers a lélek tréningje. Ungváry Ildikó beszélgetése Weöres Sándorral. In: EM, pp. 141-142.

Vajda, Miklós 1987: The Poetic World of Sándor Weöres. In: The New Hungarian Quarterly 107. autumn 1987, pp. 43-50.

Vargyas, Lajos 1966: Magyar vers – magyar nyelv. Verstani tanulmány. Budapest.

Várkonyi, Nándor 1976: Pergő évek. (Tények és tanúk) Budapest.

Ward, Keith 1987: Images of Eternity. Concepts of God in Five Religious Traditions. London.

Warren, Henry Clarke 1972: Buddhism in Translations: Passages Selected from the Buddhist Sacred Books and Translated from the Original Pāli into English by Henry Clarke Warren. New York.

Wellek – Warren 1966: The Mode of Existence of a Literary Work of Art. In: Theory of Literature, pp. 142-157.

Weöres, Sándor 1975: Egybegyűjtött írások. 1-3. 3. bővített kiadás. Budapest.

– 1990: Weöres Sándor levele Babits Mihálynak. In: MO, pp. 64-65.

– 1993a: Megfejtés a "Rejtelem"-re. Nyilatkozat. In: EM, pp. 41-49.

– 1993b: A reménytelenség könyve. Nyilatkozat. In: EM, p. 368.

– 1993c: Önvallomás. In: EM, pp. 58-59.

– 1994: Weöres Sándor: Tűzkút. Domokos Mátyás sorozata. Beszélgetőtárs: Parancs János. In: Forrás. 1994:5, pp. 77-86.

WW = Weörestől Weöresről.

Weörestől Weöresről. A kötetet összeállította: Tüskés Tibor. Budapest, 1993.

Wåhlin, Christian 1995: Allmän och svensk metrik. Lund.

Photo and Figures

Photo
Photo 1   Sándor Weöres

Figures